THE COMPLETE IDIOT'S GUIDE® TO

Teaching the Bible

By W. Terry Whalin

ALPHA
A member of Penguin Group (USA) Inc.

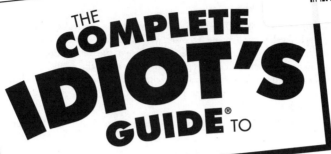

International Standard Book Number: 1-59257-064-X
Library of Congress Catalog Card Number: 2003106904

05 04 03 8 7 6 5 4 3 2 1

Interpretation of the printing code: The rightmost number of the first series of numbers is the year of the book's printing; the rightmost number of the second series of numbers is the number of the book's printing. For example, a printing code of 03-1 shows that the first printing occurred in 2003.

Printed in the United States of America

Publisher: *Marie Butler-Knight*
Product Manager: *Phil Kitchel*
Senior Managing Editor: *Jennifer Chisholm*
Senior Acquisitions Editor: *Renee Wilmeth*
Development Editor: *Suzanne LeVert*
Copy Editor: *Krista Hansing*
Illustrator: *Jody Schaeffer*
Cover/Book Designer: *Trina Wurst*
Indexer: *Julie Bess*
Layout/Proofreading: *John Etchison, Ayanna Lacey*

Contents at a Glance

Contents

Foreword

Throughout the world, teachers use a variety of textbooks. Even in our New Life Clinics, we recommend a variety of different books from which to learn. If I had to choose just one book to teach and learn from, it would be the Bible, which is the greatest book ever written. In the pages of Scripture, we learn that God created a plan for the recovery of broken people and creation. We meet numerous individuals whose hurting lives are mended through the wisdom and power of God. We meet the Lord of the universe, who is waiting with arms outstretched for all of us to turn back to him, seek after his ways, and recover the wonderful plan he has for us. Spiritual renewal and recovery is a consistent theme throughout the Bible.

Yet how does the Bible spring to life and become more than a book we only carry to church and use rarely? Small groups, individuals, families, co-workers, and neighbors can learn to take the next step in their spiritual growth with *The Complete Idiot's Guide to Teaching the Bible*. A longtime student of the Bible, Terry Whalin uses simple steps to teach at least 12 different methods of Bible study. If you are stuck in a rut or haven't begun the spiritual journey to learn from the Bible, you now have in your hands one of the best new tools to begin this process. Besides including step-by-step instructions for the individual, Terry has added insights for the teacher to use in developing his or her skills. For a shot of adrenaline and energy, consider the various teaching tips as something to try even at the last minute.

In our fast-paced world, it can be a struggle to find the time to prepare for studying the Bible. What if you are called at the last minute to substitute for your Bible teacher or Sunday School class? I'd encourage you to use the fourth part of this book, in which Terry provides complete lessons using each of the major teaching methods along with starter questions to ask the group and insights into the parts of the Bible under study. It's the complete starter package for you to begin teaching the Bible and encouraging others to take the journey toward healing and newfound strength.

Studying the Bible and constantly growing in our spiritual relationship with God are essential parts of life. These actions involve the simple but challenging process of daily seeking God's will for our life instead of demanding to go our own way. It allows God to do for us what we cannot do for ourselves, while taking the steps necessary to draw us closer to our Creator and Redeemer. We all need to take part in this process; it is an inherent part of being human. These teaching insights will help you in this spiritual journey.

Stephen Arterburn

Stephen Arterburn, M.Ed., is the founder and chairman of New Life Clinics, the largest provider of Christian counseling and treatment throughout the United States and Canada, and is also the host of the daily "New Life Live!" national radio program heard on more than 100 outlets and at www.newlife.com. Arterburn is the creator of the Women of Faith Conferences and the best-selling author of more than 30 books, including the executive co-editor of the *Life Recovery Bible* (Tyndale House Publishers) and *Every Man's Battle* (Waterbrook Press).

Introduction

One of the great people in the pages of the Bible is Moses. Raised in the courts of Pharaoh, Moses spent 40 years in Egypt and then fled Pharaoh and spent 40 years in the desert of Midian. In his final 40 years, Moses led the people of Israel. During those final 40 years, Moses had an assistant named Joshua. The name of this assistant rarely appears in the first five books of the Bible. As Moses heads toward the mountain to receive the Ten Commandments, he goes with Joshua. When Moses sends out 12 spies into the Promised Land, one of those spies is Joshua. In the final days of Moses' life, this great leader is to pass along his leadership to someone named Joshua. The young assistant, who has watched Moses for years, takes the mantle of leadership and guides the children of Israel.

You've opened this book to learn how to teach the Bible. The most significant book on your bookshelf is God's message to man, and it's through the pages of the Bible that we learn God's promises for our lives. After the death of Moses, the Lord gave Joshua insight into how to be successful. The key to success and God's presence was tied to studying the Bible. Joshua told the people …

> Be strong and very courageous. Obey all the laws Moses gave you. Do not turn away from them, and you will be successful in everything you do. Study this Book of the Law continually. Meditate on it day and night so you may be sure to obey all that is written in it. Only then will you succeed. I command you—be strong and courageous! Do not be afraid or discouraged. For the Lord your God is with you wherever you go. (Joshua 1:7–8, NLT)

Toward the end of the Book of Joshua, after the people had conquered some of the Promised Land, Joshua again exhorts the people, "But if serving the Lord seems undesirable to you, then choose for yourselves this day whom you will serve, whether the gods your forefathers served beyond the River, or the gods of the Amorites, in whose land you are living. But as for me and my household, we will serve the Lord." (Joshua 24:15, NIV)

When we look at our bookshelves, most of us have books that we'd like to read someday. Activities at home and work compete for our time and attention. One book on your shelf contains God's message for man about how to live in today's world: the Bible.

How to Get the Best Value from This Book

Whether you are preparing to teach the Bible to a small group in your home or gathering your family to teach the Bible, you will need to take some time for preparation. The first part of this book provides answers to such questions as these: What are the benefits of teaching? How do I ask good questions? What if I gather everyone and no one talks? With simple, step-by-step instructions, you will be prepared to teach the Bible. The second part of the book looks at some basic Bible study methods, including the Devotional Method, the Chapter Summary Method, the Bible Character Quality Method, and the Bible Theme Method.

After you learn the basic teaching methods, the third portion of the book helps you add depth and variety to your Bible teaching with eight more ways to teach the Bible. The final portion of the book returns to these various methods with detailed practical examples of each one. An example from the Old Testament and another from the New Testament are included.

If you are called at the last minute to teach a Bible lesson, you can turn to these practical examples and draw from them for your own teaching. And when you begin each method, it's a great idea to turn to these practical examples to make sure you understand how to accomplish each of these various methods of Bible study and teaching.

Extras

Scattered throughout the book are sidebars that provide some extra help and insight into the process of teaching the Bible.

Potent Quotables

These tidbits offer key Bible verses related to teaching the Bible and to understanding the book.

Proceed with Caution

Here, you'll receive warnings about potential teaching problems or pitfalls.

Just in Case

If you need more ways to get your group involved with a particular method or a longer teaching note, you might be able to find them here.

Teaching Tips

In these sidebars, you'll find ideas for teaching in various situations or clarifications of the teaching points discussed in the chapter.

Acknowledgments

I would like to thank my editors, Renee Wilmeth (senior acquisitions editor), Suzanne LeVert (development editor), Nancy Caine (technical editor), and Christy Wagner (senior production editor). I love to work with professional editors whose valuable work improves every page of the book. Also with thanksgiving, I acknowledge my agent, Scott Waxman. Without you, Scott, I never would have been involved in this tremendous project. Thank you.

To a small group of writer friends (you know who you are) who stayed behind the scenes but consistently wrote notes of encouragement, cheering the completed chapters and bathing the entire writing process in prayer and praise: thank you.

Finally, I want to acknowledge my wife, Christine, who has endured many late nights and evenings without my companionship as I have worked diligently on the details of this book. Thank you, Christine, for your encouragement, patience, and support, which have been critical to this book. You're remarkable, and I'm privileged to be married to you.

Special Thanks to the Technical Reviewer

The Complete Idiot's Guide to Teaching the Bible was reviewed by an expert who double-checked the accuracy of what you'll learn here, to help us ensure that this book gives you everything you need to know about teaching the Bible. Special thanks are extended to Nancy Caine.

Trademarks

All terms mentioned in this book that are known to be or are suspected of being trademarks or service marks have been appropriately capitalized. Alpha Books and Penguin Group (USA) Inc. cannot attest to the accuracy of this information. Use of a term in this book should not be regarded as affecting the validity of any trademark or service mark.

Part 1

On Your Mark, Get Set, Teach

Teaching the Bible to others can be the most fulfilling and rewarding time that you spend all week. Instead of talking with people about the weather or the current news events, you interact with others about the best-selling book of all time, the Bible. The Bible contains God's message to mankind about how to live and triumph through everyday events.

As you begin to teach the Bible, you have to start with the preparation stage. The following chapters look at why you'd want to teach the Bible instead of something like a Shakespeare play or a classic novel. We also examine the type of study tools you need to teach the Bible and detail some of the benefits of teaching.

Chapter 1

Why Teach the Bible?

In This Chapter

- Why study the Bible?
- Finding opportunities to teach the Bible
- Developing your skills as a teacher
- Study tools and how to use them

Although the Bible never appears on best-seller lists, it is a perennial best-seller, with millions of copies sold annually. More than 90 percent of American homes contain a copy of the Bible, and some 47 percent of Americans claim to read part of it at least once a week. Yet a Gallup survey also reveals that only 49 percent of Americans can name the first book of the Bible, and only 34 percent can name the person who delivered the Sermon on the Mount.

Making the Choice to Teach

While most people own a copy of this spiritual book, few study or read it on a regular basis. And unless you take your Bible from the shelf and crack open the pages, it's hard to know the contents. George Barna and his company, the Barna Research Group, have researched and compiled many statistics about the religious marketplace. In a December 17, 2002, news release, he wrote:

> Most adults read the Bible during the year, and a huge majority claims they know all of the basic teachings of the Bible. How, then, can most people say Satan does not exist, that the Holy Spirit is merely a symbol, that eternal peace with God can be earned through good works, and that truth can only be understood through the lens of reason and experience? How can a plurality of our citizens contend that Jesus committed sins and that the Bible, Koran and Book of Mormon all teach the same truths?
>
> In a sound bite society, you get sound bite theology. Americans are more likely to buy simple sayings than a system of truth that takes time and concentration to grasp. … Hopefully, once Christian leaders and teachers comprehend this, we can be more devoted to effectively challenging the superficial spirituality of our nation. As Paul wrote in the letter to the Galatians, we are only fooling ourselves; God will not be mocked.

Periodically, Jay Leno on *The Tonight Show* takes a microphone and heads out to interview people. One night, Jay stopped two college students and asked, "Can either of you name just one of the Ten Commandments?" One student paused and then responded, "Oh, yes, freedom of speech."

Turning to the other student, Leno asked, "Who was it in the Bible who was swallowed by a whale?" Immediately, the student answered, "Pinocchio?"

Not successful with either answer, Jay decided to try a fill-in-the-blank answer with a well-known Bible verse, "He who is without sin …" The other person replied, "… has a good time."

Although these answers may bring smiles, they also show that we live in a time of biblical illiteracy. Never before has the Bible been more available to the Western world, yet such a famine of God's Word. We have Bibles in hotels, doctors' offices, libraries, and most homes in America; yet most people are ignorant of what the Scriptures really have to say.

Potent Quotables

"Surround me with your tender mercies so I may live, for your law is my delight." (Psalm 119:77, The New Living Translation [NLT])

The Bible teaches us that you cannot be a disciple of Jesus Christ if you do not maintain a regular intake of the Word of God. On one occasion, Jesus said to his followers, "You are truly my disciples if you keep obeying my teachings. And you will know the truth, and the truth will set you free." (John 8:31–32, The New Living

Translations [NLT]) As you look back through the history of the Christian church, you will find that the common element of every great man or woman of God is that they knew the Bible and spent consistent, regular time studying the Scriptures.

As you teach the Bible, make sure you present spirituality as a journey and a series of choices rather than something you have or don't have. Too many people see their single decision to trust Christ as Savior or their salvation decision as the only thing they need to make for Jesus. Help them discover that most of their day-to-day decisions have the potential either to honor or disgrace Jesus. They can talk kindly to a friend or slam her. They can choose to solve problems or get revenge. When the Holy Spirit nudges them with guilt, they can change the behavior that caused it or angrily ignore the guilt. They can talk with God to find out how to cope with sadness, or they can wallow in self-pity. They can encourage their opponents during competitive activities, or they can win at all costs.

Finding Your Students

Because of an increasing interest in spirituality in today's culture, many people would like to learn more about the Bible. This book provides step-by-step tools to help you both study the Bible and to teach it to others. Once you learn the methods outlined in this book, your choice of how to apply them is restricted only by your own desires and creativity. Here are just a few people who might benefit from what you'll learn in this book:

- **You.** Independently from any particular church or Bible study group, you can begin to learn the different ways to study the Scriptures.
- **Your family.** Sometimes the ones we love the most are the most difficult to teach about spiritual truth from the Bible on a consistent basis. Talk about it with your spouse and children, set a realistic schedule for studying the Bible together, then stick with it.

Teaching Tips

Guide the members of your Bible group to embrace spirituality as if it were a steering wheel, not a spare tire. Often people feel powerless even though they have the power of God at their fingertips. God wants to work through each person, although this truth is a revelation to many people. Help the individuals in your group decide to draw on the power of the Holy Spirit. Challenge them to watch each day for one good that God gives them opportunity to do, and then to do that good. Invite them to share the best part of their week and explain how they drew on God's power to make that good thing happen. Invite them to share a temptation that God helped them resist that week, and how he did it.

- **Your church or Sunday school class.** Discuss your desire to teach with the leaders in your church. Volunteer teachers are almost always needed, and it will give you a consistent place to teach the Bible.
- **Your co-workers.** Teaching the Bible and talking about spiritual matters in the workplace could be a good way to grow closer to your co-workers. However, keep in mind that it can be a bit risky in some work environments. Make sure you arrange to meet before or after work, or at lunch time, and preferably meet away from the workplace.
- **A nonprofit group.** A number of these groups, such as Mothers of Preschoolers or Promise Keepers, often look for people to lead small groups in a variety of activities, including teaching the Bible. Volunteers are constantly needed, and your help would be welcomed.
- **A neighborhood Bible study group.** Spirituality is a key topic of discussion and is more common in the media and our culture. As you reach out to your neighbors and offer to teach them the Bible, you may be surprised at the interest.

As you can see, there are many opportunities to teach the Bible.

Proceed with Caution

Introduce three class rules: First, no one can slam another member's comment, question, or concern. Instead, everyone must encourage each other toward Christlikeness. Second, there are no stupid questions. No sincere question is a dumb question, and every comment makes sense when you hear what's really said. Finally, no talking when another talks, so that everyone can hear and cherish each other's pearls of wisdom.

Learning How to Teach

After you select your group for teaching the Bible, it's common to feel insecure about your own abilities. A number of practical resources will help you to continue improving your abilities as a spiritual leader.

- **Books.** The book you're reading now is a great place to start. Your local bookstore might be able to recommend other titles designed to help you improve your teaching skills and give you new ideas for teaching.
- **Cassette tapes.** Many teaching tapes are available from a variety of Bible teachers. Well-known national pastors and pastors of large churches often record

their Bible study teaching. If you are studying a particular book or portion of the Bible, it is often helpful to listen to a particular Bible teacher you admire for additional insight, and also to watch and learn from his or her teaching techniques.

- **Personal experience in Bible studies.** Often we learn from our participation in a small group Bible study. How does this leader guide the discussion and the group? How are the various studies selected for study? What methods work or fail to work? You can benefit and grow as a teacher by watching and thinking about the groups in which you've been a participant.
- **Conferences.** Various denominations or Christian publishers hold Sunday school conventions occasionally. Study the program for these events, and look in particular for skilled workshop leaders who teach techniques for teaching the Bible.
- **One-on-one mentoring.** This final suggestion might be one of the most effective tools for personal growth as a teacher. Find someone in your church or your local area you admire as a teacher. Then approach him or her and ask for a regular meeting to talk about teaching techniques. Then, when you get together with this person, discuss the methods that have and have not worked for you. Proverbs 27:17 says, "As iron sharpens iron, a friend sharpens a friend." (NLT) Take advantage of this focused time with someone else to learn and grow from his or her teaching experiences and techniques.

Garnering the Tools of the Trade

One of the best-kept secrets among Christians is the availability of practical Bible study resources. Many excellent reference tools are available that make studying and teaching the Bible possible and exciting. If you don't use these tools and teach your students to use them, you'd be like a carpenter who tries to build a house by hand without using a hammer and a saw during the construction process.

As Christians in the Western world, we have an abundance of helpful books designed to aid us in our personal Bible study and make use of the latest archaeological finds, word studies, and research of great Bible scholars. These Bible study tools don't replace the Bible, but they do help us study it.

Indeed, Bible study is a skill that requires practice in order to develop. Most skills require tools. Plumbers need their wrenches, artists need their brushes and paints, and carpenters need their hammers and saws. The serious Bible student will want to take advantage of the availability of reference tools to help in searching the Scriptures effectively. If a person tries to study the Bible systematically without using good tools, that person will find the task tedious and difficult.

Some people are hesitant and afraid to use Bible reference tools because they don't want to become too dependent on these books. They piously proclaim, "All I need is the Bible." Although that statement is true, the tools in the following section are designed to help you get into the Bible. Don't be afraid of using these reference resources, because most of the books represent the lifelong studies of dedicated men of God. The insights they received from the Scriptures can enrich your Bible study and provide information about people, places, and events that you can't find if you only use the Bible.

As a leader and Bible teacher, you should acquaint the people in your group with these books. A practical way for you to "prepare God's people for works of service" (Ephesians 4:12, New International Version) is to familiarize them with these Bible study tools.

For instance, a thorough, contemporary Bible handbook provides students with important information, including the occasion and purpose of each Bible book or each part of the book. For example, a handbook will explain what prompted Paul to write his first letter to the Corinthians, where Paul was at the time, and what was going on with the Corinthians. Although a careful reading of 1 Corinthians often reveals the historical and factual background, it's often very helpful to add to your knowledge by consulting a Bible handbook.

Let's examine eight types of reference tools that are used in connection with the different Bible teaching methods presented and explained in this book.

Study Bibles

One of the most important tools is a good study Bible. Usually the term *study Bible* is referenced on the cover of the book. It should have print large enough for you to read for long periods of time without causing eyestrain, and it should have paper thick enough for you to make notes without the ink running through the paper to the next page. Wide margins are helpful because they allow room for making personal notations. Finally, a study Bible should have a good cross-referencing system.

Quite a number of study Bibles are out there, but not all are objective—that is, most are oriented to a particular brand of theology. Two that I recommend are available in various translations. One is *The New Open Bible* (Nelson, 1975; Expanded Edition, 1990) (King James Version, New American Standard Bible, New King James Version). Among its features are outlines, lengthy book introductions, and a "Biblical

Cyclopedia Index" (a 300-page topical Bible/concordance). It also provides alternative translations and cross-references at the end of each verse. However, the space limitations of this format result in a small reference system. Because of the variety of features and its availability in three popular translations, this Bible is growing in popularity.

The *Thompson Chain-Reference Bible* (Kirkbride, 1908, 5th Improved Edition, 1988) (King James Version, New International Version, New American Standard Bible, New King James Version) is another excellent study Bible. The heart of this work is its unique chain-reference system. Thompson developed a "Chain Index" of more than 4,000 biblical subjects that forms a 196-page "Topical Bible and Dictionary" (KJB edition) immediately following the biblical text. Then, rather than simply sprinkling the margins with cross-references, Thompson lists the specific topics in each verse with their index number and often identifies the next biblical reference in the chain. By turning to the numbered topic in the back or following the references through the text, a person is led in a well-organized thematic study. This Bible contains more than 50 additional features in its 8 "departments," including introductions and outlines of each book, character studies, dozens of historical and topical charts and diagrams, an archaeological dictionary, and a concordance (a list of the main words of the Bible and some key references plus a phrase from the particular verse), all of which are keyed by number to the text and index. Because of its valuable cross-reference system and its availability in four of the top five translations, the *Thompson Chain-Reference Bible* remains a popular study Bible choice.

During the last 10 to 15 years, many other study Bibles have become available. Here are some of the features you want to consider when choosing a study Bible that's right for you:

- **Translation.** Many modern translations, such as the New International Version (NIV), the New Living Translation (NLT), or the New King James Version (NKJV), fall into this category. You want to consider the accuracy of the translation, the readability of the translation, and the number of reference books that support this particular translation. The NIV has the greatest number of reference books that support the translation.
- **Introductions and outlines.** These pages usually provide the reader detailed information about the author of the book, the audience or readers of the book, the date it was written, original use of the book, and a summary of the contents of the book and overall outline. These introductions and outlines differ in length and thoroughness in each study Bible, and they also differ in theological perspective. Some might be more conservative or nonconservative.

- **Cross-references.** One of the most useful features in a study Bible for analyzing the biblical text is a cross-reference system, which appears in a column beside the text or between two columns of text. Often a verse in the Bible will be similar or connected to a different verse in the Bible (either in the same book or a different book) and these verses are called cross-references.

- **Notes.** Many times the notes simply add explanation regarding meaningful words or obscure definitions in the text, explanations of customs, historical background, and similar information. Like the introductions, these notes often betray an alignment with a particular theological or critical approach to the text.

Proceed with Caution

Don't buy a study Bible with type you can't read! When you choose a study Bible, scan a few pages to evaluate how readable the text is for you. A growing number of study Bibles are available in large-print formats. Consider also whether the extra features interfere with readability. Study notes, cross-references, and testimonials can actually make the Bible less readable if they are poorly integrated into the text. Make sure the format is not overly distracting.

- **Concordance and index.** Just as the cross-reference system connects key words, phrases, and concepts through the biblical text, the concordance or index lists such connections in a separate section. The index is sometimes called a "Topical Index" or a "Subject Index" and will list the term and various Bible references. A concordance deals with specific words and, in addition to the Bible reference, will include a phrase with the context of the particular word.

- **Dictionary.** A Bible dictionary defines key technical words found in the text. While most of the information is drawn from the biblical text, information from historical, archaeological, and other biblical reference works often supplements the definition.

- **Maps.** Almost every Bible has a set of maps in the back. Many Bibles include an index of the maps so the reader can easily locate countries, cities, and natural landmarks.

- **Charts.** These visual elements gather and display biblical and historical data in a clear form. Some study Bibles spread these charts throughout the text, while others gather them in a section in the back of the Bible.

Teaching Tips

People who considered Christ's words to be more inspired originally developed the practice of putting his words in red. While we know that "all Scripture is God-breathed" (2 Timothy 3:16), highlighting Christ's words in red can help pinpoint the flow of the Gospel passages at a glance.

- **Special essays and articles.** Most study Bibles have special articles on subjects such as the history of Bible translation, theological themes, how to understand the Bible, and outlines of biblical history and archeology. Look at the articles in the table of contents when evaluating a study Bible.

Understanding Bible Translations

During the past 70 years, many new translations of the Bible have appeared in contemporary English. Although weaknesses exist in every translation, each one makes a unique contribution to a better understanding of the Bible. Many people have tried the King James Version and were put off by the archaic language and the difficulty of understanding the Bible. Now many of those people have returned to the Bible and have begun to read and study it because the more recent translations have made it so much more accessible and easy to read and understand. Often you can derive great benefit from simply comparing various versions to discern the many possible meanings and usages of a word. Here are some of the most popular and reliable modern translations:

- **The New International Version** (NIV) (Zondervan). This translation has gained wide acceptance in the last 25 years.
- **The New Living Translation** (NLT) (Tyndale). First introduced in 1996, this translation is growing in popularity and has replaced the Living Bible, which was a popular and widely used paraphrase of the Bible and introduced by Dr. Kenneth N. Taylor in 1971.
- **The New American Standard Bible** (NASB) (Moody). This translation is recognized as one of the most accurate that is faithful to the original languages.
- **The New King James Version** (NKJV) (Nelson). Introduced in 1982, the NKJV retains the elegant style of the King James Version but is easier to read.
- **The Contemporary English Version** (CEV) (Zondervan). This Bible, first published in 1995, has the pope's imprimatur. In general, it uses natural and uncomplicated English.
- **The Message** (TM) (NavPress). The full Bible was released in 2002 and is a highly colloquial and interpretive translation/paraphrase by Eugene H. Peterson that is growing in popularity. As this version was being translated, the New Testament was introduced in 1993, then other books were added as they were translated such as the prophets or the wisdom books. Now the entire Bible is available in this version.

An Exhaustive Concordance

One of the most important tools for studying the Bible is a concordance, which is an index of words contained in the entire Bible, both King James and New International. Many Bibles have a limited concordance in the back that lists only a few of the major words and names. An exhaustive concordance lists every usage of every word in the Bible and provides page numbers where that word may be found.

Just in Case

The two most commonly used exhaustive concordances are *Strong's Exhaustive Concordance* (many publishers) and *Young's Analytical Concordance* (many publishers). Both are keyed to the King James Version of the Bible. For the New International Version, you can get *The NIV Exhaustive Concordance* (Zondervan). A complete concordance, as opposed to an exhaustive one, lists every reference to most words (omitting words like *the*). An abridged concordance lists many, but not all, references to a given word.

A Bible Dictionary and/or Encyclopedia

A Bible dictionary explains many of the words, topics, customs, and traditions in the Bible, and also gives historical, geographical, cultural, and archaeological information. Background material is also given for each book of the Bible, and short biographies are presented for the major people of both testaments. A Bible encyclopedia is an expanded Bible dictionary with longer articles that explain more subjects in greater detail.

A Topical Bible

This reference tool is similar to a concordance, except that it categorizes the verses of the Bible by topic instead of by word. This tool is helpful for the Bible student because a verse often deals with a topic without ever using the specific word. If you had to rely on your concordance alone, you might miss an important verse relating to a particular topic. For example, if you were to look up the subject "Trinity" in Nave's Topical Bible, you would find 83 references listed, even though the actual word *Trinity* never appears in the Bible.

Another helpful feature of a topical Bible is that the verses under each topic are written out in full, which allows you to scan the key verses on a topic quickly without having to look up each one in your Bible. Please note that a topical Bible is not exhaustive and does not list every verse related to a particular topic. The standard topical Bible is *Nave's Topical Bible* (available in KJV and NIV). Billy Graham has said that, apart from his Bible, this book is the one he uses more than any other.

A Bible Handbook

A Bible handbook is part encyclopedia and part commentary in concise form. You can use it for quick reference while reading through a particular book of the Bible. Instead of being arranged by topic alphabetically, handbooks are designed to follow the order of the books of the Bible. This resource offers background notes, a brief running commentary, maps, charts, archaeological notes, and many other helpful elements.

There are several excellent choices when it comes to Bible handbooks, including *Zondervan Handbook to the Bible*, edited by David and Pat Alexander (Zondervan), and *Halley's Bible Handbook with the New International Version*, by Henry H. Halley (Zondervan).

A Set of Word Studies

Word studies allow today's Christians to benefit from the work of Bible scholars. They allow you to study the original words of the Bible without knowing any Hebrew or Greek. Some people have spent their lives searching out the full meanings of the original words and then writing about them in simple, comprehensible language.

From a good set of word studies, you will learn the following information: the original root meaning of the Greek or Hebrew word, the various uses of the word throughout the Bible and in similar nonbiblical literature of that historical period, and how often the word occurs in the Bible.

Word studies reference tools range from inexpensive one-volume dictionaries to very expensive 12-volume sets. Here are several recommended books:

- *Word Study: New Testament and Concordance* (two-volume set), edited by Ralph Winter (Tyndale)
- *Vine's Expository Dictionary of Old and New Testament Words Super Value Edition*, by W. E. Vine (Nelson)
- *Word Studies in the Greek New Testament* (4-volume set), by Kenneth S. Wuest (Word Publishing)
- *New Wilson's Old Testament Word Studies: Keyed to Strong's Exhaustive Concordance, Keyed to the Theological Wordbook of the Old Testament*, by William Wilson (Kregel)

Commentaries

A commentary is a scholarly collection of explanatory notes and interpretations on the text of a particular Bible book or section of the Bible. Its purpose is to interpret and explain the meaning of the biblical message by analyzing the grammar and syntax of the words used and the historical background of the book. Each book includes an introduction to introduce the book and the relation of that particular book to the rest of the Bible.

Used properly, commentaries can greatly increase your understanding of the Bible. However, you generally should not refer to a commentary until after you have done your own study.

Because commentaries are written by human beings, they are flawed. Sometimes equally able commentators disagree on interpretations of the same biblical text. Therefore, don't rely on them to provide you with perfect answers; instead, compare their observations and comments with your own. Beware of buying and using commentaries written by people who do not believe or regard the Bible as the Word of God. Often this type of information on the author's perspective is contained in the introduction of the book.

> **Proceed with Caution**
>
> Commentaries can be extremely valuable if you resist the temptation to let them do your study for you and if you select them wisely. A commentary is only as good as its author is wise and learned. *How to Read the Bible for All Its Worth*, by Gordon D. Fee and Douglas Stuart (Zondervan), includes an excellent chapter on how to select a good commentary. They suggest reliable commentaries for each book of the Bible.

Creating a Reference Library

When someone begins personal Bible study, they need only a few basic tools to get started, including the following:

- A study Bible
- Two recent Bible translations
- An exhaustive concordance
- A Bible dictionary

- A topical Bible
- A Bible handbook
- A one-volume commentary

When you and the other members of your study group grow more confident and proficient in your personal Bible study and feel comfortable using the reference tools in the basic library, you might want to begin to add advanced tools. In addition to the previous seven tools, the following are recommended:

- Additional versions of the Bible and paraphrases
- A Bible encyclopedia
- A set of word studies
- Individual commentaries on books of the Bible
- A Bible atlas
- Old and New Testament surveys
- Other Bible reference books listed in other places in this book

Right now, you're probably thinking, "That's a lot of books!" You are absolutely right. But consider these books to be a long-term investment in your spiritual life. You probably read most books you buy just once, but you'll use these reference books over and over again as you study the Bible. If you're serious about Bible study, then you'll want to acquire these tools regardless of their cost.

Of course, you can save some money by borrowing at least some of them from the library until you can afford your own copies. If you buy just one reference book a month, you'll have a respectable and valuable collection of reference tools within a year. You might also consider asking for these books as Christmas or birthday gifts. A book that you use is a gift that lasts a lifetime.

Finally, encourage your church to set up a section of Bible study reference tools in its library. The church could purchase one or more of the more expensive tools, such as the encyclopedias, word studies, and commentary sets, in order to make them available to the membership. Because the Bible is God's Word, Bible study must be a top priority. With these tools, you will be able to effectively study the Scriptures, which is an all-important endeavor that will change your life.

The Least You Need to Know

- The Bible is the most important book in any home. There is no "best" translation, but different types of translations meet different needs.
- Many excellent reference tools to help in Bible study are available to help you to teach and help the members of your group grow in their faith.
- A basic library includes a study Bible, two recent Bible translations, an exhaustive concordance, a Bible dictionary, a topical Bible, a Bible handbook, and a one-volume commentary.

Chapter 2

The Benefits of Teaching

In This Chapter

- Inspire learning, facilitate feedback, and motivate members with your teaching
- Accept the existence of different views on the same Bible stories
- Find the truth about the Bible from history and from the Bible itself
- Bible organization basics

Whether you've chosen to teach the Bible or a church leader suddenly has volunteered you for the task, there are wonderful benefits from teaching the Bible to others. Also, as a teacher or individual, it's important to understand why there are different perspectives on the information in the Bible and the role of archaeology to validate this information. This chapter concisely provides this information so you will be prepared to shine in these Bible discussions.

Finding God's Timeless Truth

Bible teaching takes place in a variety of contexts. Do you teach adults or teens? Possibly you huddle near your cozy fireplace with a small, fellowship-oriented group, or maybe you gather 25 or 30 people in a church classroom. Or maybe you want to teach an evangelistic Bible study at your office during the lunch break, or perhaps you could lead an intense Bible study with mature Christians.

Whether your setting is a church facility, a house, an office, or a classroom, and whether your learning environment is tightly regulated or informal, what takes place during a teaching session is largely a discussion that you lead. As applied to Bible teaching, discussion is a cooperative search for God's timeless truth and the bearing it has on our lives. All Bible discussion should be done in prayerful reliance on the Holy Spirit to illuminate God's Word and to guide the interaction among members of the group.

Beyond these elements, a successful Bible discussion has at least six components:

- A teacher or facilitator who originates and directs the conversation
- One or more questions to inspire thought in the participants
- A meaningful, specific goal for verbal interaction
- Two or more interested participants
- An authoritative source of truth (the Bible)
- A supportive learning environment

Teaching Tips

Involve your group members rather than simply informing them. If you wanted the group to feel the exhilaration of, say, climbing a mountain, would it be better to simply say "The results are worth the climb" or to take them with you on the climb in the first place? Which experience would make a greater mark and would impact life more deeply? Which would motivate them to climb the mountain again? It's the same with Bible study: The more the individuals do for themselves, the more meaningful their learning becomes.

Potent Quotables

"So make every effort to apply the benefits of these promises to your life. Then your faith will produce a life of moral excellence. A life of moral excellence leads to knowing God better." (2 Peter 1:5, NLT)

Any Bible teacher can increase his or her effectiveness by simply learning to ask the right questions of the group members and thus instigate a relevant discussion. Here are some of the benefits members derive from such a discussion:

- **Discussion motivates.** Teachers who weave questions into the fabric of their Bible studies provide incentives for learning. The opportunity to participate in the learning process helps to enhance students' motivation. Teens and adults who investigate and report on the Bible feel valued. One high school student was happy to conclude "What I think matters." Students of all ages appreciate hearing what others think.

Teaching Tips

According to the authors of *The Act of Teaching,* discussion meets several inherent needs of learners:

- The need to seek diversion and change
- The need to give others information
- The need to attract a certain amount of attention to oneself
- The need to receive feedback in the form of praise and commendation
- The need to form associations and friendships

Possibly you aren't comfortable meeting all of these needs in the Bible study setting. That's okay, but don't ignore the pluses of varying your methods and giving learners a moment in the spotlight.

- **Discussion facilitates feedback.** Show me a group or class in which verbal interaction thrives, and I'll show you a leader who's receiving helpful information from and about his learners. Discussion methods allow teachers to become students of their learners. When the participants in your Bible study group answer your questions or ask their own questions, you'll find out how well they are grasping the concepts set forth. By their questions and answers, you can determine whether they are digesting the material or whether you should proceed at a slower pace. You discover the level of their Bible study skills. And you may be able to detect attitudes or emotional baggage that can affect their receptivity to the Scriptures. If, as a Bible teacher, you aren't interested in feedback, the learners will know it. A teacher appears insensitive to people's needs when he or she relies excessively on lecture. As one college student reported, "When teachers lecture the whole time, it shows they aren't concerned about how I'm understanding the material."
- **Listening rather than lecturing aids the discussion.** The person who talks is the person who learns. When you ask questions and make assignments, let the individuals talk more than you do. Let them show and tell you the Bible truths they discover, rather than you showing and telling them. They'll find it easy to let lectures go in one ear and out the other, but they'll remember what they themselves say. Then they live what they commit to.

Proceed with Caution

Direct rather than dictate. Your group members may ask some hard questions, such as "Is watching this television program good for me?" "What is sin?" "How can I know the will of God?" Rather than tell your group members what to do, guide them to Bible verses that address their questions. As the individuals make their own choices, they gain confidence in their ability to read and understand the Bible for themselves. And they grow close to God, who authored the Bible.

- **Discussion fosters fellowship.** When the members of your group talk together, it not only acquaints you with your group, but it also helps the members get to know each other better. By responding to questions, people reveal their beliefs, attitudes, and personal experiences. Participants may then be able to identify with each other's comments and sympathize with personal needs. Whether verbal exchanges occur on an intellectual or emotional level, discussion requires self-revelation. And self-revelation is a catalyst for creating community.

- **Discussion elicits encouragement.** John and Carol led eight couples through a "Parenting from Proverbs" course. During a session on disciplining children, Bill constantly furrowed his brow and fidgeted in his seat. Clearly something was bothering him. When John asked for examples of how to correct a child, Bill vented his emotions. Earlier that day, he had jumped to conclusions and spanked his seven-year-old son. Later, Bill discovered that a sibling had committed the offense. Bill told his son to forgive him, and knelt by the boy's bed to seek the Lord's forgiveness. "The incident demoralized me," Bill admitted, "I'm still feeling bad about it. I wonder if I bruised my son's spirit or drove a permanent wedge between us. You know, you hear about how kids remember something like that the rest of their lives." After a half-minute of silence, Sam, an older man with three children, spoke up: "Bill, I commend you for serving as a positive model to your son. I don't think he'll remember the unjust spanking. But he'll never forget his dad's tearful apology. And the sight of you kneeling by his bed, seeking God's forgiveness, is burned into his memory forever. You modeled how to handle sin. I'd be worried only if you had been too proud to admit you blew it." That fresh perspective buoyed Bill's spirit and enabled him to forgive himself. Sam's remarks reminded Bill that God wants moms and dads to model Christian living, not perfection. Ask good questions, and you will enhance mutual concern and encouragement.

Give the group variety rather than the same entrée. People of various ages like to learn in different ways. As the individuals in your group express Bible truths in ways that are comfortable to them, learning takes on special meaning. This doesn't mean that singers must always sing to learn, but it means your class sings for the singers some of the time. Then you doodle for the doodlers the next week, dramatize Scripture for the actors, and discuss for the talkers. You choose methods for which each member has to respond, even if it's not their favorite way. Rather than fret over who learns which way, relax with the truth that everyone learns best when you vary your methods—just like Jesus did.

- **Discussion increases insight.** Those who participate in a discussion learn from one another, not just from the designated leader. It's the two-heads-are-better-than-one principle applied to exploring the Scriptures. Imagine a teacher-centered context in which the leader holds impressive credentials and prepares extensively. Even in this setting, when the teacher poses a question, somebody much lower on the knowledge totem pole may offer a valid, fresh insight on the Bible text. And the teacher may even learn something! Effective discussions allow teachers to become learners, and learners to become teachers. There is one qualification with this key point. The extent of this benefit often depends on the maturity level or spiritual background of group members. In general, the longer people have been Christians, the longer they have been under the influence of solid Bible teaching, and the more valuable their contributions are during a Bible study. You can use discussion principles successfully even with the unchurched in an evangelistic study. But what any participant gleans from the text will be in direct proportion to the illumination provided by the Holy Spirit. That's why the quality of discoveries increases dramatically in a group of maturing Christians.
- **Discussion increases retention.** The right questions serve as a mental crowbar, prying open the Bible passage for the participants. Group members stitch together noteworthy facts, arrive at timeless conclusions, and then articulate the truths they discover. This process requires brain activity that tucks the content deeper into their minds. Imagine that you've just seen or heard some vital information. To rephrase that information in your own words demands thinking. Research suggests that you'll more readily remember the thought you formulated than the information that prompted it. To tell the truth is a lofty calling. And so is discussion leadership that guides the participants into God's truth and then helps them remember it.

Potent Quotables

"People can get many good things by the words they say; the work of their hands also gives them many benefits." (Proverbs 12:14, NLT)

- **Discussion strengthens study skills.** Individuals who stick with a discussion-oriented group for at least a few months will begin to polish their Bible study skills. Week after week, they hear questions that lead them to the Bible for answers. Gradually, they learn how to think about a Scripture passage. Imagine that you're leading a group through Philippians. You start each session with a few probes to help people discover important facts in the text. Only then do you ask them to analyze the data for meaning. Without devoting a session to Bible study methods, you are helping people learn to base interpretations on facts. If you reserve time each week to discuss the practical implications of truths you uncover, you'll increase the likelihood that people will mull over applications when they read the Bible on their own. Teaching is one thing. Teaching people how to learn is another. A stimulating Bible discussion educates by its process as well as by its content.

As you teach, find creative ways to read the Bible passage. Begin by giving the members of your class a reason to read the Bible passage. Perhaps you'll challenge them to find the answer to a question or the names of certain people. Maybe they'll act out the passage, using the Bible as their script. Or maybe they'll play a learning game that requires them to read the Bible to find the answers. In any case, work to motivate your group members to open their Bibles.

The Bible from Many Angles

If you consider the Bible across history and time, it's clear that coming to an agreement on one view of the Bible is a difficult task. If there were only one way to interpret it, we would have only a handful of Jewish and Christian denominations instead of the hundreds that currently exist. The Catholics would never have split from the Orthodox. The Protestants would never have split from the Catholics. The Baptists, Episcopalians, and African Methodist Church members would all be worshipping side by side. All of these groups seem to agree that the Bible provides God's truth for our lives, but how to interpret that truth is another question.

Which interpretation holds the "correct" answer? Perhaps each one is right. An old legend tells about five blind men who examined an elephant, and each was convinced that his perception was the correct one. One man compared the elephant to a tree (feeling the leg), another to a rope (feeling the tail), another to a fan (feeling the ear), another to a hose (feeling the trunk), and another to a wall (feeling the side). Each man was absolutely correct to the extent of his knowledge. The problem was that not a single man saw the elephant in entirety, and instead they preferred to argue about the little they did know.

People approach the Bible from different points of view and arrive at a number of various beliefs and interpretations. In most cases, the differences are not huge, yet they tend to be significant enough to divide rather than unite. I understand that for every opinion I express, there are likely to be hordes of dissenting opinions. My challenge is to help you interact with the whole animal, or the entire Bible, rather than one particular interpretation.

In *Archaeology and the Old Testament*, Alfred J. Hoerth wrote:

> Ideally, one is never content with one's present level of Bible knowledge. Thoughtful study of the biblical text often engenders questions concerning cultural attitudes and historical actions. Archaeology can provide some answers. Further, a more accurate understanding of history and culture allows deeper insight into theological issues. For instance, now that the Canaanite religion is more fully known, one can better appreciate why it was so fiercely condemned in Scripture, and the consequences of a faith in violent opposition to the biblical teaching become more obvious.

The Historical Truth

It's been said that God kept two copies of the historic records of his special dealings with man and his revelation to man. One record was the Bible, which had been written on parchment, and through great effort God placed it in the hands of man. The other record was written among the ruins and in strange languages of the lands from which the Bible came. For many years, man had access to the first record and could read and live his life according to the Bible. There were few records from the ruins. This situation has changed over the last 200 years through some significant discoveries, such as the Rosetta Stone found by Napoleon's engineers at Rosetta, Egypt. Many people tried to read this stone, which was written in two different languages, but it wasn't until 1822, after the young Frenchman Jean Campollion had dedicated 23 years of his life to deciphering the mysterious stone, that a complete translation was published. As interest grew in archeological discoveries, governments, universities, museums, and influential individuals began to finance expeditions. This work helped to connect the ruins of ancient civilizations with the stories in the Bible. Today an army of learned scholars has picked up the threads of ancient life from thousands of city mounds and woven them into a pattern that corresponds almost exactly to the recorded lives and deeds of Bible characters. Thousands of these "outside" evidences have come to light and corroborate Scripture narratives.

Teaching Tips

As you teach, make sure the individuals in your class apply the facts to their everyday lives. Bible knowledge means little if it never transforms lives.

The Bible's Own Validation

The Bible is a collection of 66 "books" written over a period of more than 1,500 years. In a typical printed Bible, the longest book (Psalms) takes up more than 100 pages, and the shortest book (2 John) less than a page. More than 40 different people wrote the various books of the Bible. Some of them were rich; some were poor. Among them were kings, poets, prophets, musicians, philosophers, farmers, teachers, a priest, a statesman, a shepherd, a tax collector, a physician, and a couple of fishermen. They wrote in palaces and in prisons, in great cities and in the wilderness, in times of terrible war and in times of peace and prosperity. They wrote stories, poems, histories, letters, proverbs, and prophecies.

The Bible is not a textbook or a book of abstract theology meant to be analyzed, discussed, and understood only by highly educated theologians and experts. It is a book about real people and about the God who is real. The Bible is the inspired Word of God. Theologians and scholars have argued endlessly over how a book written by so many authors over so many centuries can possibly be inspired by God. But it is like sitting down at dinner and arguing about the recipe instead of tasting the food, enjoying it, and being nourished by it.

Teaching Tips

Are there many Old Testament manuscripts? Fragments of Hebrew Scriptures number in the tens of thousands, the majority dating between the third century B.C. and the fourteenth century A.D. The greatest validation of the Hebrew Old Testament is the manuscripts found in the Dead Sea Scrolls, which mostly date from the third century B.C. to the first century A.D.

As "the proof of the pudding is in the eating," so is the proof of the Bible in the reading—as long as you do so with an open mind and an open heart. Such a reading will reveal that the Bible is a divinely inspired, interwoven message from God (compare John 7:17).

Because it was written so long ago, some things in it we who live in the twenty-first century may find difficult to understand. But our hearts and spirits can grasp what God's heart and his Spirit tell us: that we are beloved by him now and forever. Through the consistent themes and message of the Bible, it validates its own authority.

Two Testaments

If you are new to the Bible, here are some Bible basics. At first glance, the Bible appears to be an assortment of shorter and longer "articles," without any apparent organization except for the main division of two parts—the Old Testament and the

New Testament. The Old Testament takes up about three fourths of the Bible, and the New Testament comprises about one fourth. The book of Psalms is approximately in the middle of the Bible.

The Old Testament was written before the time of Christ in Hebrew, the language of the Jewish people, and it continues to be the Bible for the Jewish people. In the very early days of the church, during the first decades after Jesus' death and resurrection, the Hebrew Bible was the only Bible Christians had available. Only later, when the New Testament came into existence, did people begin to call the Hebrew Bible the "Old Testament." The word *testament* means "covenant," which is a solemn agreement or contract that establishes a formal relationship with mutual obligations. The Hebrew Bible speaks of the covenant God made with Abraham, the patriarch of the Jewish people. The New Testament is about the covenant that God made with all people through Jesus Christ.

The Old Testament looks forward to the coming of Jesus, the Messiah (or Christ). The New Testament tells the story of Jesus and contains the writings of his early followers.

Each testament contains three groups of books. The Old Testament contains historical books, poetic books, and prophetic books. The New Testament contains historical books; letters, or epistles; and one prophetic book (Revelation). Let's examine some further details about each testament.

Potent Quotables

"A wise teacher's words spur students to action and emphasize important truths. The collected sayings of the wise are like guidance from a shepherd." (Ecclesiastes 12:11, NLT)

The Books of the Old Testament

The Old Testament contains 17 historical books, arranged in chronological order. The Jewish people call the first five historical books the Torah (Hebrew for "law") because these books contain the laws God gave to Moses. These five books are also called the Pentateuch (Greek for "five books").

Between the historical books and the prophetic books of the Old Testament are five poetic books. These books contain some of the most beautiful poetry ever written, especially that of the Book of Psalms, which expresses the full range of human emotions, from depression to jubilant trust in God. The Book of Psalms has been a source of comfort and inspiration to Jews and Christians for three millennia.

The Old Testament contains 17 prophetic books. The first 5 of these books are called the Major Prophets because they are much longer than the other 12, which are called the Minor Prophets. Lamentations is a short book, which is included with the Major Prophets because Jeremiah (a major prophet) wrote it.

The four Gospels of the Old Testament represent a different kind of literature than other ancient and modern writings. They are not biographies of Christ, seeking to develop a full understanding of Jesus' life, his friendships, his family, or his mental and psychological dimensions. Nor do they recount heroic deeds or collections of Jesus' famous sayings (although some of these kinds of materials are found in the Gospel accounts). Instead, the four Gospels appear to be a new genre for which other categories are inadequate. These books record the life, works, and words of Jesus as they relate to the redemptive work of God in Jesus Christ. They are the good news from God that is manifest in the life, ministry, death, burial, resurrection, and ascension of Christ.

The New Testament Books

Four hundred years—known as the "silent years"—passed between the time of the Old Testament and the beginning of the New Testament. The New Testament contains five historical books: the four Gospels, which describe the life of Christ, and the Book of Acts, which tells the story of the early church, mostly through the work of the apostle Paul.

The New Testament also contains 21 letters, or epistles. The apostle Paul wrote the first 13 of these epistles, and they are arranged by length from the longest (Romans) to the shortest (Philemon). Other epistles were written by the apostle John (three letters), Peter (two letters), and James and Jude (one letter each); scholars disagree who wrote the letter to the Hebrews. All of these letters were written during the early decades of the church.

The New Testament has only one prophetic book: Revelation. The Greek word for *revelation* is *apokalupsis*, meaning an unveiling or uncovering. For this reason, the book of Revelation is also called the Apocalypse.

Scholars and religious leaders have worked with the Bible text for many years with volumes of books on this background information. This chapter has covered the basics and with these key elements in mind, you along with the members of your Bible study group will be ready to use one of the various methods of study covered in later chapters.

The Least You Need to Know

- Teaching the Bible and the discussion that results from asking good questions have incredible benefits for everyday life.
- Seven key benefits evolve from effective Bible discussion.
- While there are many different views and perspectives on the Bible, the key is to interact with the Bible itself rather than someone else's interpretation of the Bible.
- The Bible is organized into two testaments (Old Testament and New Testament). Within each Testament, the 66 books of the Bible are organized and grouped into understandable units.

Chapter 3

General Principles for Teaching the Bible

In This Chapter

- Learn to ask the right questions
- Personally prepare to teach the Bible
- Understand the ultimate goal: application, not interpretation
- Discover the value of systematic teaching
- Use the Jesus principles of teaching
- The four principles for teaching truth

Whether someone else has "volunteered" you to teach at the last minute or you've been planning to teach for a long time, the following pages will lay out the tools you need for effective teaching.

The Right Questions

When teaching the Bible, the ultimate goal is for the participants to grow in their understanding of the Scriptures and ultimately to improve or change their lives. As any skilled journalist will tell you, the combination of listening and then asking key questions at the right time will reveal critical information and garner insight for the group.

The ability to ask the right questions is a skill you can develop. This book contains a variety of teaching methods, and one of the key differences between each method is the type of questions the teacher asks. As you grow in your proficiency in Bible study, you will develop the art of asking questions. The more questions you ask about the particular text your group is studying, the more you and your group will get out of it. You will realize that you can ask an unlimited number of questions about a particular Bible text. As you ask these questions and respond to the answers from your group, you will begin to develop a more inquisitive mind and gain many insights into the text that you missed in the past. It will be like you've been given a new pair of eyes. Suddenly new truths from the Bible will leap out of the text.

Potent Quotables

Someone came to Jesus with this question: "Teacher, what good things must I do to have eternal life?"

"Why ask me about what is good?" Jesus replied. "Only God is good. But to answer your question, you can receive eternal life if you keep the commandments."

"Which ones?" the man asked.

And Jesus replied: "Do not murder. Do not commit adultery. Do not steal. Do not testify falsely. Honor your father and mother. Love your neighbor as yourself." (Matthew 19:16–19, NLT)

As you ask good questions, your group will be able to make personal application to their lives from the Bible. There are two essential steps in this process: observation and application.

Observation

Observation is defined as the act of seeing and, by doing so, increasing your awareness so that you notice things as they really are. Observation requires two key attitudes: a willing spirit and an open mind.

It's necessary to have a willing spirit because if someone is protecting or holding back an area of his or her life, that person is hindering his or her understanding and growth. For example, the woman who refuses to admit vanity in her life will probably not see the passages in the Bible that condemn vanity. Similarly, a husband who is firmly convinced that his marriage doesn't need to change will not even see his responsibilities as the husband in the relationship. Are you or anyone in your group approaching teaching from the Bible with a preconceived notion? Some people say, "Don't confuse me with Bible facts because my mind is made up!" For effective Bible teaching and study, all participants must have open minds.

In order to make accurate observations, you and the others in the group must read the Bible with inquisitiveness, thoughtfulness, diligence, and purpose. As you read through a particular passage, make sure you keep an open mind and heart so you'll hear the message the Scriptures offer.

Teaching Tips

Sir Arthur Conan Doyle created Sherlock Holmes with an eagle eye and keen observation skills. One day a stranger visited Holmes's office and the detective looked at his visitor for several seconds. Then he spoke to his associate, Watson, "Beyond the obvious facts that this gentleman has at some time done manual labor, that he dips snuff, that he is a Freemason, that he has spent time in China, and that he has done a considerable amount of writing lately, I can deduce nothing else."

Watson was amazed that Holmes knew so much about the visitor after such a cursory glance and wondered why he himself hadn't noticed the same things. "I believe my eyes are as good as yours," he said.

"Quite so," replied the famous detective. Then he pinpointed the difference: "You see, but you do not observe." The ability to observe, not merely see, is as important to Bible teachers as it is to crime investigators.

Asking, and then attempting to answer, these important questions will help you make accurate observations.

- **Who?** Who are the people involved?
- **What?** What are the results? What ideas are expressed? What happened?
- **Where?** Where does this particular story or event take place? What is the setting?
- **When?** When did it take place? What is the stated reason?
- **Why?** Why did it happen? What is the purpose? What is the stated reason?
- **How?** How are things accomplished? How effectively? By what method?

Applying God's Word

As you put God's word into practice in your life—a process called *application*—then you begin to recognize the Bible as God's personal message to you and the others in your group. The psalmist wrote, "When I took a long, careful look at your ways, I got my feet back on the trail you blazed. I was up at once, didn't drag my feet, was quick to follow your orders." (Psalm 119:59–60, The Message)

While this book offers effective methods for teaching the Bible, the key benefit from reading the text of the Bible derives not from using a particular method or technique, but instead from taking what you learn and putting it into practice in your everyday life.

> **Teaching Tips**
>
> **Application** is the joint effort of identifying lifestyle changes and attitude that spring logically from Bible truths. Together you ponder how God's truth should affect participants' relationships, decisions, emotions, and priorities. Probes that prompt participants to link a lesson to life are application questions.

The following five questions will help your group apply the Scriptures to everyday life. You can remember them by using the acronym SPECK:

S	Is there a *sin* for you to avoid?
P	Is there a *promise* from God for you to claim?
E	Is there an *example* for you to follow?
C	Is there a *command* for you to obey?
K	How can this passage increase your *knowledge* about God and Jesus Christ?

Now that you've learned the importance of observation and application, it's time to prepare to teach the Bible to a group of students. You usually can't rush into teaching the Bible. Effective teaching demands some preparation. There are four important aspects to consider for effective preparation: scheduling time to study, remembering the ultimate goal of application, discovering the three essential attitudes, and using Jesus' principles of teaching. Let's take them one by one.

Making Time to Study

It's difficult to teach the Bible without making and keeping a commitment to study yourself, independent from teaching. Set aside a specific amount of time each week. If you don't schedule regular Bible study time in your weekly schedule, either you'll never make time for it or it will be shallow and sporadic. How much time do you spend studying the Bible? The answer will be different for every person, but first you must distinguish between studying your Bible and taking personal quiet time. Many people take time each day for personal time with God. Often this quiet time includes a short devotional period (from 10 to 30 minutes) during which you read the Bible, then spend a few minutes meditating or thinking about what you've read, and then praying. The purpose of your quiet time is to draw close to Christ.

During your quiet time, don't try to perform any in-depth Bible study. Nothing will squelch your quiet time faster than attempting serious Bible study during a devotional period. Use your quiet time to enjoy God.

When it comes to Bible study, however, you're going to need a bigger block of time, about two to four hours once or twice a week. That's better than trying to study a little bit each day.

Teaching Tips

When it comes to taking quiet time with God, it's better for you to do so for a short time—say, 10 minutes each day—than for a longer time only once a week.

Proceed with Caution

Turn off the television! According to the A. C. Nielsen Co. (1998), the average American watches 3 hours and 46 minutes of TV each day (more than 52 days of nonstop TV watching per year). By the age of 65, the average American will have spent nearly 9 years glued to the television. Think of how much you could learn from the Bible if you turned off the set for even a few of those hours every week.

It's also important to try to schedule your Bible study for times when you're at your best intellectually, physically, and emotionally. Also pick a time when you can be unhurried and undistracted. Are you a "day person" or a "night person"? Pick the time when you are the most alert. Always attempt to study when you are wide awake and rested, or when you are exhausted. Your personal time of study can be a rich and fulfilling experience that you can then pass along to the members of your group when you teach them the Bible.

Apply, Don't Just Interpret

Gaining an understanding of a particular Bible passage or the meaning of a passage isn't the key reason you study the Bible. The critical point of Bible study is to apply biblical principles to everyday life. The great evangelist Dwight L. Moody used to say, "The Bible was not given to increase our knowledge, but to change our lives." The Scriptures are here to change our character and bring our lives into greater conformity with Jesus Christ. If we don't change and improve as people, all of our effort in Bible study and teaching are worthless. Like James 1:22 says, "Do not merely listen to the word and so deceive yourselves. Do what it says." (NIV)

Indeed, it's possible to know the Word of God intellectually but not to know the God of the Word. One day, a congregant asked a well-known pastor what the best translation of the Bible was. The pastor answered, "The best translation is when you translate the Word of God into your daily life." The person didn't understand the pastor's response. He responded, "But I've got my *Living Bible.*" The pastor replied, "You ought to be living the Bible! The Word made flesh ought to be visible in your life."

As you study and teach the Bible, here are some questions you should ask yourself:

- What attitude do I need to change as a result of this study?
- What does this study tell me that I should stop or start doing in my life?
- What things do I need to stop believing or start to believe?
- Which relationships do I need to work on?
- Is there a ministry I should be having with others? If so, how can I begin it?

> **Potent Quotables**
>
> "Concentrate on doing your best for God, work you won't be ashamed of, laying out the truth plain and simple. Stay clear of pious talk that is only talk. Words are not mere words, you know. If they're not backed by a godly life, they accumulate as poison in the soul." (2 Timothy 2:15–16, The Message)

In every Bible study or time of teaching in the Scriptures, our goal is to get to know Jesus Christ and become more like him in our values, our actions, our speech, our thoughts, and our attitudes.

Another caution as you study the Bible: Don't go into the study session with the attitude of finding some truth that no one else has ever seen. And don't study to find something with which to impress others. Instead study the Bible to find out what it has to say to you. The key difficulty for most of us is not understanding difficult passages, but obeying the Scriptures we do understand.

The Three Essential Attitudes

As you read the Bible, either to teach others or to motivate your own personal spiritual growth, it's important to recognize that you need several intangible elements for your heart and spirit. Isaiah 66:2 captures these essentials: "I will bless those who have humble and contrite hearts, who tremble at my word." (NLT) Unless we approach our teaching and time in the Bible with humility, a contrite heart, and trembling at a Holy God, we will only reach the edges of God's truth and will never penetrate the heart of God's riches.

Start with a Humble Attitude

Humility is essential if you want to gain a proper understanding of who God is and who you are in your relationship to him. The Lord is looking for a particular attitude in our hearts as we study and teach the Scriptures, because the Scriptures represent his Word to mankind. In Isaiah 6, the prophet saw God:

> In the year King Uzziah died, I saw the Lord. He was sitting on a lofty throne, and the train of his robe filled the Temple. Hovering around him were mighty seraphim, each with six wings. With two wings they covered their faces, with two they covered their feet, and with the remaining two they flew. In a great chorus they sang, "Holy, holy, holy is the Lord Almighty! The whole earth is filled with his glory!" (Isaiah 6:1–3, NLT)

The Bible is the most complete revelation from God, who is divine, eternal, holy, and personal. God gives his Word the highest place of honor. Our human mind can't fully grasp the thoughts, character, and person of God.

Bill and Sally came to Christ in middle age. As new believers, they were unfamiliar with the Bible, so they wanted to initiate a Bible study that would take them from the beginning to the end of the Bible. To get started, they bought a children's Bible to study to prepare them for tackling an adult Bible.

Teaching Tips

Deliberately cherish each member of your group to affirm that each person is a valued member of the Body of Christ. The Bible says that each believer has a critical role in the good of the whole group. As the members of your group sense their place in your segment of the body of Christ, they eagerly explore how to be spiritual and how to honor God.

After Bill and Sally established a personal relationship with Jesus Christ, they took a hard look at who they were and, more important, the character of God. As they saw themselves in their sinfulness and God in his holiness, it left them with little confidence in their abilities to understand the thoughts of God. They began to take baby steps of faith and learn humility.

Or consider the story of Carol; her first attempt at Bible study ended in tears. She couldn't answer the questions posed and felt she had no ability to comprehend the sections. Carol read and reread the Bible passages, but her efforts were futile and fruitless. She thought, "Why can't a reasonably intelligent woman understand a single question?" The next morning, Carol cried out to God and prayed, "Lord, please help me to understand." When Carol tried again, she was able to understand and the words on the page came alive.

Bill, Sally, and Carol aren't role models of humility, but they did admit that they were ignorant. Each of them read the Bible with humility and was aware that they couldn't approach God as equals in character, experience, or intellect.

God calls us to mirror this spirit of humility and hunger for him, whether we are accomplished students or new Christians. While intelligent, careful, and diligent study is important, the Bible doesn't offer its bounty to polished exploratory skills and high IQs alone. In many ways, the Bible is like any other book, yet it is also absolutely unique. Scripture says, "We speak of God's secret wisdom, a wisdom that has been hidden and that God destined for our glory before time began." (1 Corinthians 2:7, NLT) Wisdom is what no eye has seen "but God has revealed it to us by his Spirit." (1 Corinthians 2:10, NLT)

Potent Quotables

"Take my yoke upon you. Let me teach you, because I am humble and gentle, and you will find rest for your souls. For my yoke fits perfectly, and the burden I give you is light." (Matthew 11:29–30, NLT)

Truth from the Bible isn't discovered: It is revealed, interpreted, explained, and taught by the Holy Spirit. Let us cry out to God like the psalmist: "Help me understand the meaning of your commandments, and I will meditate on your wonderful miracles." (Psalms 119:27, NLT)

Go Forward with a Penitent Spirit

The Bible also insists that we approach God with a penitent spirit. Someone who is penitent has a contrite and remorseful attitude, as well as a keen awareness of his or her own failings. Yet a penitent person balances this attitude with gratitude for God's grace and mercy.

Be aware that the sharp contrast between our own lives and God's character will cause you to feel bruised. Like the psalmist, we can feel these words: "The Lord is close to the brokenhearted; he rescues those who are crushed in spirit." (Psalm 34:18, NLT) As the words of Jesus tell us in the Beatitudes, or Matthew 5:3–4, "Blessed are the poor in spirit, for theirs is the kingdom of heaven. Blessed are those who mourn, for they will be comforted." (NIV)

As you study the Bible, it will bruise you as well as bless you. If you begin studying the Bible with a self-sufficient, self-satisfied attitude, God's blessing can't penetrate your armor of self. God's Word must pierce your thick skin, must strike stinging blows at times, and must hold a mirror before your face so you can see what sin does to you. The Bible must wound before it heals. A penitent spirit welcomes God's work because it reveals who he or she really is. A penitent spirit limps to the throne of grace to receive the healing balm.

Apart from the Holy Spirit's enlightening ministry to our spirits, we accept or reject God's thoughts according to our reasoning. While we are barely aware of it, to each Bible study we bring our own baggage. We must face our own defects and acknowledge that we have barely begun to face them. As we study the Bible, we must come as open-minded and open-hearted as we can, yet with the full realization that we are wearing human skin and are entangled in our humanity. Then we grieve, and this is a penitent or remorseful spirit.

Tremble at the Scripture

God also wants us to study the Bible with a trembling spirit. To tremble at God means to fear him and consider the Bible as a serious book for study. James 2:19 says, "Do you still think it's enough just to believe that there is one God? Well, even the demons believe this, and they tremble in terror!" (NLT) The demons tremble because they understand that the Scriptures are alive, powerful, and dangerous. Hebrews 4:12 tells us, "For the word of God is full of living power. It is sharper than the sharpest knife, cutting deep into our innermost thoughts and desires. It exposes us for what we really are." (NLT) The Bible brings us into direct contact with Jesus Christ. As the demons know, the Scriptures are not something to be taken for granted.

Teaching Tips

Often young people will not participate in class because they don't want to look stupid in front of their peers. Even the school-smart may not know their Bible as well as their algebra. To keep from looking dumb, students will pretend they don't hear the question, will cut up, will refuse to participate, or will deliberately act dumb. Meet this need to look smart by structuring the session so that the students have success with the Bible. Begin with questions that come directly from the passage, and proceed to questions that require deeper application. Show students that their attempts to answer spiritual questions will be accepted even when the answers are not quite right, and that people won't laugh when they try. When young people look smart in church, they tend to trust God and the Bible, citing God as the source of their competence.

One model of a trembler from the Bible is King Josiah. During his reign, the priests found the long-neglected Book of the Law in the temple. When Josiah heard the message of the book and realized the extent of the nation's disobedience and the pending judgment of God for them, the king tore his clothing and wept in anguish. (2 Kings 22:23) Josiah approached the scrolls with a prior commitment to obey them with all of his heart and soul. He reinstituted the Passover and began a vigorous campaign to rid the land of false gods. His responsive action characterizes a man or woman who takes the Bible seriously.

A trembling heart prepares us for greater intimacy with the Bible. As a teenager, E. Stanley Jones, a Methodist missionary to India for 50 years, pressed his lips to passages that spoke to his heart. Jones's holy kiss seems to express the same spirit of the writer of Psalm 119, who wrote: "I have rejoiced in your decrees as much as in riches" (verse 14, NLT); "Your decrees please me; they give me wise advice" (verse 24, NLT); "How sweet are your words to my taste; they are sweeter than honey" (verse 134, NLT); and "My heart trembles only at your word." (verse 161, NLT)

When we take the Bible seriously, we open the Scriptures to study or teach or read with great anticipation. The Bible tells us that God's Word is the necessary bread that will satisfy. (Isaiah 55:1–3, Matthew 4:4) It is like snow and rain that falls down from heaven for a purpose. God's Word comes to nourish and refresh and make fruitful and effective. We can expect something to happen as we study the Scriptures and then teach them to others. A spirit of anticipation banishes a blasé approach to Scripture.

Using Jesus' Principles of Teaching

There wasn't a more serious teacher than Jesus Christ. He taught in many different ways and showed many principles for teaching the Bible.

Jesus invited other people to talk by saying, "Who do people say that I am?" (Mark 8:27, NIV) In his invitation to speak, Jesus moved from the general to the specific or from others' opinions to his own. This process helped other people get comfortable before Jesus asked the tougher questions or the personal question, "Who do you say that I am?" (Matthew 16:15, NIV)

Jesus used questions in his teaching primarily in three ways. First, Jesus asked questions to validate his ministry. Many times Jesus asked a question to prove that what he said made sense. Notice the significant statement that Jesus made in Matthew 6:25: "So I tell you, don't worry about everyday life—whether you have enough food, drink, and clothes." (NLT) Then, to validate his teaching, Jesus continued with a series of questions: "Is not life more important than food, and the body more important than clothes?" "Are you not much more valuable than they?" "Who of you by worrying can add a single hour to his life?" (NIV) When we face Jesus' questions with honesty, we can't help but agree with his original statement. Other examples of validating questions appear in Luke 6:27–32 and 9:23–25.

Second, Jesus asked questions to challenge false ideas. He lived in a religious culture where false ideas flourished—not very unlike our world today. Jesus used questions to challenge these ideas. In Luke 13:1–2, Jesus challenged the Jewish understanding of suffering. The Jews considered any time of suffering to be a direct result of sin (see John 9). After hearing a report of a tragedy involving some Galileans, Jesus challenged these Jewish assumptions. "Do you think those Galileans were worse sinners than other people from Galilee?" he asked. "Is that why they suffered?" (verse 2) The piercing question from Jesus forced his listeners to reconsider their views. Other examples of challenging questions from Jesus can be found in Matthew 15:1–3 and 16:13–15. These questions confront our traditional and sometimes wrong views of God.

Third, Jesus asked questions to deepen people's faith. Often before Jesus performed a miracle, he asked a question like, "Do you want to get well?" (John 5:6, NLT) The question seems too obvious because of what we assume the answer will be: "Of course I want to get well!" Maybe Jesus intended to help the person identify the object of his or her faith and, in this process, deepen that person's faith in Jesus. In addition, Jesus asked faith-building questions after incidents that demonstrated a lack of faith. For example, in Matthew 14:31, Jesus rescued Peter after his walk on the water, asking, "Why did you doubt?" (NIV) This question from Jesus Christ probably rang in Peter's ears for the rest of his life and provided strength in difficult situations.

Twenty Questions from Jesus

Now that you have some understanding of Jesus' teaching principles, it's time to test that understanding with the following exercise. Following are 20 samples of Jesus' questions recorded in the Gospels. Classify each one as being either a validating, challenging, or faith question. Keep in mind that some of them can fall in more than one category.

- "And why worry about a speck in your friend's eye when you have a log in your own?" (Matthew 7:3, NLT)
- "You parents; if your children ask for a loaf of bread, do you give them a stone instead?" (Matthew 7:9, NLT)

- "Who is my mother? Who are my brothers?" (Matthew 12:48, NLT)
- "How long must I put up with you?" (Matthew 17:17, NLT)
- "Which is greater, the gold or the Temple that makes the gold sacred?" (Matthew 23:17, NLT)
- "How many loaves of bread do you have?" (Mark 8:5, NLT)
- "Who do you say I am?" (Mark 8:29, NLT)
- "Why are you calling me good?" (Mark 10:18, The Message)
- "Why berate her for doing such a good thing to me?" (Mark 14:6, NLT)
- "My God, my God, why have you abandoned me?" (Mark 15:34, The Message)
- "Do you think you deserve credit merely for loving those who love you?" (Luke 6:32, NLT)
- "So why do you call me 'Lord,' when you won't obey me?" (Luke 6:46, NLT)
- "Didn't I heal ten men?" (Luke 17:17, NLT)
- "What do you want me to do for you?" (Luke 18:41, NLT)
- "Wasn't it clearly predicted by the prophets that the Messiah would have to suffer all these things before entering his time of glory?" (Luke 24:26, NLT)
- "Would you give me a drink of water?" (John 4:7, The Message)
- "Are you going to leave, too?" (John 6:67, The Message)
- "Where are your accusers?" (John 8:10, NLT)
- "Are there not twelve hours of daylight?" (John 11:9, NIV)
- "Shall I not drink from the cup the Father has given me?" (John 18:11, NLT)

Teaching Tips

Often Jesus didn't answer his own questions. Instead he used questions to lead his listeners toward truth.

Notice how each of these questions from Jesus couldn't be answered with a simple yes or no. Instead they stirred the reader to think about the situation and move toward the truth.

Four Principles for Teaching Truth

We will discuss many different Bible study methods throughout this book. No method is necessarily more helpful than another; they all can lead to meaningful study of the Bible. However, you must follow several key steps no matter which study method you choose.

- Discover a creative way to read the Bible passage of the lesson. Give the members of your group a reason to read the passage. Perhaps you will challenge them to find the answer to a Bible question or to identify the names of certain people. You could have the various members of the group read as if reading a play. Or you might make up a learning game, posing questions that the Bible can answer. The goal is to motivate your group to be excited about the Scriptures.
- Get the facts. Make sure your lesson spells out the Bible facts for the group. Unless they examine the facts, they will have no basis for comments or conclusions. Perhaps you will pose a different question to each student that guides your students to find a different fact. Or maybe they'll use their Bibles to put the facts in order.

Proceed with Caution

It's important as a teacher to understand and acknowledge your own limitations. Ask God to help you throughout your search, and pray this type of prayer:

> Father, I'm responsible for striving for life change in my teaching. During both the preparation and the presentation phases of each Bible lesson, there are things I can do to encourage application. Yet I'm aware of my own limitations. Only you can turn a person to hate sin. Only you can instill joy in a heart that's hurting. Only you can reconcile family members who haven't spoken to each other in years. Only you can mold a person's will until he wants to obey your Scriptures. So if life change is going to occur among the members of my group, you must soften their hearts. You must encourage behaviors, attitudes, and thoughts in line with the lesson. I'll do my part and commit the group time to probe possible applications. But the last thing I want to be, Lord, is cleverly ineffective. In the name of the one who prayed for the people he taught. Amen.

- Understand the facts. Guide the members of your group so they understand the facts using one of the numerous methods in this book. Bible understanding contains two critical elements. First, the students need to understand the meaning of facts as they related to people in biblical times. Then they need to understand the meaning of the facts in the Bible in our lives today.
- Apply the facts. How do the Bible facts apply to the personal lives of the group? Without personal application, having knowledge of the Bible means very little.

Whether you use the pattern of Jesus' questions or ask your own leading questions, it's important to get others talking. The only person who learns in a situation where people sit around and hang on every word from the teacher is the teacher. Your challenge as a teacher is to talk less and ask piercing questions which draw the members of your group into the discussion. As each person talks, they begin to individually wrestle with the truth in a particular passage from the Bible; then they can apply that section to their own situation. In the next chapter, we turn and examine specific problems that occur in the classroom. For example, what happens if you ask the leading questions and there is complete silence? The answer will come in the next section.

The Least You Need to Know

- Create questions that are designed to trigger observation and application.
- Take the time to study the Bible on a personal level as well as trying to teach it.
- The ultimate goal isn't simply to interpret the Bible, but rather to apply it to your everyday life—and to help your study group members to do likewise.
- Maintain an attitude of humility, have a penitent spirit, and tremble at the Scriptures.
- Use Jesus' principles when you teach.
- Get the facts, understand the facts, and apply the facts inherent in the Bible.

Chapter 4

Practical Concerns and Answers

In This Chapter

- Fostering a teaching-friendly climate
- Flourishing with active participatory teaching methods and absorbing visitors into your group
- Making class participants feel welcome
- How to lead the discussion (Is silence okay?)

Does standing in front of a group make you tremble and sweat? Or do you love to be in front of a group? Whether you love leadership or loath it, this chapter gives you some much needed principles to guide you in teaching the Bible.

Handling the Dreaded Silence

Almost everyone has either led or been in a class in which the teacher bounces into the class with enthusiasm and receives absolutely no response from the participants. Even when the teacher phrases and rephrases the material in repeated questions, he or she still gets no answers.

To avoid this problem, start by laying down three ground rules with your students. First, no one can slam another person in the group or laugh at anyone else's question, comment, or concern. Ask your students to follow the guidelines in Hebrews 10:24–25: "Think of ways to encourage one another to outbursts of love and good deeds. And let us not neglect our meeting together, as some people do, but encourage and warn each other, especially now that the day of his coming back again is drawing near." (NLT) Encourage each member of the group toward a Christlike attitude and not to put down or slander the others in the group.

Second, there is no such thing as a stupid question. Anything can be asked during the session because no sincere question is a dumb question; every comment makes sense when you hear what is really being said. When teaching his disciples, Jesus Christ said, "Keep on asking, and you will be given what you ask for. Keep on looking, and you will find. Keep on knocking, and the door will be opened." (Matthew 7:7)

Just in Case

You want to foster spiritual growth through your teaching. Recognize that some people don't necessarily believe what they say. They may be voicing a viewpoint that they heard someone else say, or they have seen an idea in the Bible and verbalize one of God's ideas to see how it works. Listen, understand, and gently guide them to compare what they say to what the Bible says. Let them discover and voice the truth. For example, in a class of youth, a student named Harry reacted against the passage that said "Obey your parents." (Ephesians 6:1a) Rather than say something like "Who are you to question God's Word?" The teacher said, "You must have a good reason to react so strongly. Tell me why you feel that way." An honest discussion revealed that his dad had abused Harry's sister, and Harry's dad wanted to keep it a secret. Harry rightly concluded that God would not want him to obey this request.

Finally, no one should talk when another person is talking. This polite guideline allows each person to hear one another and cherish the insight provided. 1 Peter 2:17 says, "Show respect for everyone. Love your Christian brothers and sisters. Fear God." (NLT)

Fostering the Right Climate

When it comes to teaching the Bible, you will be doomed to failure if you take for granted that your group has a conducive learning environment. More than any other key in this chapter, the feeling or tone of the group is critical for whether discussion will flourish or fizzle. Here are several factors that will make or break your group's climate:

- **Create a caring environment.** The television show *Cheers*, about a local bar in Boston, highlighted the importance of having a place to go where "everybody knows your name." In a bar, often people will tell the bartender their personal woes and let down their hair without fear of judgment or repercussions. While likely you will not be teaching the Bible in a bar, you do want to create a place where you're able to meet the participants' need for acceptance. Everyone is more likely to participate if they know the other people care about them. The Apostle Paul felt that an interpersonal dimension of the ministry of teaching the Bible was paramount. While recalling his ministry to the church in Thessalonica, he wrote, "We loved you so much that we were delighted to share with you not only the gospel of God, but our lives as well, because you had become so dear to us." (1 Thessalonians 2:8, NIV)

Proceed with Caution

As you teach, make sure you look past the masks of the members of your group. At first, your participants will smile all the time, talk with heavenly lingo, deny struggles, and appear to be perfectly fine. As they begin to feel safe, they will be able to show both happy and sad times, talk more openly, and attempt to conquer struggles and face guilt head on by avoiding the wrong that causes it. They will become free to grow in Christ.

- **Be on a first-name basis.** Learn the names of everyone in the group, and make an effort to use their names regularly when you teach the class. You can also take pictures of everyone in the class and display them in the room so the others in the class can quickly learn the names.

- **Express yourself in writing.** Write short but encouraging notes to each member of the group. Express thankfulness for someone's encouragement. Or salute someone who is enthusiastic about the group. In general, encourage the participants to reach their potential for increased learning in the group. Or follow up on a prayer request that was voiced during the group.

- **Bond with laughter.** When people enjoy being together, humor naturally surfaces. Therefore, don't feel obligated to collect a bunch of jokes to use with your teaching each week. If you can, use a humorous anecdote in a lesson if you can connect the concept to the Bible lesson. Researchers have discovered a principle about humor that relates to teaching the Bible. Laughter that isn't associated with satire, ridicule, or other forms of sharp put-down humor can act as a social lubricant in the learning environment. On the other hand, the lack of humor indicates poor social bonding. Another researcher discovered that student satisfaction with learning improves when humor is part of the process, and that humor has a liberating effect on the flow of ideas.

- **Perform "get-to-know-you" exercises.** For instance, during the first session of the group, you might pass out 3×5 cards and have each person describe a pleasant experience from recent months. Tell the participants not to reveal their identity on the card. After the writing, scramble the cards and give everyone a card (not their own). Then have them find the person whose experience is recorded on the card. Or ask everyone to think of three words that end in "-ing" and reveal some personal information. For example, one person who likes to cook would choose "cooking." Have every member of the small group share their words with others. Or consider making "designer" name tags. Distribute name tags and ask each person to print or write his or her name in the shape of a personal attribute, hobby, or current interest. For example, someone who likes pick-up basketball could write his name in letters to form a circle. Or someone who is considering making a job change or who has unanswered questions about the future could arrange the letters of his or her name in the shape of a question mark. Explaining the meaning of the shapes helps people get to know each other.

Teaching Tips

Help your group imagine and embrace spirituality as a turning wheel, not as a spare tire. Often individuals feel powerless, yet every person has the power of God at their fingertips. The fact that God wants to work through people is a revelation to many people. Help the members of your group live out this revelation by deciding to draw on the Holy Spirit's power. Challenge them to watch each day for one good that God gives them opportunity to do—and then to do that good. Invite them to tell about the best part of their week and how they drew on God's power to make that happen. Invite them to tell about a temptation God helped them resist that week and how he did it. Encourage each participant to be decisive for Jesus.

Later, let the name tags become a part of the teaching process as well as help you remember the participants' names. If the designer name tags don't work for you, here are some other choices:

- Pass out preprinted tags with a verse that you'll emphasize during the study.
- Invite students to make their own name tags related to the study.

- Ask the group members to tear their name tags into the shape of a symbol of the Bible passage. For example, if the study involves Acts 18:1–4, a student might fold the tag into the shape of a house, to remind him to invite people home to study like Priscilla and Aquila did.

Connecting Through Prayer

Theologian Dietrich Bonhoeffer said, "Intercessory prayer is the purifying bath into which the individual and the fellowship must enter every day." As you teach the Bible to others, it's critical to make time to pray for other group members and to reserve meeting time to pray for one another. This commitment and priority acknowledges your dependence on the Holy Spirit. As the group prays for one another, it moves the individuals closer together as a community. When people bear each other's concerns and burdens, they feel freer to ask questions or respond to questions during the Bible teaching.

I encourage you to take your cue in this area from the Apostle Paul and the way he prayed for the people in Ephesians 3:14–19 and Philippians 1:3–5. His prayers were specific for individuals and their needs in these locations.

Potent Quotables

"A yes on earth is yes in heaven; a no on earth is no in heaven. What you say to one another is eternal. I mean this. When two of you get together on anything at all on earth and make a prayer of it, my Father in heaven goes into action. And when two or three of you are together because of me, you can be sure that I'll be there." (Matthew 18:18, The Message)

You don't have to set the same time for prayer in every session; instead, you can change the routine and keep it fresh. Here are some ideas about how to connect through prayer:

- Link your time of prayer with the lesson application. Particularly if you have a close-knit group, each person can huddle with one or two others, brainstorm the application, and pray for each other's follow-through.
- Add the following questions to the end of your Bible teaching: What personal needs has the Holy Spirit exposed during this study? How can we pray with you about those needs?
- Lead a Bible study on the theme of intercessory prayer. Look at the biblical basis for this expression of group life and discuss ways to exercise intercessory prayer for one another.

In case you need it, here's a short study on intercessory prayer:

Have your group read Nehemiah 1, the chapter which could bear the title, "The Ministry of Intercession," and then ask these questions:

- What need prompted Nehemiah's intercession? In chapter 1, look at the record of Nehemiah's behavior and his words. What character qualities does he possess? Why are these particular traits prerequisites for the ministry of intercession?
- What principles of intercession can you glean from Nehemiah's prayer (verses 5–11)?
- What insights from Nehemiah 1 are most applicable to our relationships within this group?
- How can we prevent the promise "I'll pray for you" from becoming just another church cliché?

Encouraging Participation

Discussion about the Bible will flourish in a study group or class where encouraging the group to participate is the norm, not the exception. As you consistently involve learners in your group, any attempts at discussion will be more successful. If you pop a question out of the blue in a group accustomed to straight lectures, you'll probably receive limited responses. But if you mix up the way you teach and ask a question during a lecture, you might just find that the room buzzes with dialogue. Involve your group members by using a variety of teaching methods included in the remainder of this book, and watch the learning atmosphere warm up.

Professional educators have investigated hundreds of classroom sessions and compared student attitudes and outcomes to the methods employed by their teachers. The results of their findings reveal the value of using a variety of learning activities. The more predictable a teacher's style and method are, the lower the impact is on the students. The less predictable the methods are, the greater the impact is.

> **Teaching Tips**
>
> Jesus used everyday experiences and objects to explain spiritual truth—we call them parables. After studying one of Jesus' parables, invite the participants of your group to tell their own parables about a theme using an everyday object.

How do you choose which Bible-teaching method to use? If you want your students to always participate, which discussion format should you employ? Do you stick with a simple question-and-answer approach?

When is it appropriate to frame a session around research assignments you've distributed to the members of the group in advance?

It isn't difficult to select an appropriate study method and specific methods are detailed in the remainder of this book. After praying for wisdom, consider the following criteria. The various key words and evaluative questions will help you make good choices.

- **Message.** What teaching methods will accurately and clearly convey the message of this Bible passage? Is the material so controversial or complex that you need to provide background through a brief lecture so a fruitful discussion can follow?
- **Environment.** How does the physical environment of the class or study group affect the choice of learning activities? What techniques does the physical setting or lack of equipment eliminate? What procedures, such as dividing into smaller groups, does the space or room layout prevent?
- **Time.** Which methods are realistic for the time frame? Should one discussion strategy be substituted for another that will conserve some precious minutes?
- **Hospitality.** What approaches to this lesson will help create a warm, hospitable learning atmosphere? Which discussion format will promote research in text from the Bible and build relationships?
- **Objectives.** Which Bible-learning activities will best meet the stated lesson objectives? How can the discussion be structured to accelerate understanding of Bible truths?
- **Discovery.** What methods will propel group members into the Bible passage so they can discover truths for themselves? How can your questions best highlight the most important facts and principles in the text? Do any questions encourage speculation instead of investigation and analysis of Bible content?
- **Students.** In light of the number of people in the group, what techniques are the most appropriate? How should the participants' ages and levels of spiritual maturity influence the choice of methods? What teaching styles did previous leaders of the group use effectively? How will the way the group was taught previously affect the students' receptivity to teaching strategies?

Potent Quotables

"I have not spoken in secret,
from somewhere in a land of darkness;
I have not said to Jacob's descendants,
'Seek me in vain.'
I, the Lord, speak the truth;
I declare what is right." (Isaiah 45:19, NIV)

The first letters of these seven methods spell the word *methods*. As you use these guidelines, you will be able to select the appropriate method to teach your group the Bible.

Provide a Welcome (and Welcome Back) Mat

It's very likely that people outside your group will hear about your work and want to join you. How well will someone new be absorbed into the group? Honestly answer these questions:

- What percentage of guests attending your class or group return?
- How frequently do newcomers drop out after a few weeks or a month?
- What words describe the behavior of the "regulars" toward newcomers?
- What strategies do you use as a leader to create a sense of belonging and improve visitor absorption?

> **Teaching Tips**
>
> A common question from young people about Bible lessons is "So what?" You may be hearing this question in your group (young or old). So ask "So what?" during the Bible study to prompt your members to tell you why a Bible truth works in real life situations. Their answers to these questions are where in the everyday a person's faith becomes active in life.

A local church wrestled with these questions and decided to create a position of "class host" for each adult class. They recruited couples with exceptional relational skills to introduce the visitors to the class, call first-time guests during the week, and generally enhance fellowship among the group. The class host position removes this responsibility from the teacher or leader and delegates it to someone else in the Bible group. Because the class host is focused on this responsibility, it leads to increased effectiveness for the entire group.

Here's a job description of the "class host." Try to adapt it to your group, and it will improve how visitors are absorbed into your class.

Faith Church Adult Class Hosts

Goal: To help class participants feel welcome through the establishment of an atmosphere of warmth and acceptance.

Requirements:

- Evidence of genuine Christian conversion and growth.
- Membership in Faith Church.

- Regular attendance in Faith's worship services.
- Attendance in at least 80 percent of class sessions during the year.
- A one-year commitment to this ministry.
- Willingness to work as a team. Two people should fill this position, one male and one female. A married couple is preferred.

Assets:

- A spirit of hospitality, enjoying making people feel welcome and valued.
- An affinity for meeting and greeting new people.
- Faithfulness in handling details and keeping records.

Responsibilities:

- Learning the names of every participant and calling them by name each week.
- Greeting visitors and introducing them to others in the class.
- Contacting every visitor by phone within one week of their first time in the group.
- Developing a class roll of regular members, including addresses and phone numbers.
- Planning, promoting, and implementing at least one fellowship/social activity for the class every three months. Seeking to cultivate relationships and improve the assimilation of visitors into the life of the church.
- Coordinating weekly provision of coffee/refreshments.
- Arranging for someone else to serve as class host when they plan to be absent.
- Consulting with the teacher regularly concerning the groups activities and the amount of time related to host-related duties.

Proceed with Caution

Be aware that talking about spiritual matters is difficult. It requires that group participants reveal themselves and their personal relationship (or lack of it) with God. To venture into talking about such sacred things, the various members have to feel safe and smart talking about simple things. They must see how the Bible relates to even the simplest worry and pleasure. They must have success with answering Bible questions and opportunities to explore how spiritual truth impacts their life.

Come Across as Real

Sometimes a good Bible discussion turns pivotally on the leader's transparency, or willingness to share aspects of his or her own life—sometimes very intimate aspects. Often the teacher or leader will share a personal illustration or ask the others in the group to pray for a particular personal need. What happens when you add this personal aspect to your teaching? You send these positive messages to the others in your group:

- "The Bible passage we are studying encouraged (or convicted) me."
- "This lesson was prepared in my heart, not just in my head."
- "I'm not self-sufficient. I need to lean on Jesus Christ daily. And I need others in the body of Christ."

When you genuinely identify with the others in your group, you come across as real and you've found the opening to their hearts. Even the highly respected Apostle Paul modeled transparency before the people when he taught:

> I think you ought to know, dear brothers and sisters, about the trouble we went through in the province of Asia. We were crushed and completely overwhelmed, and we thought we would never live through it. In fact, we expected to die. But as a result, we learned not to rely on ourselves, but on God who can raise the dead. And he did deliver us from mortal danger. And we are confident that he will continue to deliver us. (2 Corinthians 1:8–10, NLT)

Don't feel like you have to expose all of your failings to the group. Before choosing what personal things to talk about, think about these guidelines:

- Will my personal anecdote accelerate Bible learning and clarify a truth in the lesson?
- Will my personal illustration show the benefits of obeying a particular truth or the painful consequences of neglecting it?
- Will my self-revelation encourage others to share needs and prayer requests?
- Will self-disclosure meet a genuine need in my life for emotional support and prayer?
- Will my illustration portray family members or friends in a negative manner?
- Have I received permission to tell my story from people who could be embarrassed by it?

While you will need to be selective about what you tell the group and your degree of transparency, these actions confront the superficiality and hypocrisy in a group. Beyond your own transparency, you want to promote transparency among the members of your class or group.

When Is Silence Golden?

What happens when you ask a question of the group? Chances are, your behavior with the class immediately after you ask the question will be the critical factor in determining the direction of the discussion. Your tone in response will either expand or constrict the number and the quality of responses. This aspect of teaching is one of the most difficult parts of leading a group.

You can respond to your students' reactions to your questions in a number of ways: displaying enthusiasm, showing sincerity, and waiting with patience for someone to be ready with an answer.

Display Enthusiasm

Providing participants with positive reinforcement is one of the most successful means of garnering support and enthusiasm. When you express excitement over fresh and new insights, the excitement of the entire group grows.

Therefore, what you say right after someone contributes is crucial. If the point made seems elementary to you, you may be tempted to gloss over it with something like, "Who else?" But your verbal reaction should express fascination at the discovery that the participant made, even if it seems like an obvious one to you. I'm not advocating that you be mushy in your response, but do congratulate and support the person who opens up to you and to the group enough to make an observation. By doing so, you'll keep people digging in the Bible for answers that only God's Spirit can reveal.

Teaching Tips

People often learn by speaking about the issues presented, so your job as a leader should be to encourage discussion. Resist the temptation to answer your own questions if the group members take "too long": Wait at least 10 to 20 seconds. Because you have been thinking about the question since you prepared the lesson, the answer is on the tip of your tongue. But your group members have just heard it, so they need time to think about it. If no one answers after 20 seconds, rephrase the question or tell participants to look up a specific verse. If you asked the question to a specific student, keep rephrasing the question until that student answers. Don't let others jump in, or the chosen student will miss having the learning experience.

Show Sincerity

At the same time, you should tailor the level of your enthusiasm to the quality of the answer. Reserve high praise for the best answers or for feedback that reveals critical thinking about the particular issue under discussion. Also be sure to praise participants for raising thought-provoking questions and for input that shows an honest effort to understand the Bible text.

Value Silence by Waiting

When you raise a question, how long do you wait before rephrasing it or answering it yourself? How many seconds do you wait before you feel like you should keep things moving? Is silence a threat or an opportunity for people to spend some quality time thinking about the answer?

Research has shown that when a teacher increases his or her wait time from one second to three or five seconds, significant changes occur in the classroom. Students offer longer answers, they volunteer more appropriate answers, and they fail to respond less frequently.

Good Bible study questions jump-start the mind, sparking thoughts about the passage and its practical implications. But when we show disrespect for silence and expect instant replies, discussion sputters.

Conquer Discussion Trouble Spots

Your group may not have any trouble spots. If so, skim or skip this next section. Almost every group at one time or another will run into some of the difficulties in this section, though. Possibly you have a resident theologian in your group who always locks horns with relatively new yet enthused students of the Bible. In the next few pages, we'll show you ways to manage a participant who monopolizes the study, how to control controversies, how to avoid the pool of ignorance, and how to rescue the possible rabbit trails of discussion.

Control a Monopolizer

Sometimes a member of your group will feel obligated to jump into the conversation after only a second of silence. Even though most monopolizers are passionate learners, their continual verbal intrusions can cause other people to become passive and not participate in the discussion.

If you have a problem managing a monopolizer, discuss the answers to these questions with a fellow Bible study leader:

- What motives or factors prompt someone to monopolize a Bible discussion?
- What effect does a monopolizer have on others in the group?
- Which technique for muzzling monopolizers impresses you the most, and why?
- In what additional ways can we increase the percentage of group participation?

Because "iron sharpens iron" (Proverbs 27:17), your work with another leader may help provide fresh insight into this situation.

Here are some ideas about how to increase the percentage of people who participate, thus putting the brakes on those who would monopolize the discussion:

- Introduce a study question with a qualifying remark. You will be able to get a lot of mileage out of this method: "The next question should be answered by someone who hasn't contributed yet today." (Obviously, this technique will not work in a small group of two or three people.)
- Set specific conditions required for someone to respond. Examples: "I appreciate the responsiveness of the ladies in the group. Men, now it's *your* turn to answer the next couple questions." "The next question must be answered by someone on my left" (or someone in the last three rows, whose birthday falls in the summer, etc.).
- Select a couple group members who don't monopolize the conversation, and give them a question or assignment a week in advance. At the appropriate time during the following Bible lesson, ask them to report on their research. Choose people who possess a high regard for the Bible and whom you can count on to follow through with the assignment. If you choose teens or new Christians, maintain quality control by assisting them in the assignment.
- Plan for a variety of discussion forms or strategies. For example, divide a large class into smaller groups. Give the smaller groups a time limit and a specific Bible text assignment. Tell every small group to appoint a recorder who will later summarize the findings of the group for the entire class. When you mix this question-and-answer approach with other forms of discussion, it broadens participation and may silence the monopolizer.
- Speak one-on-one with the monopolizer. If the person's talkative style is prompted by enthusiasm for learning, make comments like, "Harry, you're the kind of learner I'd like to photocopy and put in every chair! But I need your

help in getting others as involved in discussions as you are. Because they expect *you* to respond, they're shifting into a passive mode and aren't wrestling with the questions. I want you to keep participating. But could you delay your answers to some questions and compel your peers to get more involved?"

Control Controversies

When it comes to biblical perspective or theology on contemporary issues, Christians don't always see eye to eye. If you have disagreements that crop up during your discussions, there are several strategies to make that dissent work for you and the group:

- Anticipate participants' questions. As you prepare each Bible lesson, look at it from the various group members' perspectives. What questions are they likely to have about the interpretation or application of the thorny issues in the text? Use this principle of anticipation to answer a question—in your mind—before it comes up. Your preparation and anticipation will help you to clarify and cut off potential disagreements.

> **Teaching Tips**
>
> If your group is stalled on a difficult passage, you may need a lecture to provide an interpretative framework. Try giving the two or three most recognized explanations of a passage and the rationale for each. Then point out the interpretation you or your church prefers.

- Set the stage for discussion by giving a lecture addressing the issues. Even in a more informal discussion group, some topics or passages need an explanation that derives from background research. If you present a few minutes of historical context or another form of scholarly spadework, it doesn't overly formalize the Bible study. Instead, it keeps participants from fruitless verbal exchanges and the snare of speculation by giving them some facts upon which to base their discussion.
- Agree to disagree. No matter how convincing an explanation may seem to you, not everyone will adopt your interpretation of a difficult passage. Yet you don't want the Bible discussion to bog down. A good approach for this situation is to admit the complexity of the content with something like, "For centuries, sincere Bible scholars have viewed this doctrine in different ways. Though it's an important issue, we aren't going to resolve this controversy to everyone's satisfaction today. Perhaps the wisest approach is to 'agree to disagree' and move on to other material." If you use this strategy, it will help you with the next one.
- Set a strict time limit for group coverage of the subject matter. When a sticky point surfaces in the context of a passage that offers a lot of other important

truths, remember that the guiding mechanism for your lesson is the main theme or basic teaching of the passage, not one problematic phrase or verse. It's easy to spend an inordinate amount of time on an area of disagreement and neglect the practical instruction that isn't up for debate.

- Minimize misunderstandings. In rare situations, small group participants or a class gets hot under the collar when discussing a social issue or doctrine. When one person throws a verbal jab at another, before you know it, emotions erupt and impede logical thinking. Your group suddenly moves from disagreeing to being disagreeable. The atmospheric thermometer plunges, and folks who have enjoyed friendly fellowship suddenly act like frosty foes.

Sometimes folks quarrel because they don't listen to each other. What they think is a disagreement may actually be a misinterpretation. Don't allow personal attacks or harsh tones of voice. If the topic merits the class time, ask the opposing viewpoints to prepare talks on their respective positions to be given at the next meeting. Set a time limit, with questions from other group members. If you stage an informal debate, it may result in a more restrained, rationale discussion of different opinions. In the final analysis, you will want to encourage everyone to agree to disagree.

Potent Quotables

"If you bad-mouth the Son of Man out of misunderstanding or ignorance, that can be overlooked. But if you're knowingly attacking God himself, taking aim at the Holy Spirit, that won't be overlooked." (Luke 12:9, The Message)

Avoid the Pool of Ignorance

Some people avoid attending groups related to the Bible because they believe they degenerate into a pool of ignorance. Here are a few ways to guard against uninformed conclusions from time in the Bible:

- **Prepare the participants.** When all the participants commit to taking the time outside of the study to study and read the Bible passage, ignorance evaporates. Determine a reasonable amount of "homework" time and ask the group members to sign a covenant. Devoting 30 minutes to the passage before the meeting won't turn them into scholars, but it may prompt them to give up some preconceived notions. Then when you meet to cover the Bible lesson, they will have some rapport with the biblical text.

- **Qualify the questions.** As you ask questions about the Bible text, narrow the scope of possible answers by wording the questions in a way that directs the members of the group to turn their attention to the Bible text. By using this approach, you let the text be the teacher and guide your discussions.
- **Enlist the experts.** Some passages in the Bible are difficult to interpret without looking at the insight from a good Bible commentary or other reference books. Instead of asking the group's opinion, do your homework and lecture for several minutes. Otherwise, you put out the welcome mat to ignorance and usher it to the front-row seat in your class. It's important for any leader to study the Bible passage independently and avoid depending too much on someone else's research. Yet at the same time, a leader must not rely completely on his or her own findings and ideas alone. As the saying goes, "A leader who learns only from himself has a fool for a teacher."

If you are afraid that the members of your group will drown in the deep waters of uninformed conclusions, then drain the pool using the strategies listed earlier. You will manage to pull the plug by preparing the participants, qualifying your questions, and enlisting the experts.

Steer Clear of Detours

Sometimes a participant will steer a discussion way off course. If a member of your group darts after the proverbial white rabbit, the direction of the discussion gets derailed. Any remark that takes a different direction than the slant of the study may take you too far off track. Here are some suggestions to keep the discussion focused:

- **Search for a slant.** From a single Bible lesson, your group may create numerous truths. As you prepare and as you lead the discussion, don't examine the various points in isolation from the big picture of the passage. Your observation and analysis of the passage should help you identify overarching and unifying themes. As you clearly communicate the broad theme that governs the passage, the participants will be less likely to steer conversation away from it. Connect the facts and principles to a comprehensive subject slant, and group members' ideas or illustrations will usually mesh with it.

Teaching Tips

Here's a quick way to find that unifying theme: Pluck a resource book or published curriculum off the shelf of a Christian bookstore. Let the scholars trumpet a theme for you, and then organize your questions around it. No matter who gives birth to the basic teaching or big idea, it keeps everyone on track.

- **Polish your probes.** Do your queries show the participants the main idea of the Bible passage? To what extent do your questions unify the lesson? Does the wording of questions on a specific passage connect those insights to the big picture?
- **Create a way back.** Imagine that you are deep in the middle of a Bible discussion. Someone inserts a personal illustration or comment that seems off the track. While the connection may seem unclear to you, something in the Bible text or prior discussion likely sparked this contribution. Why else would the group member add this material? How can you affirm the person's remarks and still convey the importance of sticking to the particular subject at hand?

Here is another way to get the discussion back on track. Try asking the person who got off track to build a verbal bridge back to the passage or topic. Perhaps his or her explanation of what triggered this extra thought will reveal the connection to everyone. These examples should get you started: "Gary, what you said is interesting, but tell us how it relates to the topic (or Bible passage) we're discussing. What connection do you see?"

"Jane, thanks for contributing. But I'm curious: What part of the Bible passage triggered your comment?"

"Cindy, thanks for the transparent nature of your illustration. What made you think of it? Was it something one of us said? Or a verse we examined?"

As you tactfully ask these types of questions, it won't always result in the verbal bridge back to the topic at hand. Yet your efforts will train the group participants to evaluate their contributions for pertinence.

The Least You Need to Know

- You can foster an environment in which people care about each other and feel comfortable talking.
- Bond using laughter and prayer with the people you teach.
- Be open about your own life and difficulties, plus real, as you teach.
- Be enthusiastic and sincere, and value silence through waiting.
- Control the monopolizer, calm controversies, and stay on track.

Part 2

Start with the Basics

The writer of the Book of Hebrews described many people in today's church: "You have been Christians a long time now, and you ought to be teaching others. Instead, you need someone to teach you again the basic things a beginner must learn about the Scriptures. You are like babies who drink only milk and cannot eat solid food." (Hebrews 5:12, NLT)

If you're new to teaching the Bible or are leading a group of people new to the Bible, you'll want to start with this part of the book.

This part covers the four basic methods of Bible study: the Devotional Method, the Chapter Summary Method, the Bible Character Method, and the Bible Theme Method. Each of these methods requires only a good Bible, and each is easy to understand.

Chapter 5

Application Through Devotion

In This Chapter

- Meditating on text for deeper understanding
- Application is the key
- Following the steps of the Devotional Method

The Devotional Method is one of the easiest means for a group to study the Bible. This way to study is practical, and it encourages everyone to participate. In this chapter, you'll learn how to apply and teach this method. Then in Chapter 15, you can explore the method further by reading an example of it.

Applying Scripture to Everyday Life

The goal of the Devotional Method is to take seriously the content of the Bible and "do what it says." (James 1:22) The Devotional Method of studying the Bible involves prayerfully meditating on a large or small portion of Scripture until the Holy Spirit shows you how to apply its truth to your own life in a way that is practical, personal, possible, and measurable.

Clearly, this method emphasizes application. The Bible shows us how to have a relationship with the God of the universe and how to live our lives in his way in this world. The Scriptures were given to us to change our lives and make us more like Jesus Christ. The Apostle Paul taught that the Bible is useful for teaching, rebuking, correcting, and training the Christian in righteous living. (2 Timothy 3:16)

The Bible is a practical book because it is concerned with practical living. Bible study without personal application can just be an academic exercise with no spiritual value. The Bible was written to be applied to our lives. Howard Hendricks, the well-known professor at Dallas Theological Seminary, has said, "Interpretation without application is abortion!"

> **Potent Quotables**
>
> "And we are instructed to turn from godless living and sinful pleasures. We should live in this evil world with self-control, right conduct, and devotion to God." (Titus 2:12, NLT)

The Importance of Application

Before we can understand the method, we need to examine why application is necessary and why it is hard work. The bottom line is that application should result in changing us so that our lives are more conformed to God's will.

You can't really know the Word of God unless you apply it to your life. When Jesus was on the earth and in ministry, he had a number of encounters with the religious leaders of his time. These leaders were primarily the Pharisees, who were the acknowledged scholars of the day, and the Sadducees, who represented the liberalizing element of Jewish society.

One day the Sadducees, who didn't believe that resurrection from the dead was possible, asked Jesus a trick question:

> Teacher, Moses told us that if a man dies without having children, his brother must marry the widow and have children for him. Now there were seven brothers among us. The first one married and died, and since he had no children, he left his wife to his brother. The same thing happened to the second and third brother, right on down to the seventh. Finally, the woman died. Now then, at the resurrection, whose wife will she be of the seven, since all of them were married to her? (Matthew 22:24–28, NIV)

> **Proceed with Caution**
>
> Teaching for application doesn't refer to the attitude or behavior change itself. Instead, it's the guided process of helping learners follow through possibilities. You can't guarantee that anyone will obey God's Word, but you can reserve group time to probe a passage's practical implications. You can make sure people leave the group with application possibilities spinning in their minds.

Jesus' answer was interesting. He said to them, "You are in error because you do not know the Scriptures or the power of God." (Matthew 22:29, NIV)

These Jewish leaders had an intellectual knowledge of the facts of the Old Testament (the Jewish Scriptures), but they did not apply these principles in a personal way to their lives. You can be a walking Bible encyclopedia with your head crammed full of Bible knowledge, but it won't do you any good if you don't apply it practically in daily living. If you study the Bible without applying it to your life, you are no better off than the Pharisees and Sadducees of Jesus' day. You really don't know the Scriptures until you put them into practice.

Beware of Failing to Apply

Without application, Bible study can be dangerous because knowledge puffs up a person. The Apostle Paul said, "Knowledge puffs up, but love builds up." (1 Corinthians 8:1, NIV) In the Greek language, the word that translates into "puff up" implies that a person is so inflated with pride that it leads to arrogance. From the Bible, we know that the devil knows the Scriptures intellectually (see his temptation of Jesus in Matthew 4:1–11), and we also know that he is puffed up with pride and is arrogant. When you correctly apply the Bible to your life, you eliminate the danger of being puffed up with pride.

Bible study without application can be dangerous because knowledge requires action. If someone knows something, that knowledge should be demonstrated in everyday living. James said, "And remember, it is a message to obey, not just to listen to. If you don't obey, you are only fooling yourself." (James 1:22) The commandments from God are not optional. The Lord of the Universe doesn't say, "Please won't you consider doing this?" He commands, "Do it!" with the full expectation that we will obey his words.

Teaching Tips

During application, God's Word reaches out and touches the lives and events in you and your group. Reconsider the final phrase of the last sentence: you first, then the people you lead. The Apostle Paul emphasized the same progression in 1 Timothy 4:16a: "Keep a close watch on yourself and on your teaching." If you want to make an impression on others with something from the Bible, first let it work in your own heart.

In his most famous Sermon on the Mount, Jesus compared an obedient disciple to a wise man: "Anyone who listens to my teaching and obeys me is wise, like a person who builds a house on solid rock." (Matthew 7:24, NLT) When the trials of life came along, the wise man's life stood firm, while the foolish man's—the one who didn't practice what he knew—came crashing down. (Matthew 7:25–27, NLT)

King David was known as a man after God's own heart because he applied the Scriptures to his life and practiced what he knew. The psalmist wrote, "I pondered the direction of my life, and I turned to follow your statutes. I will hurry, without lingering, to obey your commands." (Psalm 119:59–60, NLT) Like David, you need to put what you know into action.

If you study the Bible without application, it also can be dangerous because knowledge increases responsibility. If you get serious about studying the Bible, you will be held more accountable than the average person because with added knowledge comes added responsibility. James wrote, "Remember, it is sin to know what you ought to do and then not do it." (James 4:17, NLT) If you have a deeper knowledge of the Bible, you will receive a stronger judgment if you fail to apply them. When you begin to study the Bible, God begins showing you areas of your life that need changing and calls you to greater responsibility. Although this may sound harsh, the truth is that if you are not planning to apply the lessons you receive from your Bible study, it may be better for you not to study the Bible at all. Otherwise, you'll only be heaping more judgment on yourself!

The great Christian poet John Milton allegedly said, "The end of all learning is to know God, and out of that knowledge to love him and be like him." As you and the members of your group study the Bible, be prepared to apply the Scriptures: We are to know God, to love him, and then to be like him.

If you are struggling to apply a particular section of the Bible, during your lesson preparation, keep one eye on the Bible passage and another on people's characteristics, needs, and day-to-day responsibilities. Here are a few questions to help you think of the group's application:

- What relationship does this principle have to my group members?
- In view of my group's members' life situation, what hindrances to application will they likely face?
- What kind of assistance or support system could help them apply this lesson?
- When the group meets, how can I illustrate the benefits of obeying this passage or the painful outcome of ignoring it?

Application Is Hard Work

Why is it hard to apply the Bible to our lives? At first glance, it would appear that applying the Bible to our lives would be fairly simple, but actually it is the hardest part of the process. Application isn't accidental. We have to plan for it, or it will never come about. Here are three ways that application of the Bible difficult: It requires thinking, the devil fights it viciously, and we naturally resist change.

Let's look at just how much serious thinking putting Bible teaching in action takes first. Often we must spend long periods in meditation (concentrated prayerful thinking) before we see a way to apply the truth of the Scriptures that we study. At times, it means looking beneath a temporary rule to see a timeless principle in the text. At other times, it means looking beyond a local custom to gain a universal insight. Each of these efforts takes time and concentration that we may be reluctant and hesitant to give.

Then consider how difficult it is to do anything—including applying the Bible to daily life—when a powerful force, like the devil, viciously fights it. The strongest attacks from the devil often come during your quiet times when you are trying to apply the lessons from your studies. Satan knows that as long as you are content with merely having head knowledge of the Word and fail to take action, you are not much of a threat to his plans. But as soon as you get serious about making some changes in your life, he will intensely fight you. Satan hates "doers" of the Bible. He will let you study the Scriptures all you want as long as you don't ask yourself, "Now what am I going to do with all that I've learned?"

Finally, application is hard because we naturally resist change. Often we don't feel like changing, which is exactly what true application requires. We live by our emotions rather than by our wills, for we are content to continue and do things the way we have always done them. Some Christians say they don't feel like studying the Bible, or they don't feel like praying, or they don't feel like witnessing. Feeling has nothing to do with living the Christian life, for feelings come and go. The key to spiritual maturity is to live for Jesus Christ not because it makes us feel good, but because we know it is the right thing to do. I have discovered that if the only time I study the Bible, pray, or witness is when I feel like it, the devil makes sure I never feel like it.

You should also apply the Bible to your life not because you feel like it that day or week, but because you know God expects it of you. Applied Bible study is an act of the will that leads to maturity and is the basis for stability in your Christian life.

The Steps of the Devotional Method

When you direct a group of people in the Devotional Method, use four simple steps: pray, meditate, apply, and memorize.

Step One: Pray for Insight

Teach your group to specifically ask for God's help to apply the Bible as you study and to show you specifically what he wants each person to do. You already know that God wants you to do two things: obey his instruction and tell others. In your prayer, tell God that you are ready to obey his message and that you are willing to share any revealed truth from the Scriptures with others.

> **Potent Quotables**
>
> "When I took a long, careful look at your ways, I got my feet back on the trail you blazed. I was up at once, didn't drag my feet, was quick to follow your orders." (Psalm 119:59–60, The Message)

Step Two: Meditate on the Verse(s)

Meditation is the key to discovering how to apply Scripture to your life. Teach the members of your group that meditation is essentially "thought digestion." You take a thought God gives you, put it in your mind, and think it over, over and over again. Meditation can be compared to cogitation, or what a cow does when it chews its cud. It eats some grass and sends it to its first stomach; then it lies down, brings up the grass, chews on it, and swallows it again. This process of digestion is repeated three times. Scripture meditation is reading a passage of the Bible and then concentrating on it in different ways. Here are several practical ways you can meditate on a passage of Scripture:

Visualize the scene of the narrative in your mind. Put yourself into the biblical situation and try to picture yourself as an active participant in the scene. Whether you are reading the Gospels or the Book of Acts or the historical books of the Old Testament, imagine yourself in that historical context. Ask yourself how you would feel if you were involved in that situation. What would you do? What would you say?

If you are studying Luke 7, for example, visualize yourself as the Pharisee who invites Jesus to his home and watches in horror as a woman brings expensive perfume and anoints Jesus' feet. What would you say to Jesus, and how would you feel about the "wasted" perfume? Or what would your emotions be if you were the woman who brought the perfume and anointed Jesus' feet?

Another example of visualization in meditation is to imagine yourself as the Apostle Paul in prison writing the letter we know as 2 Timothy. Picture yourself in that Roman jail, condemned to death, awaiting execution, and alone except for Luke. Feel the loneliness Paul must have felt, but also feel the triumph he must have experienced as he wrote, "I have fought a good fight, I have finished the race, and I have remained faithful." (2 Timothy 4:7, NLT) When you start visualizing a scene, Scripture comes tremendously alive to you.

Teaching Tips

The benefit of Bible study isn't derived from methods, techniques, or diligent efforts to decipher the text. The benefit is in obeying the voice of the Lord—receiving what he says and putting it into practice. Application doesn't happen by osmosis or by chance; application is by intent.

Emphasize words in the passage. Read through a verse aloud several times, each time emphasizing a different word, and watch new meanings develop. For instance, if you are meditating on Luke 1:37, you would emphasize the words as follows:

> "*For* nothing is impossible with God."
>
> "For *nothing* is impossible with God."
>
> "For nothing *is* impossible with God."
>
> "For nothing is *impossible* with God."
>
> "For nothing is impossible *with* God."
>
> "For nothing is impossible with *God.*"

You will get six different meanings from this verse as you go through and emphasize a different word each time.

Paraphrase the passage. Rephrase the verse or passage by putting your name in place of the nouns or pronouns used in the verse. For example, Psalm 23:1 would read, "The Lord is *Terry's* shepherd, *I* shall not want." This type of personalization will help you meditate on a passage and make it come alive for you.

Potent Quotables

"Study this Book of the Law continually. Meditate on it day and night so you may be sure to obey all that is written in it. Only then will you succeed." (Joshua 1:8, NLT)

Pray the verse or passage back to God. Change the passage under study into the first-person singular tense, turn it into a prayer, and then pray it back to God. The Book of Psalms is a good example of this method of meditation. Some scholars believe that King David memorized the Law of God and then personalized it and gave it back to God in the Psalms.

An example of this method of meditation can be seen in two verses from Psalms 19:7–8:

> Your law, O Lord, is perfect, reviving my soul. Your decrees, O Lord, are trustworthy, making me wise instead of simple.
>
> Your commandments, O Lord, are right, bringing joy to my heart. Your commands, O Lord, are clear, giving insight to my life.

Use the S-P-A-C-E P-E-T-S acrostic. The S-P-A-C-E P-E-T-S acrostic is a useful aid for meditation on Scripture verse. Each letter represents a question that can help you apply the passage to your life. If you memorize the nine questions represented from this acrostic, you'll have these questions available each time you want to meditate on a passage. This acrostic asks: Is there any …

- **S**in to confess? Is there some situation where I need to make restitution?
- **P**romise to claim? Is it a universal promise? Have the actions of my life met the condition(s)?
- **A**ttitude to change? Am I willing to work on a negative attitude and begin moving toward a positive one?
- **C**ommand to obey? Am I willing to do it no matter how I feel?
- **E**xample to follow? Is there a negative example to avoid or a positive one to copy?
- **P**rayer to pray? Is there anything I need to pray back to God from this passage?
- **E**rror to avoid? Is there any problem that I should be alert to or beware of?
- **T**ruth to believe? What new things can I learn about God the Father, Jesus Christ, the Holy Spirit, or other biblical teachings?
- **S**omething to praise God for? Is there something here for which I thank God for his provision or presence?

Step Three: Write Down Your Application

Write your insights about application that you've discovered through your meditation on the passage. Putting these insights down on paper will help you be specific about what you are learning. If you don't write it down, you'll soon forget it. This step is particularly necessary when you are dealing with spiritual truths. If you can't put it down on paper, you haven't thoroughly thought it through. Research shows that if you write something down, you'll remember it longer and be able to express to others what you have learned.

Teaching Tips

It's an important part of the learning process to reproduce in your own words what you have studied. The founder of the Navigators, an interdenominational nonprofit ministry, Dawson Trotman, said, "Thoughts disentangle themselves passing over the lips or through the pencil tips." If you want your group members to master the truths of Scripture, encourage them to write down those truths in their own words.

There are four key factors to writing down a good application:

- Your application should be *personal.* Write down your thoughts using the first-person singular tense. When you write out an application, use the personal pronouns *I*, *me*, and *mine* throughout your writing.
- Your application should be *practical.* Make sure the way you choose to apply a passage is something that you can accomplish. Plan definite steps you intend to take. Create a personal project that will encourage you to be a "doer of the Word." As James 1:22 says, "Do not merely listen to the word and so deceive yourselves. Do what it says." (NIV) Make your applications as specific as possible. When you write in broad generalities, you often feel helpless and it produces little action.
- Your application should be *possible.* It should be something that you know you are able to accomplish, or otherwise you will grow discouraged.
- Your application should be *provable.* You must set up some way to follow up and check on your success in doing the application. It has to be measurable so that you will know when you have completed it. This aspect involves setting a time limit on the completion of your application.

Here's an example of these four factors from Ecclesiastes 6:7. The passage reads, "Wise men and fools alike spend their lives scratching for food and never seem to get enough." (Living Bible) Writing an application using these four factors would look like this:

- **Personal:** "I need to …"
- **Practical:** "I need to lose some weight."

- **Possible:** "I need to lose five pounds."
- **Provable:** "I need to lose five pounds before the end of the month."

To aid in your ability to carry out this type of application, tell a friend or a family member about your goal. That person can then encourage you and check on your progress.

Write down your applications for your present needs and your future needs. For example, what if you find an application that doesn't apply to you at that particular time? For example, you might be studying a passage about death and how to overcome grief and sorrow, but at the moment you don't have any issues in this area. How do you apply these verses? You should make an effort to write down your application, regardless of your particular situation, for two reasons. First, you might be able to use the application soon in your own life. Second, it might help you minister to someone else who is in that situation at the moment. Ask yourself, "How can I use the application from these verses to help someone else?"

Step Four: Memorize the Key Verse

To continue thinking about the application of a passage long after you've studied it, it's important to memorize the key verse from the section.

If you or some of the members of your group are struggling to memorize Scripture, here's something different to try: memory by rhythm. Guide your group to memorize Bible verses or truths by setting them to a rhythm, musical tune, or rap pattern. Invite one of the members to start the rhythm. Prompt others to join in, and then gradually add the words to the tune, reading from Bibles for the words. Repeat until the words smoothly fit the rhythm and until volunteers can say the verse from memory. This method is excellent for anyone new to the Bible or new to church. If someone in your group has special musical talent, invite him or her to start the rhythm or rap. This person then becomes the leader in a familiar area and becomes open to the Bible.

Leading Your Group in the Devotional Method

Sometimes God will work on one area of your life for several weeks or even months. It takes time to change ingrained character traits, attitudes, and habits. New ways of thinking and habits are not set in one day. We must be aware of this factor and be willing to let God continue to reinforce a new truth in our lives. Don't be fooled into thinking that if you write down one application, it will become a magic formula that will produce an instant change. Instead, consider your application as a step along the pathway to growth. The memorized verse will help in that process because you will carry this verse of Scripture in your heart and mind.

One time James had to work on the quality of increasing his sensitivity to others. It took several months for God to build such a quality into his life because James needed to see how this quality related to the various areas of his life. God continued putting James into situations where he was tempted to be insensitive—the opposite quality. Your application process may be the same in your life. God may teach you to love others and put you in the middle of some hard to love people. You may have to learn peace in the midst of chaos, and learn patience while experiencing irritations. Through this application of Scripture, you will discover how to have joy in the middle of testing and sorrow. You will begin to understand that when God wants to build a positive quality in your life, he must allow you to come face to face with situations in which you can choose to do the right thing instead of following your natural inclinations.

Although the bulk of this chapter has described the execution of the method, you will need to go through the various steps yourself and then teach it to the members of your group. During the group session, lead a discussion about the variety of applications from a single verse. You will be surprised at how a single passage from the Bible can mean different things to different people. Focus your discussion on the personal application from the Devotional Method. It's a powerful tool to help people gain practical, everyday insight from the Bible.

The Least You Need to Know

- The Devotional Method applies Scripture so that it is practical, personal, possible, and provable.
- Application is hard work but helps promote personal growth.
- Pray for insight into the passage, meditate on the passage, write down your application, and memorize a key verse from the passage.

Chapter 6

Chapter by Chapter

- The Chapter Summary Method explained
- Why is the Chapter Summary Method important?
- Four keys as you read the Bible chapter
- Ten steps in the Chapter Summary Method
- Teaching the Chapter Summary Method to others

Believe it or not, when the Bible was originally written, it didn't have any chapter or verse divisions. In A.D. 1228, Bishop Stephen Langton added chapter divisions to make the Bible more accessible to readers. Although some of these divisions tend to interrupt the flow of the writer's message, they usually provide a good break in the text and thus help readers study smaller portions of the Bible as a unit. There are 1,189 chapters in the Protestant Bible. If you studied a chapter each day, it would take you just over three years to complete the Bible. Although I don't recommend this approach, this chapter suggests how to study a chapter in depth.

One Chapter, In-Depth

By using the Chapter Summary Method, you can gain a general understanding of the contents of a single Bible chapter. You will derive insight into the chapter if you read the chapter at least five times, ask a series of content questions, and summarize the central thoughts of the passage. If you use this method, you will begin to gain an understanding of discrete chapters of books from the Bible. For many people beginning Bible study, this method is popular because most chapters are fairly short, and thus it requires less study to understand and complete a chapter summary. Furthermore, it is easy for a teacher to impart this method of study to brand-new Christians or any people interested in performing meaningful Bible study.

Potent Quotables

Look at how the Jewish people processed the Laws of God in the book of Nehemiah: "The Book of the Law of the Lord their God was read aloud to them for about three hours. Then for three more hours they took turns confessing their sins and worshiping the Lord their God." (Nehemiah 9:3, NLT) And sometimes to us, it seems boring or a waste of time when someone reads only a short Bible passage!

Indeed, as soon as you understand the 10 basic steps outlined in the next section of this chapter, you can begin practicing this method. The study form and the example in Chapter 16 will give you further tips about using this teaching method. Another benefit of the Chapter Summary Method is that it doesn't take much time to teach or to learn. Depending on the length of the chapter you are studying, you can complete a chapter summary in about 20 to 30 minutes, especially if the chapter contains a historical narrative such as those included in the Old Testament, the Gospels, and the Book of Acts. The historical narrative sections of the Bible are easier to understand and less complicated to study. However, the Chapter Summary Method requires more time in the Psalms, the prophetic books, and the doctrinal letters of the New Testament.

Proceed with Caution

Don't try to force your students to read aloud if they feel terribly uncomfortable doing so. Sometimes people stop attending a study because they're too afraid to take part when their turn comes. Suggest that each person read only as much as they want to read. Good readers are then free to read a paragraph or two, and those less willing or able can join in only as they are ready to participate.

Another beneficial aspect of the Chapter Summary Method is that you won't need any outside reference tools. If you are teaching at a church retreat where not a lot of reference tools are available, use this method for the entire group to make discoveries about the Bible. Once you and your students understand the 10 basic steps (summarized shortly) and select a book of the Bible to study, all you'll need is a Bible and a piece of paper.

Finally, this method is a good type of study to use when you are trying to rapidly read through the entire Bible and grasp a general survey of the text. As you read each chapter, you can make some initial notes using the Chapter Summary Form.

Getting All You Can

As you prepare to begin this method, read through the Bible chapter at least five times—it's the best way to get acquainted with the content of that particular chapter. The more times you read a chapter, the more it will come alive for you. Many Christians miss the great insights of Scripture because they fail to reread a passage from the Bible.

The great Bible preacher G. Campbell Morgan was famous for his powerful, exciting sermons. When someone asked him for the secret of his ability to communicate God's Word, he replied that he made it a habit to read a chapter or passage 30 to 40 times before he began working on it for a sermon. With this type of effort in understanding the text, it's no wonder his sermons were meaningful and exciting.

Teaching Tips

Here are some alternative reading methods to try at different times with your group:

- Read the passage in unison several times, each time more quickly than before.
- Read responsively.
- Do a conversational reading (particularly with narratives like the Gospels), with the members of the group pretending to be Bible characters.

To get the most out of each reading, follow these tips and have your students do the same when they use this method of study:

- Use a clean copy of the chapter. If you use this method with a previously notated Bible, you'll have a tendency to concentrate on the same ideas over and over. Let God speak to you through the text in fresh ways and give you new insights.

- Read the chapter at least twice straight through, without stopping. During the first few readings, don't stop in the middle of a chapter, but read it from beginning to end. The goal is to get a feel for the flow of the chapter, so encourage your students not to be concerned with the details at first. Instead, have them try to focus on the central theme of the chapter and the writer's overall message.
- Read the chapter in several different modern-day translations. Each version will give you additional insights as you notice how the various translators rendered the original writing. Make notes on the interesting differences you find.
- Quietly read the chapter aloud. Doing so helps those who ordinarily have trouble concentrating. Many people find that reading aloud helps them focus better on the text.

Responsive reading is another way to read the Bible in a group setting. As the leader, you read the first verse of the passage; then the group responds in unison with the second verse. Then you read the third verse and the group responds with the fourth verse, and so on. Repeating the passage together provides everyone (readers and non-readers) with a level of comfort working together. One caution is to make sure everyone is using the same translation of the Bible, or such an exercise will sound like everyone speaking in a different language at the same time.

Ten Steps to Understanding

To make the most of the Chapter Summary Method, begin looking for the following 10 specific things as you read and reread the chapter. Write down your observations and insights on a blank sheet of paper, in any order.

Let's take one step at a time, starting with the importance of creating a simple one- or two-word title understanding the caption.

Step One: Create a Caption

Encourage your students to give each chapter they read using this method a short, descriptive title. The shorter the title is, the more likely you will remember it. In fact, if you use this method for every chapter in a selected book of the Bible, you can remember the contents of the entire book simply by memorizing the chapter titles. If possible, use one word (for instance, you could title 1 Corinthians 13 "Love") and, at the most, five words (Hebrews 11 could be "Heroes of the Faith"). Try to find the key word of the chapter and fit it into your title.

You and your students will remember your title longer if it is catchy or produces a mental picture. One creative personal gave "Well-Well" as a title for John 4. And here's why: The two key events of that chapter are the woman at the well and the nobleman's son whom Jesus made well.

Step Two: Make a Table of Contents

Summarize, describe, paraphrase, outline, or make a list of the major points you discover in the chapter. The particular method you use will depend on the literary style of the chapter and your own preference. Analytical people enjoy outlining, while other people like to summarize. Both you and your students should choose the method with which you are most comfortable and the one that is easiest for you to complete. Don't try to interpret the chapter; instead, make simple, off-the-cuff observations on its contents.

Step Three: Identify Chief People

Another way to develop a deeper understanding of the chapter is to identify and list the most important people in the chapter. Who are the main people in this chapter? Why are they included? What is significant about them? If the chapter contains pronouns (*he*, *she*, *they*, etc.), you might have to refer to the previous chapter to identify the people. Write down your reasons for choosing certain people as the chief personalities in the chapter. When you come to long genealogies (lists of people's names), don't try to list each one, but summarize the list.

> **Teaching Tips**
>
> Encourage your readers by quoting the Apostle Peter's words about the Apostle Paul: "This is just as our beloved brother Paul wrote to you with the wisdom God gave him—speaking of these things in all of his letters. Some of his comments are hard to understand ...." (2 Peter 3:15b, NLT)

Step Four: Choosing a Choice Verse

After reading the chapter a few times, select a verse that summarizes the entire chapter or one that speaks to you in a personal way. If a chapter doesn't contain a key verse summarizing the writer's viewpoint, you may want to pick a verse that will help you write your application, one that carries a message that you believe God would have you apply to your life.

Step Five: Recognize Crucial Word(s)

Write down the key word or words of the chapter. Many times the key word will be the one that is used most frequently (for instance, *love* in 1 Corinthians 13 and *faith* in Hebrews 11). Sometimes the crucial word may be the most important word but not the one used most. For example, in Romans 6, the word *count* (KJV, *reckon*) is the most important word, although it is used only once. (Romans 6:11) Also, a chapter may have more than one crucial word. Chances are, you'll know them when you see them—and when you do, write them down!

Step Six: Face Your Challenges

Often you can learn more from what you don't understand than what appears obvious to you. That's why you should make a list of any difficulties you face within the chosen passage. Are there any statements or sections that you don't understand? Is there any problem or question you would like to take additional time to study? You may even find that you'll get ideas for other types of studies you might want to do in the future. If a certain word catches your attention, for instance, make a note and take the time to study it later. A question about a doctrinal matter might motivate you do to a topical study on that particular teaching.

Teaching Tips

Choose your words carefully when one of your students contributes a comment. Your verbal reaction should express appreciation with the participant's discovery, and you should give verbal applause recognizing a person's textual investigation. Public congratulations will encourage the participants to dig into Scripture and participate in the discussion.

Step Seven: Organize Cross-References

As you study more and more of the Bible, you'll begin to see how characters and themes recur within several different chapters. If you keep a list of where and what you find, you'll be able to refer to those passage to help you clarify issues as you read them. As you read, ask the question: What else in the Bible might help me understand this chapter? Cross-references are important because they are helpful tools to interpret the meaning of a chapter. These references help you see what the Bible as a whole has to say on any given topic.

Step Eight: See Christ

The entire Bible is a revelation of the person of Jesus Christ. In fact, Jesus used the Old Testament to teach his disciples about himself. On the day Jesus rose from the dead, he appeared on the Emmaus Road and taught two of his disciples. "Then Jesus quoted passages from the writings of Moses and all the prophets, explaining what all the Scriptures said about himself." (Luke 24:27, NTL) As you study each chapter, be alert to statements that tell you something about Jesus Christ, the Holy Spirit, or God the Father. Ask yourself what you can learn about the nature of Jesus from this chapter. What attributes of God in Christ are illustrated here? Examples of such attributes are his love, justice, faithfulness, power, mercy, and holiness. This step may be one of the most difficult to complete in certain portions of the Bible, particularly in the Old Testament narratives and in passages where symbolism is used. When symbolism is involved, it's more challenging to write down what you learn about the nature of Jesus.

Step Nine: Derive a Central Lesson(s)

Write down the major principles, insights, and lessons you learned from this particular chapter of the Bible. Ask yourself why God wanted this passage in the Bible and what he wants to teach you with the chapter. What central thought is the writer trying to develop?

Step Ten: Come to a Conclusion

This is the final step of the application portion of the study. As discussed previously, it's important in each of these Bible methods to develop a plan to implement the lessons in your life. For the Chapter Summary Method, ask two questions: How do these truths apply to me personally? What specifically am I going to do about them?

As an alternative closing to your group session, read this quote from W. E. Sanger: "God's work, apart from prayer, at best produces clever ineffectiveness." Prayer is essential for God to work in your group. Close your time with intercessory prayer. As people voice their requests, ask another individual to pray for this request. Make sure you model transparency in the prayer time and your own need to seek God's wisdom each and every day.

Teaching the Chapter Summary Method to Others

As discussed, your first step is to select a book or a section of chapters. The Gospel of Mark is often a good place to begin because the stories are straightforward in language (little symbolism) and are short chapters.

After you help the group agree on a series of chapters for study, teach this method by following the contents of this chapter. First explain the importance of reading the chapter at least five times. Then go through each of the 10 steps and explain the rationale behind each step. As you complete your personal study, prepare probing questions for each of the 10 steps. Remember, part of your challenge is to guide the group to truth. You are not expected to have the answers to everyone's questions. You are expected to stimulate conversation about the content of the particular chapter.

You might want to use the detailed example of the chapter method in Chapter 16 to illustrate your various points and make them clear.

The Least You Need to Know

- The Chapter Summary Method doesn't require deep study.
- This method is particularly valuable for the brand-new Christian, but anyone interested in meaningful Bible study can benefit.
- Read the chapter at least five times and in different translations, without stopping and without taking study notes.
- Take time to learn the 10 steps of the method; then teach them to your group and guide the discussion.

Chapter 7

Understanding the Bible Character Quality Method

In This Chapter

- Defining the Bible Character Quality Method
- Concentrating on positive character traits
- Following the nine steps
- Teaching the Bible Character Quality Method

One of the main goals of Christian life is to develop Christlike character. When we replace the bad qualities in our lives with good ones, we daily grow to become more and more like Jesus Christ. Yet before we can work on developing Christlike character, we must be able to recognize that character.

The purpose of this particular method of study is to help you identify and understand these positive and negative character qualities. With this new understanding, you can work on setting aside the negative character qualities and building the positive ones in your life. By emphasizing the positive, you can become more and more like Jesus Christ.

Concentrating on Character

This method of Bible study involves discovering what the Bible says about a particular characteristic of a person and then paying special attention to how to apply those characteristics to your own personality and life. This method combines in a simplified fashion three other Bible study methods: the Biographical Method (see Chapter 9), the Word Study Method (see Chapter 10), and the Cross-Reference Method, but with important differences.

The method is distinct from the Biographical Method because here you are studying the characteristics of a person rather than the biographical facts about the person. These qualities can be negative or positive or both. The point is that we learn to recognize those characteristics in ourselves, and then avoid the negative ones and work on building the positive ones.

As these positive qualities are brought into our everyday lives, we can grow to become more like the Lord Jesus Christ. For example, the Bible admonishes you to be meek. So if you wanted to become meek, you would have to know the character qualities of meekness before you could really embrace it and make it a part of your character.

Potent Quotables

"Now the Bereans were of more noble character than the Thessalonians, for they received the message with great eagerness and examined the Scriptures every day to see if what Paul said was true." (Acts 17:11, NIV)

Proceed with Caution

To teach the Bible with clarity, avoid asking long-winded questions. A good discussion facilitator trims questions until they are crisp and to the point. Long questions hamper class participation.

This method is the first one in this book that requires the use of some Bible tools. Here are some of the reference tools you will need:

- **A study Bible.** This Bible usually has the phrase "study Bible" in the title. This reference book includes the Bible text in different translations along with some features to enhance the reader's knowledge about the Bible.
- **A Bible dictionary and/or a word study book.** A Bible dictionary is a specialized dictionary of words from the Bible. A word study book is another specialized Bible reference tool and often contains the Greek or Hebrew definitions of Bible words along with some usage guidelines for each word.
- **An exhaustive concordance.** A concordance is a large book (usually 9×12 hardcover) with almost 2,000 thin pages, and it references every single word and its usage in the Bible. Each word appears with a Bible verse reference along with a short phrase where the word is used in the Bible.

- **A topical Bible.** As the name implies, it's not your typical chronological Bible. Instead the principle verses of the Bible are organized by key words. Underneath each key word, there are the main Bible references that contain this word.
- **An English dictionary.** Another valuable reference tool, a dictionary comes in handy when you encounter unfamiliar words. Instead of skipping over these words, make a habit of looking up the word and learning the definition.

If you want to grow and develop positive biblical character qualities in your life, follow these tips:

- **Work on only one quality at a time.** Don't try to work on two or three or more—it takes concentrated effort to see how that one quality applies to every area of your life. It is far better to build one quality solidly in your life than to work on several at a time that end up being weak.
- **Don't rush it!** Developing character takes time. I've discovered that God works on an area in my own life for months (sometimes years) before that becomes a part of my daily walk with God.
- **Stick with one quality until you feel you've incorporated it into all aspects of your life.** Don't skip around trying to work on many qualities when you need victory in that one area. Remember that the quality of diligence is one quality you want to work on!
- **Be sensitive to the fact that the Lord wants to turn your weaknesses into strengths.** That means that you might think you have a negative quality when, considered in a different light, it could benefit you and others. If you tend to be legalistic, rigid, and unbending, for instance, you might use those qualities in a more positive way to enhance self-discipline. However, you would need to add compassion and concern for others to temper your more rigid and unbending nature; that way, self-discipline becomes a positive asset.
- **Trust the Holy Spirit to build these qualities into your life.** In the final analysis, it's God's power within you that reproduces the fruit of the Spirit in your

Teaching Tips

The most overlooked book for Bible study is the English dictionary. The *Funk and Wagnall's Standard Desk Dictionary* not only explains the English words of the Bible, but often gives a theological definition for terms such as *salvation, grace,* and *baptize.* An English dictionary can provide clarity when comparative study falls short.

life. God alone can change your character. "For God is working in you, giving you the desire to obey him and the power to do what pleases him."—Philippians 2:13, NLT. So let go of your own control; let God move in your life, and trust the Holy Spirit to work.

Nine Steps for Doing a Character Quality Study

If we are to believe Madison Avenue and the advertising on television, character is built upon the type of vehicle we drive and the clothing or perfume we wear. But we know that's not the truth. If we want to acquire and develop character, we begin to do so by studying these character qualities in the Bible. If you follow the steps discussed here, you'll learn how to dig these character qualities for your life from the Scriptures.

Step One: Identify the Quality

Select the quality that you want to study, and write it down. Next look up the quality in an English dictionary and write down the definition of the word or concept. Finally, make a list of any synonyms or related words that help you to understand the quality.

Step Two: Name the Opposite Quality

After you identify the quality you want to study, try to identify its opposite. Once you have, look up and write down its dictionary definition. If you need help, use a dictionary of antonyms. Keep in mind that some qualities will have a clear-cut opposite (unfaithfulness is the opposite of faithfulness, for example), and others may have more than one. In the case of "faith," for example, you could develop the following list:

- Faith and doubt
- Faith and fear
- Faith and apathy

Step Three: Perform a Simple Word Study

Locate the Bible definition of the quality you are studying by seeing the way it is used in the Scriptural contexts and then checking a Bible encyclopedia, a dictionary, or a word-study book for the ways the quality was used in biblical times and in the

Scriptures. Some of these resources will even tell you how many times the word was used in the Bible, in each testament, in the writings of different authors, and in the book you are studying.

For example, if you were studying the quality of meekness and used a Bible encyclopedia and other resources, you'd discover that the word meant "breaking something and bringing it under submission" in its original Greek. The Greeks used the word to describe the quality that horses possessed after they were trained and brought under submission to their masters. A stallion would still have all the power and strength of its wild days, but it was under the control of its master. As a Christian character quality, meekness is strength in that it allows you to be submissive to Jesus Christ.

Proceed with Caution

The process of selecting the best cross-references for the quality you choose will take some time as you look up and compare various Scriptures. But don't become frustrated. Be patient; once you have chosen your dozen or so best passages, stop. There's no need to wander endlessly through the Bible searching for one more tidbit of truth.

Step Four: Locate Cross-References

When it comes to interpreting Scripture, the Bible is the best source. Use your topical Bible and concordance to find all the verses you can on this quality. Using cross-references will help you derive additional insights from other portions of the Bible. Look up the word and its synonyms in the topical Bible and concordance, write the cross-reference on the appropriate section of the character quality form (see Chapter 17, and give a brief description of that verse. Then ask the following questions about the quality you are studying as you meditate on the cross-reference verses:

- What benefits can this trait bring to you?
- What are some of the bad consequences this trait can bring to you?
- What are the benefits this trait can bring to others?
- What are some of the bad consequences this trait can bring to others?
- Is there a particular promise from God related to this trait?
- Does God give any warning or judgment related to this trait?
- Is there a command related to this trait?
- What are the factors to produce this trait?
- Did Jesus have anything to say about this quality? If so, what?

- What writer talked about this quality the most?
- Is this trait symbolized by anything in the Bible? Is that significant?
- Is this trait listed with a group of qualities? What is the relationship between them? What does this suggest?
- Which Bible verses tell us directly what God thinks of this trait?
- Do you want more or less of this trait in your life?

After you ask this series of questions, plus others that you create on your own, you might want to write a brief summary of the Bible's teaching on this quality. You might list any lessons or principles that you learned from this mini-topical study, or you might paraphrase a few key verses on this trait.

Teaching Tips

When you ask questions, take your lead from Jesus. His questions were often provocative but understandable. The pages of The Gospels are filled with examples of his compelling probes. The following examples spurred thought among those listening to Jesus:

"How could evil men like you speak what is good and right?" (Matthew 12:34, NLT)

"Who do people say that the Son of Man is?" (Matthew 16:13, NLT)

"Why do you call me, 'Lord, Lord,' and do not do what I say?" (Luke 6:46, NIV)

"Will you lay down your life for me?" (John 13:38, NIV)

Always be sure to write down any difficulties you have with the verses you looked up and the questions you would like to have answered. Possibly they will be points of discussion during your teaching time with your group. You may also discover the answer to your questions in another verse you study at a later time.

Step Five: Create a Brief Biographical Study

Once you've identified your cross-references, return to your Bible and locate at least one person (or more, if possible) who demonstrated this character quality in their life. Briefly describe this character quality and write down the Bible verses that refer to it. As you complete this portion of the study, ask these questions:

- What shows this quality in this character's life?
- How did this quality affect his or her life?

- Did the quality help or hinder the character's growth to maturity?
- What result did it produce in his or her life?

Here's an example of this step: Joseph, the son of Jacob, manifested different qualities of the fruit of the spirit (Galatians 5:22–23) in different incidents from his life, including this passage from Genesis: "As they discussed who should be appointed for the job, Pharaoh said, 'Who could do it better than Joseph? For he is a man who is obviously filled with the spirit of God.'" (Genesis 41:38, NLT)

Just in Case

Good general resources for conducting word studies are W. E. Vine's *Expository Dictionary of New Testament Words* (Zondervan Publishing House, 1982) and Lawrence Richards's *Expository Dictionary of Bible Words* (Zondervan Publishing House, 1991). Both are inexpensive resources based on the English text, yet they give Greek and cultural information that is understandable to anyone.

Here are some qualities we discover in the life of Joseph:

- He showed self-control during a difficult temptation. (Genesis 39)
- He exhibited patience and industry in difficult circumstances. (Genesis 39:19–40:23)
- He displayed faithfulness during a difficult task. (Genesis 41:37–57)
- He showed kindness, goodness, and gentleness in difficult family reunions. (Genesis 42:50)
- He showed love in a difficult family situation. (Genesis 47)

Often a particular quality will be compared to the manners of certain animals, particularly in the Book of Proverbs. For example, a diligent person will be compared to an ant or a lion's roar to a king's rage. (Proverbs 19:12) When you discover these qualities, write them down.

Teaching Tips

A prolific pastor of the nineteenth century, Charles Spurgeon knew that Bible truths overshadowed illustrations in importance. Yet Spurgeon realized that folks are more likely to remember and to obey a truth that's illustrated. What he told aspiring preachers also is relevant to discussion facilitators and classroom teachers: "Examples are more powerful than precepts."

Step Six: Select a Memory Verse

Using the passages from your biographic portion of the study or your cross-references, write down a memory verse that speaks to you and that you intend to memorize during the following week. When God provides an opportunity for you to work on this character quality in a specific way, this verse will come in handy. When you memorize a Bible verse, God will bring this verse to your mind in prayer or during temptation or other situations where you need encouragement and are away from your physical Bible.

Step Seven: Choose a Situation or a Relationship to Work On

This step begins the application portion of a character quality study. Think of an area in which God wants you to work on this character quality—avoiding it if it's negative, and building it in your life if it's a positive trait. The application can involve either an interpersonal relationship or a personal situation.

If it is an interpersonal relationship with a spouse, a neighbor, or someone else you deal with, determine ahead of time how you will respond in your interactions with that person. For example, possibly you need to be more patient with this other person. Study the character quality of patience throughout the Bible and learn how it can help your life. Look for opportunities to work on this character quality in your relationship with the person or persons. Your goal is to have more mature relationships.

If it is a personal situation, anticipate in advance what you will do when the situation occurs. For example, let's say you feel that you are lazy, and your study on laziness has convinced you to get rid of this quality in your life. Plan ahead—think of situations that bring out this side of you and determine ahead of time how you will respond. For example, if getting up early in the morning is difficult for you, set two alarm clocks on the other side of the room to force you up and out.

Step Eight: Plan a Specific Project

This step is the practical part of your application; you'll actually implement the plans you made in Step Seven. For example, one time I was working on the quality of gratitude. My specific project was to write five letters of thankfulness each week to people who had been a blessing in my life. In each letter, I wrote "I'm grateful to you because …." Remember, each application should be measurable, possible, personal, and practical.

As the leader for your group, you set the stage for the lesson response, but the group members are the ones who actually speak about the application section. They are responsible to God for reforming their relationships, reversing sinful patterns, and meeting the needs around them as the Bible passage teaches them.

One method you can use is to reserve group time to discuss a truth's implications. You can testify about the power of a passage in your own life. You can help people picture the difference a precept would make if they followed it in their daily routines. You can ask them for anecdotes that illustrate the benefits of obeying and the consequences of disobeying God's Word. You can probe for possible responses that fit the maturity levels and needs of the participants.

However, do keep in mind that you cannot apply the Bible to anyone but yourself. Because of your teacher role in the group and the personal relationship you have outside of the group setting, you will be tempted to try and apply the Scriptures to the lives of others. Don't do it, because the only person you can change is you. A learner's heart is either prepared to respond to the Scriptures or too hardened or afraid for God's truth to penetrate and change the heart.

It's natural enough to feel frustrated at how limited you are in helping others apply God's word, but here's one healthy way to deal with that frustration: Pray for your group members. When you pray for them, you're acknowledging your dependence on the Holy Spirit. You're admitting that transferring truth from the head to the heart is a divine matter, not something that a human can accomplish. You're asking God to accomplish what even excellence in teaching cannot fulfill: to prick their consciousness, to alter their attitudes, and to bend their wills in the direction of biblical standards. This reliance on God for life change in your group reminds us of something theologian W. E. Sanger said: "God's work, apart from prayer, produces clever ineffectiveness."

Step Nine: Write Down a Personal Illustration

A few days after you have completed the first eight steps of this study, write down an illustration of how you were able to work on this quality. Remember, this is the "measurable" portion of your application. Be specific—write down where you have succeeded and where you might have failed. In just a short time, you should be able to develop a whole set of personal examples of how God is working in your life, getting rid of negative qualities and building positive ones.

These written illustrations will serve a number of purposes. When you feel discouraged, you'll be able to review your illustrations and recall how God has worked in your life. You can also use your illustrations to teach a new Christian and encourage that person to examine his or her own experiences and create his or her own illustrations. Finally, when you share these illustrations with your group, add personal statements to your presentation like, "Here's how God worked in my life."

Often God builds character in our lives by putting us in situations in which we are tempted to do the wrong thing. For example, God may teach you honesty by placing you in a situation where you are tempted to be dishonest.

Teaching the Character Quality Method to Others

In order to teach the Character Quality Method to others, begin going through the lists of qualities found in New Testament passages. Some of the positive ones are listed here:

- Matthew 5:3–12: The Beatitudes
- Galatians 5:22–23: The fruit of the Spirit
- Philippians 4:4–9: Admirable qualities
- 2 Peter 1:5–8: Qualities that should increase in our lives

Also, don't neglect to study the negative qualities so you can work on ridding these features from your life. Here are some negative qualities:

- Galatians 5:19–21: A list of the works of the flesh
- 2 Timothy 3:1–5: Qualities you should have nothing to do with

Here are some other specific qualities taught throughout the Bible that you should study and work on:

Positive Qualities

- Contentment
- Sincerity
- Discipline
- Cooperativeness
- Fairness
- Loyalty
- Generosity
- Forgiveness
- Teachability
- Availability
- Faithfulness
- Diligence
- Determination
- Humility
- Honesty
- Servanthood

Negative Qualities

- Apathy
- Bitterness
- Lustfulness
- Fearfulness
- Worry
- Impatience
- Dishonesty
- Inability to love
- Gossip
- Rebelliousness
- Disrespectfulness
- Unfaithfulness
- Selfishness
- Pride
- A critical spirit
- Laziness

There are many other character qualities found throughout the Bible, but these should start you and your students on a remarkably enriching journey.

The Least You Need to Know

- Bible character studies help you identify positive and negative character qualities and understand them so you can become more like Jesus.
- The method involves a simple, nine-step process.
- Several key passages are listed for positive and negative traits in the New Testament for additional study.

Chapter 8

Understanding the Bible Theme Method of Teaching

In This Chapter

- Defining the Bible Theme Method
- Using questions to reveal themes
- A shorter way to the heart of the matter
- Asking the right questions
- Teaching the Bible Theme Method

One of the keys to good Bible study is learning to ask the right questions. For the Bible Theme Method of study, you determine a set of questions to ask about the chosen theme before you look in the Bible. Your questions should be based on what Rudyard Kipling called his "honest serving men" in *The Elephant's Child* from *The Quotations of John Bartlett* (Little, Brown and Company, 1951):

> I keep six honest serving men
> They taught me all I knew.
> Their names are What and Why and When
> And How and Where and Who.

As you prepare the questions, use Kipling's serving men as your guiding light for thematic study. Ask these vital questions: What? Why? When? How? Where? Who?

Exploring Themes to Reveal Meaning

The Bible Theme Method involves approaching a biblical theme with a set of no more than five questions in mind. Next you trace this theme through the Bible or a single book by asking only those questions, and then summarizing your conclusions and writing out a personal application.

> **Potent Quotables**
>
> "My heart is stirred by a noble theme as I recite my verses for the king; my tongue is the pen of a skillful writer." (Psalm 45:1, NIV)

The Bible Theme Method is similar to the Bible Topic Method (Chapter 9), but it differs in two key ways. First, the Theme Method takes less time than the Topical Method because you study fewer verses. In addition, while one topic may have many different themes running through it, a theme is, by definition, more prescribed. For example, the topic "prayer" could involve several themes, such as "The Prayers of Jesus," "The Prayers of New Testament Writers," "Conditions for Answered Prayer," "Prayer Promises," "Intercession for Others," and many others—and you examine every possible Bible verse that relates to the overall topic. When you do a thematic study, however, you concentrate on just one theme and only on those Bible passages that deal with that theme.

The second way a thematic study differs from a topical study is in the number of questions that you ask. In a topical study, you ask as many questions as you can because your goal is to discover as much as possible about the topic. The thematic study limits the questions to a maximum of five carefully chosen questions. After creating a list of all the verses that relate to the theme, you examine each verse, asking only the questions that you prepared.

The reason for limiting the number of questions is that a theme may have 100, 200, or more references. If your set of questions gets too long, you'll get bogged down and grow discouraged. You'll become tired of the study before you finish it.

As you and your group begin this study, ask the Holy Spirit of God to guide and enlighten your study. Approach the Bible with a prayer like that of the psalmist: "Open my eyes that I may see wonderful things in your law." (Psalm 119:18, NIV) Pray with expectancy because a new experience is waiting for you.

The Benefits of the Bible Theme Method

The purpose of the Bible Theme Method is to discover what you can about a chosen theme with a specific set of questions, prepared beforehand, that you ask for each verse chosen for study. This method, too, will require some study tools, but there are some great advantages to its use and several practical tips for using it. For this method, you will need to have a study Bible, an exhaustive concordance, and a topical Bible.

Some of the advantages of the Bible Theme Method include the following:

- You don't need many reference tools. You can do a limited study if you have only a topical Bible. But because a topical Bible doesn't list all the references on a particular theme, you will benefit by also using an exhaustive concordance. With the concordance, you can make a list of every word that relates to the theme, and then look up each word in the concordance and select the verses that deal specifically with the theme you have selected.

Teaching Tips

Some people in your group might never have seen an exhaustive concordance. This reference tool lists every occurrence of each word in the Bible. For instance, if your topic or theme is grace, you can use the concordance to find every page in the Bible that mentions grace. If you remember that one of the psalms talks about "thirsting for God like a deer," you can use a concordance to track down the psalm by looking up the words *thirst* or *deer.* You can even find information about the Hebrew or Greek words behind the English translations. The two most commonly used exhaustive concordances are *Strong's Exhaustive Concordance* and *Young's Analytical Concordance.* Both are keyed to the King James Version of the Bible. For the New International Version (NIV), you can get *The NIV Exhaustive Concordance.* You can purchase any of these books online, in the reference section at a Christian bookstore, or in the religious section at a regular bookstore.

- You can use this method when you don't have time to do a full-scale topical study.
- This method is a good way to preview a topic because it allows you to review the high points of its subordinate themes before attempting a regular topical study of the subject. Or you can use this approach when you are interested in having only certain questions answered on a particular theme. By using this method, you can discover exactly what you want to find out without spending valuable time on unrelated matters.

- This method makes turning the material into a Sunday school lesson or sermon very easy. After completing your personal study, make each of your questions a major point in your talk. Add personal illustrations, and then share the biblical answers with your group, class, or congregation.
- If you're mentoring new Christians or other students, this method is a good one to use. It is simple enough to grasp even for someone who has not done any personal Bible study.

From a single Bible lesson, your group may glean numerous truths. As you prepare the lesson and as you lead the discussion, try not to examine other points unrelated to the theme. Your observation and analysis of the text should help you identify an overarching, unifying theme. Clearly communicate the broad theme that governs the passage, and the participants will be less likely to steer the conversation away from it. Connect the facts and principles to a comprehensive slant, and group members' ideas or illustrations will usually mesh with it.

Practical Tips: The Bible Theme Method

Because of the simplicity of this particular method and the danger of "getting carried away," some practical tips and words of caution are necessary.

First, don't use too many questions. Even a discrete theme under a major topic may be so vast that it could have hundreds of references. If you list too many questions, you will not be able to effectively accomplish the study. On a major thematic study, you should ask no more than five questions.

Sometimes you can complete a study with the Bible Theme Method using only one question. Here are some examples:

- According to Solomon (in Proverbs), what brings poverty?
- What traits of a fool are given in the Book of Proverbs?
- What are the things we should "consider" as Christians?
- According to the New Testament, what things should we "endure"?
- What things does God hate?

Many times you will not find the answer to every one of your questions in the same verse. When this happens, just leave a blank space on your paper and go on to the next question.

Proceed with Caution

Whether you teach a teen Sunday school class, lead a Bible study in a women's prison, or facilitate a discussion with mature adults, your cardinal goal is accuracy. The same holds true whether you circle metal chairs in the corner of a gymnasium, sit on the plush carpet of a multimillion-dollar educational facility, or huddle around the fireplace in your den; and whether you use a wide assortment of creative methods or you stick to plain old question-and-answer. When it comes to Bible study, what group members conclude about a passage should match its God-intended meaning.

If you are not finding the answers to any of your questions in your verses, it probably means that you need to revise your questions. You may be asking the wrong questions. Possibly, you are asking questions that God does not care to answer. Check the verses to see what God is really saying, and fit your questions to what he wants to tell you in those passages. Or maybe you are asking a question that is answered elsewhere.

If you want to know everything God has said about a certain subject in the Bible, you will have to use an exhaustive concordance and look up every one of the words related to your theme. This task can become a massive project. Remember that topical Bibles are not exhaustive, and you will have to use either Strong's or Young's concordance.

Six Steps to Studying a Theme

Before you begin the Bible Theme Method of study and look up Bible references, create a series of questions. These questions should include some of the six great investigative relative pronouns: What? Why? When? How? Where? Who? When used in various combinations, these words will give you an unlimited supply of questions to use in your Bible study. For example, if you were to do a study on "Anger in the Book of Proverbs," you could ask these types of questions:

- What are the characteristics of an angry man?
- What causes anger?
- What are the results of anger?
- What is the cure for anger?

Each of these four questions begins with the word *What*, but you could have created just as many other questions using the other five pronouns.

Step One: Selecting a Theme

Choose a theme that you would like to study. If this is your first time using this method, choose a relatively simple theme. Here are a few ideas to get you started, including some sample questions—feel free to create your own, though.

One potential theme is "Praising the Lord in the Psalms." Notice that we're limiting the theme to the Book of Psalms. Words that relate to praise include *praise*, *thanksgiving*, *adoration*, and *joy*. Among the questions you can ask are these:

- How can I praise the Lord?
- Why should I praise the Lord?
- When should I praise the Lord?
- What are some results of praising the Lord?

If you choose obedience as your theme, you might look for words like *obey*, *obedience*, *commandments*, *do*, and *keep*. Among the questions you can ask are these:

- How am I to obey God?
- Why is obedience important?
- What are the results of obedience?
- What are the results of disobedience?

Here's another theme you and your students might study: "The Prayers of Jesus." Examine this theme in a topical Bible and look up the words *pray* and *prayer* in a concordance, choosing only those words that appear in the Gospels and for when Jesus is praying. Here are some suggested questions, but you should be able to write many others:

- How often should I pray?
- When did Jesus pray?
- Why should I pray as Jesus did?
- To whom should I pray?

Another theme you and your students could study is "Knowing God's Will." If you look in a concordance, you'll find references to God's will, the will of God, the will of the Lord and the Lord's will, and many other related words and phrases. You could ask the following questions:

- What specific things are God's will?
- Why am I to do God's will? (such things as results and motives)
- How am I to do God's will? (such things as actions and attitudes)

Step Two: Listing Verses to Study

Using your three tools—the study Bible, the exhaustive concordance, and the topical Bible—create a list with all the Bible verses related to your selected theme. Make sure you consider synonyms and other similar words and concepts when using the concordance. Choose from this list the Bible verses that are most important to your theme, unless you are trying to discover everything the Bible has to say about your theme.

Step Three: Determining Questions to Ask

How do you know which questions to ask? Write down questions that interest you most. What are some things you would like to learn about your chosen theme? Make a list of no more than five questions. Remember that sometimes you may need to ask only one question. Write your question(s) on a blank sheet of paper.

Teaching Tips

As you teach your group, the participants will ask you many tough questions, such as "Is God real?" Be assured that God has the answers to all of these difficult questions. You should know one important truth: You can't give the answers to the members of your group. Instead, direct them to seek their answers in the Bible. Members must search for their own answers and embrace what they discover as they study the Scriptures. You're not the "answer person," but rather someone who guides members to discover the truth.

Step Four: Asking Questions

Read through your references and ask your set of questions for each verse that you read. Write your answers on a blank sheet of paper. Sometimes you will be able to answer all of the questions in a given verse, but usually you will answer only one or two of them. Occasionally, a verse may not answer any of your questions. If a question does not have an answer, leave that part blank. If you're not getting any answers to your questions, start over and write a new set of questions.

Step Five: Drawing Conclusions

After you've read through all the references and answered your questions from them, return and summarize the answers to each of the questions. You might organize your study into an outline by grouping similar verses together and turning your questions into major divisions of the outline. This organization will make it easy for you to explain your insights with a Bible study group, class, congregation, or another individual.

Step Six: Apply the Theme

To implement what you have discovered and make it practical in your life, write down a personal application that is measurable, practical, and possible. Refer to the steps suggested in Chapter 5 if you need help in developing an effective application.

Just in Case

Sometimes the group may get stalled just asking the questions. What do you do to break out of the routine? Here is an idea:

Enlist a member of the group to tape-record the questions for that day's passage. Ask that the questioner leave a few seconds of silence between each question. During the Bible study, direct the group to pass the recorder, play one question, answer it from the Bible, and pass it to the next person. The novelty of the tape recorder invites the group's attention and interest. Sometimes members get carried away trying to discover who is speaking. If this happens, spend a few moments guessing until the identity of the speaker is confirmed.

Teaching the Bible Theme Method

The Bible Theme Method is one of the simplest study methods to teach to others. You emphasize the vital journalistic questions of who, what, when, where, and how as the centerpiece of the study. One of the keys to a successful Bible Theme Method study is to teach the group how to ask simple yet effective questions. Then help the group to use a study Bible, exhaustive concordance, and topical Bible to locate the answers. The first session should include demonstrating the use of these tools and helping the group learn how to use them to study on their own or within the group

Potent Quotables

"Do your best to present yourself to God as one approved, a workman who does not need to be ashamed and who correctly handles the word of truth."
(2 Timothy 2:15, NIV)

setting. As a leader, part of your task is to choose a limited topic that each person can easily accomplish. Because you have completed the study yourself, you will be able to use questions to guide the others in this study method.

The Least You Need to Know

- This method is one of the easiest types of personal Bible study to use for turning the material into a Sunday school lesson or sermon.
- The Bible Theme Method limits the questions to a maximum of five carefully selected ones.
- The theme selected should be limited or short.
- You and your class use only three reference tools with this method: a study Bible, an exhaustive concordance, and a topical Bible.

Part 3

Prevent Boredom

Variety is the spice of life and can definitely be applied to Bible study. You've consistently taught the Bible to a group of people, and for variety, you've tried each of the four methods in Part 2. Now you are ready to increase the challenge and the spiritual growth for the people in your group.

Through the chapters in this part, you will learn about eight additional methods of Bible study: the Biographical Teaching Method, the Topical Teaching Method, the Word Study Teaching Method, the Verse-by-Verse Teaching Method, the Book Background Method for Bible study, the Overview Book Survey Method, the In-Depth Bible Chapter Method, and the comprehensive study of a particular Bible book.

Teaching the Bible to others has progressed from simply using the Bible and asking questions, to more complicated methods that involve use of study tools like a Bible handbook, commentaries, and other resources. Each of these methods will help you and your group to grow spiritually and become better students of the Bible.

Chapter 9

The Biographical and Topical Teaching Methods

In This Chapter

- Gaining insight by learning about the people in the Bible
- How to apply biblical character traits to your own life
- Tracing a topic through the Bible
- Teaching the Biographical and Topical Teaching Methods

Two of the most meaningful types of studies are detailed in this chapter. First, what made the people in the Bible tick? You can learn these details through the Biographical Teaching Method. If you want to know how to trace a topic through the Bible, you'll find out by reading the second part of this chapter on the Topical Teaching Method.

Using Biography to Discover Truth

The Bible contains numerous stories of men and women and their relationships with the loving God who created them. We can learn both what to do and what to be by looking at the positive attributes of hundreds of people who fill the pages of the Bible. We also can gain vast wisdom and knowledge through observing the tremendous failures and negative aspects in the people's lives mentioned in the Bible—and learning to avoid them in our own lives.

Potent Quotables

"Remember how the Lord your God led you through the wilderness for 40 years, humbling you and testing you to prove your character, and to find out whether or not you would really obey his commands." (Deuteronomy 8:2, NLT)

The Bible has made clear that people are important to God. Mankind was made in the image of God and his likeness and the Bible is a record of God's dealings with men and women. The Scriptures are also a revelation of God himself, both to the people and through people. To understand the Bible fully, you must get to know the prominent people of the Bible. The Biographical Teaching Method of Bible study focuses on what makes an individual's life a spiritual success or failure. When you do a biographical study, you attempt to become thoroughly acquainted with the inner life of the person you are studying. Ask God to help you think and feel as the individual thought and felt. In that way, your study can become a life-changing experience. You can apply what you've learned when you examine your own life in light of the study and ask God to help you make positive character changes in your weak areas. This application in your life will result in growth and maturity.

The majority of the Old Testament is written in story form, describing in detail the lives of many people. The whole book of Genesis, for example, revolves around six great people—Adam, Noah, Abraham, Isaac, Jacob, and Joseph. The Apostle Paul told us that God gave us the stories in the Old Testament to be examples to us and said that we can learn valuable lessons for living every day for God in our world. He wrote, "Such things were written in the Scriptures long ago to teach us. They give us hope and encouragement as we wait patiently for God's promises." (Romans 15:4, NLT) Paul also said, "All these events happened to them as examples for us. They were written down to warn us, who live at the time when this age is drawing to a close." (1 Corinthians 10:11, NLT)

While the New Testament is largely a book of instructions, the Old Testament concentrates on illustrations, although both testaments contain both illustrations and instructions. New Testament truths are also contained in the Old Testament. One of the best ways to study the Old Testament is to study its people. Through this type of biographical study, the older Scriptures spring to life.

In greater or lesser detail, the Bible mentions more than 3,000 people. Once you've learned this method of study, you'll have opened a door to a lifetime of exciting, fulfilling Bible study. Biographical studies are fun to do and also one of the easiest means to find personal applications.

Tools to Bring Biography to Life

You will need these four tools to use with the Biographical Teaching Method: a study Bible, an exhaustive concordance, a topical Bible, and a Bible dictionary or encyclopedia. To have a meaningful biographical study, you need to keep these tips in mind:

Choose someone in the Bible with a relatively few number of references for your first biographical study. Some biblical people can be studied in a few hours; others take weeks or even a lifetime to study. Do not start with, say, Jesus, Moses, or Abraham; instead, choose a minor but important person, like Andrew, Barnabas, or Mary of Bethany.

If you need an introduction to the biographical study, here's a possible starter idea for you: The Scriptures are alive with personality. The Bible includes numerous accounts of the lives of individuals, and we can read about their relationships both to one another and to God. This inspired record has been preserved for centuries and continues to be a source of great teaching for us today. The Apostle Paul wrote, "For everything that was written in the past was written to teach us, so that through endurance and the encouragement of the Scriptures we might have hope." (Romans 15:4, NIV) These Bible characters were real, everyday humans like us. Even Elijah, one of the great prophets in the Old Testament, is described in this way: "Elijah was a man just like us." (James 5:17, NIV) His life lived in obedience to God made Elijah great. There is much to learn studying how the lives of these individuals were touched by God, how they responded to God, what kinds of persons they became, and what mark they left on their times.

The secret of a good biographical study is to live with that person during the study. Walk in his or her sandals. Try to get inside the person's mind and see how the person thought, felt, and responded to circumstances. Attempt to see things from this person's point of view. Look through the person's eyes, hear with his or her ears, mingle with his or her friends, and fight with his or her enemies. While you are studying the person, become this person. Such transformation is possible only if you spend a lot of time with this person, reading and rereading each of the Bible references about him or her. Be careful not to confuse different people who have the same name when you look up references about them. You have to be certain that the verse is talking about the same person you have selected to study. You wouldn't want to confuse John the Apostle with John Mark or John the Baptist. Each of these is a different man. The context of your verses will usually identify the exact person. For example, the Bible shows us that the following names were popular and refer to different people:

- Zechariah: 30 men
- Nathan: 20 men
- Jonathan: 15 men
- Judas: 8 men
- Mary: 7 women
- James: 5 men
- John: 5 men

Potent Quotables

"Moral character makes for smooth traveling; an evil life is a hard life. Good character is the best insurance; crooks get trapped in their sinful lust." (Proverbs 11:5–6, The Message)

In addition, because the Bible was written in a Hebrew-Aramaic-Greek context, some people's names are different depending on the language used, both in the Old Testament and in the New Testament. For example, the Apostle Peter is sometimes known as Peter, Simon, Simeon, and Cephas. Daniel's three friends Hananiah, Mishael, and Azariah are better known as Shadrach, Meshach, and Abednego. Sometimes a name change occurs when a person's character develops, which was the case when Jacob's name was changed to Israel. Jacob wrestled all night with God, then God changed his name to Israel. (Genesis 32:22-32) Be aware of these types of changes, and be sure to find all of the names used for the same person in your Bible study.

In general, it's best to stay away from other books written about biblical people until after you have exhausted every Bible reference about that person and have squeezed every possible insight out of those texts. Don't let a Bible commentator rob you of the joy of personal discovery or prejudice your views on a person. Do your own work first; then check other sources.

Ten Steps for a Biographical Study

Are you ready to begin to learn the details of a single person from the Bible? In 10 simple steps, you will gain insight into this person's life and apply the material to your own life.

Step One: Pick a Person

You might begin by selecting someone who has either a weakness that you would like to get rid of in yourself or a strength that you would like to develop. Choose a person whose life will provide you with some valuable insights into how you can conform more to God's standard for living and become more like Jesus Christ.

Step Two: Find Your References

Use your reference tools to locate all the places in the Bible that concern the person you're studying. Locate the text about the person's birth and other major life events, the person's accomplishments, what others said about the person, and the person's death. You may not be able to get all the necessary "vital statistics" about every person you study, but find out as much about him or her as you can.

Teaching Tips

Generally, smaller is better when it comes to the size of Bible study groups. A group of between two and eight people is best; a group of more than eight could become unwieldy.

Also look up any references that deal with the historical background of your chosen person's life. If you were studying Daniel, for instance, it would help you to explore the Babylonian Exile, which provided the backdrop for Daniel's life. If you were studying the Apostle Paul, you would have to study his missionary journeys.

Step Three: First Impressions

Read through the references you've listed and write some notes about what you first thought when reading about the person under study, as well as any basic factual information you've learned. Finally, list any problems or difficulties you encounter or questions that arise as you read these references.

Step Four: Chronology Counts

If you're studying a major biblical person, read all the references again and make a chronological outline of the person's life. Doing so will help you gain a good perspective on his or her life, and you might be able to see how different events relate to one another. Later, when you study these events, you will know in what part of the person's life they occurred. For minor biblical people or those whose lives have few details in the Bible, read the references and make an outline on the basis of the information you have available.

Teaching Tips

As an alternative exercise for biblical character study with your group, play the game called "I Was There." Direct a member of your group to answer questions from the point of view of a character in the passage you are studying. Perhaps during the fiery furnace incident, the character might be Shadrach, Meshach, Abednego, the angel, a soldier, an onlooker, or King Nebuchadnezzar. (Daniel 3) Call on the group members to tell what they see, feel, think, and, in some cases, smell and taste.

Try to read all the references in one session and in a modern translation. This exercise will help you feel the flow of the person's life. As you read, look for any natural, major divisions in the person's life. Then look for and write down any progressions and changes of attitude in that person's life as time goes by. For example, a well-known division of Moses' life is as follows:

- Forty years in Pharaoh's Court learning to be somebody
- Forty years in the Midian Desert learning to be a nobody
- Forty years in the Wilderness learning that God is somebody

This process is a real key to studying the characters of the people involved. See how God slowly molded and changed the person—or how Satan brought him or her down.

Step Five: Gain Insight

Go back over the references again, and look for possible answers to the questions suggested in Appendix A. By answering some of these questions, you should get some helpful insights into the character of the person you are studying.

Step Six: Identify Character

As you review the references once again, use the suggested list of positive and negative characteristics in Appendix C as a checklist. List on your paper each quality—good or bad—that shows up in the person's life. Give a verse reference that shows each characteristic you have observed.

As you study a particular character, ask each member of the group to explain what he or she likes or dislikes about this character. This process will lead your group members to discover ways to either avoid or incorporate that quality in their own lives. Post a pair of questions like these examples, and direct each person to complete them:

- I am like Adam/Eve because …
- But I am not like Adam/Eve because …

During the discussion, frequently point out the truth that Christianity is more like a journey than an instant bestowal of perfection. (Philippians 3:12) Daily we struggle to become more Christlike in our actions and attitudes.

Step Seven: Identify Examples of Bible Truths

Examine the person's life to see how it illustrates truths taught in the Scriptures. For example, does his or her life show the principle of "you will reap what you sow"? Look for illustrations of some of the proverbs in this person's life, as well as principles taught in the Psalms. For example, you might ask, "Does his life illustrate the promise 'Take delight in the Lord, and he will give you your heart's desires'?" (Psalm 37:4, NLT) Find the cross-references that illustrate what the Bible says about some of the characteristics you found in this person's life.

Step Eight: Summarize the Main Lesson(s)

In a few sentences, write down what you consider the main lesson that is taught or illustrated through this person's life. Does a single word describe this person's life? What was his or her outstanding characteristic?

Proceed with Caution

Whether you are engaged in casual conversation with a group member or are leading a Bible study, your communication comes across through three modes: actual words, tone of voice, and nonverbal cues. A wise communicator realizes that his message travels on all three avenues of expression. To maximize effectiveness, he packages his message in a way that utilizes all three modes. Make sure you are aware of nonverbal cues when you work with the members of your group.

Step Nine: Apply the Trait

Refer to Chapter 5 if you need to learn how to write an application. In addition to the principles in that chapter, you might ask yourself these additional questions:

- Did I see anything of myself in this person's life?
- Did this person show some of my weaknesses?

- Did this person reveal to me some of my strengths?
- What impressed me most about this person's life?
- Where do I fall short in this area?
- What do I intend to do about it?

Step Ten: Transfer Your Study

Condense what you've learned into a simple outline that will help you remember it and enable you to tell others about your conclusions. Make it "pass-on-able." Ask yourself, "What can this person's life mean to others? What have I learned that would help someone else?"

Divide the information into natural sequences of time and events and lessons learned. Use the progression that you have found and recorded. Then think of some easy-to-remember ways to title each section. Keep these titles true to the major content of each section, making use of rhymes, alliterations, and other memory devices. Use your imagination with this last step!

An illustration of a transferable outline of the life of Barnabas looks like this:

- He invested money in the lives of church members. (Acts 4:36–37)
- He introduced Saul (later Paul) to the apostles. (Acts 9:26–28)
- He was the inspector of the new church at Antioch. (Acts 11:22–24)
- He was an instructor of new Christians, including Paul and Mark. (Acts 11:22–26; 15:39)
- He was the initiator of the first missionary journey, which he began as the team leader but ended as a team member. (Acts 13–14)
- He was an interpreter of the doctrine of salvation and God's plan for the Gentiles. (Acts 13–14)
- He was insistent on giving Mark another chance to be trained in the Gospel ministry. (Acts 15:36–39)

Be sure to have realistic expectations about application in your group setting. Application refers to the participants' responses to God's Word, so the group meeting is usually the setting where obedience occurs. After group members break up the meeting, they choose to follow or ignore the Holy Spirit's direction from their study.

When you teach for application, it doesn't refer to the attitude or behavior change itself. Instead, it's the guided process of helping learners identify follow-through possibilities. No one can guarantee that anyone will obey God's Word, but you can reserve group time to probe a passage's practical implications. You can make sure people leave with application possibilities swirling in their minds.

Topics, Topics, Topics

Examining a topic of the Bible is one of the most exciting ways to study it. The Topical Teaching Method is similar to the Bible Theme Method (covered in Chapter 8), but, as discussed in Chapter 8, there are some important distinctions. A topical study usually takes longer because you study more verses. It also usually has several minor themes running through it. In a topical study, you consider all of the related themes rather than concentrating on one theme at a time, as with a theme study. Another distinction is that you don't decide before the study which questions you want to ask. Instead, you examine each verse without predetermined guidelines and record all of the insights you discover. Furthermore, you don't limit your study to just finding the answers to four or five questions as you do with the Thematic Method.

The Topical Method of Bible study involves selecting a biblical subject and tracing it through a single book, the Old or New Testament, or the entire Bible in order to discover what God says about the topic. It uses extensive cross-referencing, and the questions you ask of a given text are limitless.

> **Teaching Tips**
>
> If your group selects a topic that is quite broad, such as love, you can easily divide it into several studies, such as "The Nature of Love," "Love of a Neighbor," "The Love of God," and "Man's Love for God."

The Topical Method enables you to study the Bible systematically, logically, and in an orderly manner. It gives you a proper perspective and balance regarding biblical truth. You get to see the whole of a biblical teaching. This method enables you to study the great doctrines of the Bible. It allows you to study subjects that are of particular interest to you. It lends itself to good and lively discussions. The results of a topical study are always easy to talk about with others. It gives you variety in your lifetime commitment to personal Bible study. The number of topics in the Bible for study is almost limitless.

As with several of the other study methods, the Topical Method requires some reference tools. If you want to do a thorough study on a selected topic, you will need these tools:

- A topical Bible
- A study Bible
- An exhaustive concordance

In *The Master Bible* (J. Wesley Dickson & Co., 1953), the great Bible scholar and teacher Dr. R. A. Torrey gives three suggestions to help you perform a topical Bible study:

- **Be systematic.** Don't try to study the Bible in a haphazard, undisciplined manner. Make as complete and comprehensive a list of all the things related to your topic as possible. Then take up these items one at a time, studying them in a systematic and logical order.
- **Be thorough.** As much as possible, find and study every verse that relates to your topic. The only way to know all that God has said on a topic is to go through the entire Bible, finding passages on that topic. Use your concordance to do this.
- **Be exact.** Try to get the exact meaning of every verse you study. Be sure to examine the context of each verse, to avoid misinterpretation. The biggest mistake you must avoid is taking a verse out of its context.

Potent Quotables

"Every part of Scripture is God-breathed and useful one way or another—showing us truth, exposing our rebellion, correcting our mistakes, training us to live God's way." (2 Timothy 3:16, The Message)

Six Steps for a Topical Study

Before starting a topical study, select a topic that you are interested in studying. It may be specifically mentioned or merely implied in the text, but it should be important both in content and in personal interest. When you are beginning this method of study, pick a topic that is not too vast or time-consuming. You might restrict your topic to references found in a testament or a single book of the Bible.

Step One: Compile Topic Words

Make a list of all the related words (antonyms and synonyms), events, phrases, and anything else that could have something to do with your chosen topic. If you are studying the topic of pain, for example, you will want to list words such as *anger*, *affliction*, *suffering*, *chastisement*, *grief*, *health*, *sorrow*, *trials*, and *tribulation*. If you see that your topic has become too broad, narrow it to a manageable size.

Step Two: Collect Bible References

Begin to use your reference tools to locate every verse you can find on your topic. Look up each related word in your concordance. Make a list of all verses that relate in any way to the topic. You will also want to use your topical Bible to find verses for study.

Step Three: One at a Time

Look up, read, and study each individual reference, and write down your observations and insights about them. Be sure to check carefully the context (the surrounding verses) when you study a verse so that you interpret it correctly. Ask as many questions as you can about each verse you study. Remember to use what, why, when, where, who, and how questions. Don't forget to define all key words you come across.

Proceed with Caution

Make sure your group understands that the process of selecting the best passages from the Bible takes some time and that they shouldn't become frustrated. Encourage your students to stop their study once they've found about a dozen or so good passages.

Step Four: Compare and Group References

After carefully studying each verse individually, you'll probably notice that some of the references naturally complement each other and deal with the same areas of the topic under study. Categorize these references on a separate piece of paper.

Step Five: Condense Your Study into an Outline

Using the categories you identified in Step Four, outline your study. This step will organize your study for you and enable you to explain it to others. Do this by grouping related or similar references into natural divisions. Then organize these divisions into a logical pattern.

Potent Quotables

"Be prepared. You're up against far more than you can handle on your own. Take all the help you can get, every weapon God has issued, so that when it's all over but the shouting you'll still be on your feet. Truth, righteousness, peace, faith, and salvation are more than words. Learn how to apply them. You'll need them throughout your life." (Ephesians 6:13, The Message)

Step Six: Conclude Your Study

In a two-part conclusion, first summarize your findings in a brief paragraph and then write out a practical application drawn from your conclusions. Remember to be practical and personal when you write this measurable application.

Teaching the Biographical Teaching Method and the Topical Teaching Method

Whether you are studying a person (the Biographical Teaching Method) or a topic (the Topical Teaching Method) from the Bible, emphasize the importance of application. Your individual time and the group time in the Scriptures is more than an exercise to gain more knowledge; instead, it's an experience that can be applied to everyday life.

The Least You Need to Know

- Two of the most meaningful types of Bible studies are about people and specific Bible topics.
- Through the Biographical Teaching Method, you learn the positive and negative qualities about people from the Bible. The Bible mentions more than 3,000 people for possible study.
- The Topical Teaching Method of Bible study involves selecting a particular Bible subject and tracing it through a single book, the Old Testament or the New Testament, or the entire Bible to find out what God says about a topic.
- No matter which method you use, the key aspect is to apply the lessons from the Bible character or topic to your everyday life.

Chapter 10

Digging Into the Details: The Word Study and Verse-by-Verse Methods

In This Chapter

- Using language to understand truth
- Working through a Word Study
- Studying the Bible, verse by verse
- Teaching the Word Study and Verse-by-Verse Methods

Originally the Bible was written in Hebrew, Aramaic, and Greek. Even though the average Christian doesn't know these languages, it's still possible to do word studies and verse-by-verse studies because of the availability of many excellent translation and reference tools.

In the past, people who were interested in doing personal Bible study had to learn the original languages. Only those people who had spent years learning Hebrew and Greek were able to enjoy the insights that come from studying the original languages. However, today the riches from word studies and verse-by-verse studies are available to everyone who knows how to use certain invaluable reference tools.

Finding Just the Right Word

The Word Study Method of Bible study takes a microscopic look at the origin, definition, occurrences, and uses of a particular word, especially as this relates to the context of a passage of Scripture. The purpose of this type of study is to learn as comprehensively and precisely as possible what the biblical writer meant by the word he selected.

The great Bible teacher Irving Jensen said, "Just as a great door swings on small hinges, so the important theological statements of the Bible often depend upon even the smallest words, such as prepositions and articles" (*Enjoy Your Bible*, Moody Press, 1969). Most of the great doctrines of Scripture revolve around a single word, such as *faith*, *atonement*, or *grace*. To understand the deepest meaning of the Bible, we must study the specific words that were used.

A correct interpretation of the words used to convey these truths depends on a correct understanding of the words. In the Psalms, David declared, "And the words of the Lord are flawless, like silver refined in a furnace of clay, purified seven times." (Psalm 12:6, NIV) In a similar fashion, a writer in Proverbs said, "Every word of God proves true. He defends all who come to him for protection." (Proverbs 30:5, NLT)

Just in Case

If you need another method to introduce the importance of words to your group, use this example: The French author Anatole France wrote, "The finest words in the world are only vain sounds if you cannot comprehend them." Though words are the simplest building blocks for language and community, they can be perplexing because of their various shades of meaning and usage. For example, the *Oxford English Dictionary* lists more than 70 different meanings for the word *round*. A deeper look at Scripture eventually involves the study of words and their variant meanings. The encouraging part of word studies is that they can be as simple or as involved as a person wants to make them.

Yet these flawless words were written in a language other than our own, and their full meanings are not always transmitted completely through a translation. In fact, no translation is perfect because no two languages correspond exactly. Word equivalents do not always exist between languages, so in studying the Bible we may have to search out the full meaning of a word that the translators were unable to squeeze into the chosen text.

Consider this fact: As Bible teacher Irving Jensen points out, when the original text of the Bible was translated into English, some 6,000 different words were used, but in the Hebrew, Aramaic, and Greek original, 11,280 words were used. So how do you fit 11,000 words into 6,000? By translating several different original-language words into one English word. For example, in the New Testament, the English word *servant* is the translation of seven different Greek words, each of which had a slightly different shade of meaning for a servant. Our language, a later one, is unable to completely give the full meaning of the original biblical languages.

When doing a word study, keep two things in mind. First, word studies must be based on the original-language words, not on the English words. Second, we must always allow the context to indicate the ultimate meaning of the word being studied, no matter what may be the equivalent word in English.

Teaching Tips

A good general resource for word studies is W. E. Vine's *Expository Dictionary of New Testament Words* or Lawrence Richards's *Expository Dictionary of the Bible*. Both are inexpensive resources based on the English text, yet they give Greek and cultural information that is understandable to anyone.

Tools of the Word Study Trade

For this method of Bible study, you will need more reference tools than you have used with the other study methods so far. The necessary tools are listed here:

- A study Bible is important for this method. Numerous Bibles will say on the book cover, "study Bible" and they are available in different translations.
- Several recent modern translations. These various translations enable you to see the words different translators selected. Some modern translations such as the Living Bible are noted on the cover as a "paraphrase." For this type of study, don't use a paraphrase translation.
- An exhaustive concordance.
- A Bible dictionary and/or encyclopedia.
- A good English dictionary.
- If you have taken some Greek, *The Englishman's Greek Concordance of the New Testament* (Hendrickson Publishers, Inc., 1996) will be useful.
- The two-volume set *The Word Study Concordance* and *The Word Study New Testament*, by Dr. Ralph Winter (William Carey Library, 1979).

Keep in mind that sometimes one Greek or Hebrew word is translated several ways in English. In order to overcome this difficulty, you will have to carefully study each of the different renderings of that original word using your exhaustive concordance. For example, the Greek word *koinonia* is translated five different ways in the King James Version: (1) "communication"—once; (2) "communion"—4 times; (3) "contribution"—once; (4) "distribution"—once; and (5) "fellowship"—12 times.

Potent Quotables

"When you got the Message of God we preached, you didn't pass it off as just one more human opinion, but you took it to heart as God's true word to you, which it is, God himself at work in you believers!" (1 Thessalonians 2:13, The Message)

Here are several ways to use this procedure to solve this difficulty:

- List the different ways the word is translated.
- List how many times it is translated each way.
- Give examples of each translation (if possible).
- Write down how the different meanings might be related.
- Determine whether the writer of the book is using the word you are studying in a single sense or is giving it a multiple meaning.

In other cases, several Greek words are translated with just one English word. We have already noted that the English word *servant* has seven Greek equivalents, each with a different shade of meaning. Be sure to check your concordance carefully to see if this might be true of the word you are studying. Find out what each different original word meant.

Still more confusion may ensue when an original word is translated with a whole phrase in English. This difficulty will take a little more work to overcome because concordances do not list word translations phrase by phrase. You will have to compare the versions of the Bible to see how the various translators have rendered the word. For example, Paul declared to the Corinthians, "But we all, with open face beholding as in a glass the glory of the Lord, are changed into the same image from glory to glory, *even* as by the Spirit of the Lord." (2 Corinthians 3:18, KJV) The phrase "beholding as in a glass" is just one word in the original Greek (*katoptrizomenoi*), and you will discover some interesting truths when you study the origin of that word.

Getting to the Meaning Through the Words

Make sure the group understands that in studying a specific word, only one meaning may arise. That makes your job easy. But if a number of possible definitions surface, then you decide which meaning best fits the particular passage and context. Try each potential definition within the passage and ask these two questions: (1) Which meaning best fits and is consistent with the context? (2) Which meaning is compatible with other passages of Scripture?

The actual word study involves eight simple steps.

- **Step One: Select your word.** Select a single word from the Scriptures for your study.
- **Step Two: Find its English definition.** Using your English dictionary, write out the definition of the English word. List with the definition any antonyms or synonyms of the word.
- **Step Three: Compare translations.** Read the passages where this word is used in different modern translations. Write down the different renderings of the word that you find. See if any renderings are commonly used in these translations.
- **Step Four: Write down the definitions of the original word.** Discover the meaning of the original word in your exhaustive concordance or word study book, and write down its definitions. You may find that it has a number of usages.
- **Step Five: Check the word's occurrences in the Bible.** Again using your concordance, find out how and where the word is used in the Bible. Ask these questions: How many times does the word occur in the Bible? In what books does it occur? What writers used the word? In what book does it occur most? Where does the word occur first in the Bible? Where does it occur first in the book you are studying?
- **Step Six: Discover the Root Meaning and the Origin of the Word.** This step involves some research. You will want to read a fuller discussion of the meaning and origin of the word you are studying using a Bible dictionary, a Bible encyclopedia, a word study set, or a theological word book.

CAUTION

Proceed with Caution

Finding the exact lexical meaning of a word is often confusing. Instead of trying to discover the various meanings of a word on your own, let a good Bible dictionary or lexicon do the work for you. In them, you'll find information about the word's origin, history, meanings, and theology. Look up the word, briefly list its basic idea and meanings, and then try to pick the best meaning for the passage before looking at the recommendation in the resource.

- **Step Seven: Understand the context.** By studying the root meaning of the word in Step Six, you learned what the word meant originally and where it came from, but some words change their meanings with the passage of time. Also, they might have different meanings in different situations or contexts. In the final analysis, how the word is used is the most important factor in determining its true meaning. Here's how to evaluate the context of each word. First, find out how the word was used during the time the book of the Bible was written. How was it used in other writings besides the Bible? To find out what the word meant and how it was used in the culture of the day, you will have to look at extrabiblical materials (for example, histories of the time); many times, however, the word study set you are using will have this information. Advanced students and people who know the original languages may find this information in theological dictionaries and Hebrew and Greek lexicons.

  Second, find out how the word is used in the Bible. Using your exhaustive concordance, find out how the word is translated every time it appears in the Bible. Often the Scriptures define words through usage and illustrations. This is a way of finding out the Scriptural definition. You may also ask some or all of the following questions: How does the writer use the word in other parts of the book? How does the writer use the word in other books he has written? How is the word used throughout the whole testament? Does the word have more than one usage? If so, what are its other uses? What is the most frequent use of the word? How is it used the first time in the Scriptures?

  Finally, find out how the word is used in the context of the passage. This is the ultimate test. The context will be your most reliable source for insights into what the writer really meant. Ask these questions: Does the context give any clues to the meaning of the word? Is the word compared to or contrasted with the meaning of the word? Is there any illustration in the context that clarifies the meaning of the word?

- **Step Eight: Write down an application.** Be especially careful to keep your goal of "application, not interpretation only" in mind when you do a word study. Remember that you are doing personal Bible study, not just conducting an academic exercise. Discovering the full meaning of a biblical word is not an end in itself, because

Teaching Tips

Most words have synonyms with distinctly different but very illuminating meanings from the original word. Sources like *Vine's Expository Dictionary of New Testament Words* and Richard Trench's *Synonyms of the New Testament* are helpful for finding synonyms. List each synonym with its distinctive meaning. Then evaluate the insight learned from knowing that the author chose that specific word instead of one of its synonyms.

a word study without application has little spiritual value for you. Constantly ask yourself, "How can understanding this word help strengthen my own spiritual life?" Then write down your application.

Potent Quotables

Jesus said, "Don't suppose for a minute that I have come to demolish the Scriptures—either God's Law or the prophets. I'm not here to demolish but to complete. I am going to put it all together, pull it all together in a vast panorama. God's Law is more real and lasting than the stars in the sky and the ground at your feet. Long after stars burn out and earth wears out, God's Law will be alive and working.

"Trivialize even the smallest item in God's Law, and you will only have trivialized yourself. But take it seriously, show the way for others, and you will find honor in the kingdom. Unless you do far better than the Pharisees in the matters of right living, you won't know the first thing about entering the kingdom." (Matthew 5:17–18, The Message)

Verse by Verse

The verse-by-verse analysis of a passage is a useful method when you don't have the time for an in-depth study. This method examines each verse from five viewpoints using a special verse-by-verse analysis. The five things you do with each verse are …

- Write a personal paraphrase of the verse.
- List some questions and whatever answers you find.
- Write down some insights you've discovered.
- Write a brief personal application.

The Verse-by-Verse Method involves selecting a passage of Scripture and then examining it in detail by asking questions, finding cross-references, and paraphrasing each verse. Then you record a possible personal application for each verse.

You can use this method in two different ways. First, you can substitute it for the Chapter Summary Method covered in Chapter 6 if you want to work systematically through a passage or chapter. It is particularly useful when you don't have enough time to complete a whole chapter at one sitting. Using this method allows you to select the number of verses in a passage that you want to analyze at any given time. The method is open-ended, and you may proceed at your own pace.

Second, you can use it to perform a more advanced topical study if you decide to use reference tools. The following are suggested tools for a more in-depth study:

- A study Bible
- An exhaustive concordance (for cross-references)
- A Bible dictionary and/or Bible encyclopedia
- A set of word studies

Teaching Tips

Allow everyone in your group to talk. Even the quietest person will talk when he or she feels listened to and treasured. When the various members speak, they solidify their beliefs and understand their faith. As they talk, they voice their ideas in light of the Bible, and they have opportunity to evaluate those ideas and see how well they really work. As the members share their personal experiences with friends, problems, and activities, they discover the Bible is the true source of better friendships, solved problems, and fun activities. As the group talks together about the Bible, the Bible becomes a comfortable friend and a way to listen to God.

Five Steps for a Verse-by-Verse Study

To begin a verse-by-verse study, first select the passages you want to analyze in this way. Then follow these five steps:

- **Step One: Write a personal paraphrase.** Write down the verse in your own words. Do not use the exact words from a modern translation, except to get ideas of how to do it. Stay true to the meaning of the verse you are paraphrasing, and try to condense rather than expand it.
- **Step Two: List some questions, answers, and observations.** As you study the verse, list any questions you may have about words, phrases, persons, topics, and doctrines in that verse. Write down any answers you are able to find to your questions. Also record any observations about that verse. Mark these as follows: Q = Questions, A = Answers, O = Observations.
- **Step Three: Locate cross-references for each verse.** Using the cross-references in your study Bible or from your personal Scripture memory, write down at least one cross-reference for the verse. Use a concordance if you do not have a cross-referenced Bible.

Teaching Tips

For a different type of activity, invite the members of your group to summarize the truth of the Bible passage in four words. Then guide them to summarize it in two words. Finally, invite them to name the one word that helps them remember how to live the Bible passage. For one variation, ask the first few people to use four words, the next to use two words, and the last few to use one word. For another variation, assign a different word in the passage to each person, and challenge each of them to find it and explain why it is important to the passage.

- **Step Four: Record any insights.** As you think through the words, phrases, and concepts in the verse, record any insights you derive from it, including additional observations, words, and names you've defined, or any other thought that comes to you. Let your imagination go, and be as creative as you can.
- **Step Five: Write a brief personal application.** Because of the number of verses you are studying, you will not be able to design an application project from each verse. Instead, just try to record some devotional thoughts that come to you from each verse. Later, in a devotional Bible study, you can pick one of the thoughts and plan to work on it. Or if a particular verse seems to meet an immediate need, go ahead and write out an application that is possible, practical, personal, and measurable.

Teaching the Word Study and Verse-by-Verse Methods

A popular saying is "The devil is in the details." The members of your group may want to study larger portions of the Bible, yet these two methods are excellent because each one emphasizes the details. During the word study, the members learn the importance of words and how each word in the Bible was specifically selected. In a verse-by-verse study, they see that intellectual and spiritual value can be gained if they dig into a single verse from the Bible.

One of the key ingredients for you as you teach is to help each individual learn the various steps of each method. Be sure to ask if anyone is struggling with how to accomplish the method, listen to their questions, then patiently help them through their particular issues. As each member learns to independently study the Bible, the group time will be a rich experience for every single person.

The Least You Need to Know

- Through the Word Study Method, you will learn as comprehensively and precisely as possible what the biblical writers meant when they chose a specific word.
- Most of the great doctrines and beliefs about the Bible evolve around a single word, like *grace*, *faith*, or *atonement.*
- The Verse-by-Verse Method is useful when you don't have time for an in-depth study.
- The Verse-by-Verse Method is either an alternative to the Chapter Summary Method (see Chapter 6) or a more advanced topical study.

Chapter 11

Background of the Books

In This Chapter

- Focusing on the Bible's context
- Digging deeper into the text
- Step by step through the Scriptures
- Teaching the Book Background Method

When you go to the theater, it's much easier to understand a play if all of the props and background scenes are in place. The actors perform on stage against the background of props and painted scenes. It is the same way with the Bible. God's revelation was given in the midst of history, and the various people in the Bible act out their God-given roles against the background of their times. We can understand the Scripture so much more clearly when we see it against the backdrop of the days in which it was written.

Revealing the Background

The Book Background Method of Bible study involves gaining a better understanding of the biblical message by researching the background related to the passage, person, event, or topic under study. This process involves gaining an understanding of the geography, historical events, culture, and political environment at the time that a particular part of the Bible was written.

To gain the full impact of what a biblical writer is saying, it is necessary to transport yourself back in time to learn about the background of the writer. Because you are centuries removed from the writers of the Bible, you must try to see the world through their eyes, feel what they felt, and then understand how the Holy Spirit of God used them to write what they did.

One of the primary rules of interpretation posits that since the Bible was written in the midst of history, it can be understood more fully only in light of that history. You cannot interpret the Bible correctly if you ignore the influence of the times in which it was written. A serious Bible student will always want to know the geographical, historical, cultural, and political backgrounds of the passage or book he or she is studying.

Teaching Tips

Whether telling about David's affair, Peter's denial, Noah's drunkenness, or Jacob's deceit, the Bible spares no detail as it candidly reveals the shortcomings of God's children. Aren't you glad your story doesn't appear in the Bible? But God had a good reason for recording the failures of his faithful ones. Romans 15:4 (NIV) explains, "For everything that was written in the past was written to teach us, so that through endurance and the encouragement of the Scriptures we might have hope." As you teach your group about the Book Backgrounds Method, make sure you emphasize why you need to understand the background of Bible times—to increase understanding for our world today.

Furthermore, before we can understand how to apply the message, we must understand how it was applied when it was written. If we try to interpret and apply the Bible according to our own age and culture, we will quickly run into many difficulties. Often people of another culture or time will interpret a statement, word, custom, or event in a completely different way than we would in this country today. Because of the tremendous archeological discoveries in the past century, today we have a much better understanding of the cultures and historical backgrounds of biblical times. Most of the information is available to you through excellent research tools. You will definitely have to use research tools when you use this particular Bible study method.

Digging Up the Past

Many people believe that archaeology is a dry and boring science. Thanks to the patient work of many skilled archaeologists of many nations, we know much more today about Bible times than Christians knew even just half a century ago. *National Geographic* and other popular magazines have publicized the discovered Ebla tablets, which provided us with tremendous new information about the Near East of 2000 to 2500 B.C. Thanks to the science of archaeology, we now can understand the Bible more than ever before.

In their entry on archaeology in the *Interpreter's Dictionary of the Bible*, (Abingdon Press, 1981) editor George A. Butterick, and archaeologist G. W. Van Beek wrote:

> No one can understand the Bible without a knowledge of biblical history and culture, and no one can claim a knowledge of biblical history and culture without an understanding of the contributions of archaeology. Biblical events have been illustrated, obscure words defined, ideas explained, and chronology refined by archeological finds. To say that our knowledge of the Bible has been revolutionized by these discoveries is to understate the facts. After some 200 years of archeological research, it now can be said that a large army of people has picked up the threads of ancient city life from a thousand mounds and woven them into a pattern that agrees almost perfectly with the lives and recorded deeds of Bible characters. Thousands of pieces of archeological evidence that corroborate biblical narratives have come to light.

Just in Case

When it comes to purchasing Bible reference books, make sure your group members understand that many different titles are available in each type of reference book category. Only the individual can decide which of the many good options is best for his or her particular needs—this is limited only by the person's desire, stamina, and, of course, financial resources.

Tools of the Trade

This method of Bible study is totally dependent on tools, so you will have to obtain some of these or borrow them from your public or church library. Don't be afraid of them. Instead, take advantage of the information scholars have spent their lives discovering for you. The following tools will provide helpful background material:

- A Bible dictionary and/or Bible encyclopedia
- A Bible handbook
- A Bible atlas

In addition to these basic tools, you may want to consult some of the following reference books that deal with geography, history, culture, and everyday life of the times:

- *Archeology and the New Testament*, by Merrill F. Unger (Zondervan, 1962)
- *Archeology and the Old Testament*, by Merrill F. Unger (Zondervan, 1954)
- *The Bible and Archaeology*, by J. A. Thompson (William B. Eerdmans, 1962)
- *The Biblical World*, by Charles F. Pfeiffer (Baker, 1964)
- *Everyday Life in Bible Times* (National Geographic Society, 1977)
- *Great People of the Bible and How They Lived* (The Reader's Digest Association, Inc., 1974)
- *Harper's Encyclopedia of Bible Life*, by Madeleine S. Miller and J. Lane Miller (Harper & Row, 1996)
- *The Wycliffe Historical Geography of Bible Lands*, by Charles F. Pfeiffer and Howard F. Vos (Moody Press, 1970)

This list is only representative of the many reference works available today. Visit your local public library, your church library, and/or your local Christian bookstore to look them over. Select the ones that most appeal to you, and use them for this method and many other methods of study. Archaeologists are constantly updating their findings through new discoveries, so be sure to obtain the latest edition of each reference tool.

Teaching Tips

Tell your group members that Bible dictionaries and encyclopedias are extremely useful in studying backgrounds, events, and people of the Bible. For example, to dig deeper into the background of Genesis 25, you could study hunting, foods, oaths, and covenants in these reference tools. If the group members aren't acquainted with these books, bring the materials into the session and spend a bit of time showing how to use each one.

Performing a Book Background Study

It is your challenge as the teacher to make history and culture and Bible background come alive for the members of your group. One way to break up this type of study is to play a game in which you interview Bible people. It will take a bit of preparation from each group member. Assign parts ahead of the actual meeting, and arrange interview questions to match the story. For example, with Mary, the mother of Jesus, your group could ask, "What did you and your cousin Elizabeth talk about when you discovered both of you were carrying special babies?" (Luke 1:39–45) and "What song did you write after learning you would be the mother of Jesus?" (Luke 1:46–56) The participants can dramatize the events, but make sure they quote from the Bible rather than speculate.

The Book Background Method has eight steps to follow:

- **Step One: Select the subject or book of the Bible.** Select the subject, person, word, or book of the Bible you want to study, and begin gathering reference materials with which to do your research. The availability of reference tools will largely determine the scope of your study.
- **Step Two: List your reference tools.** Listing all the reference tools you have gathered for this study will help you remember which books are most useful now and in the future.

Potent Quotables

"But don't take any of this for granted. It was only yesterday that you outsiders to God's ways had no idea of any of this, didn't know the first thing about the way God works, hadn't the faintest idea of Christ. You knew nothing of that rich history of God's covenants and promises in Israel, hadn't a clue about what God was doing in the world at large. Now because of Christ—dying that death, shedding that blood—you who were once out of it altogether are in on everything." (Ephesians 2:11–13, The Message)

- **Step Three: Explore your geography.** You will need to become familiar with the geography of the Near East in general and Palestine in particular, including the types of land found there, the major mountains and hills, elevation and rainfall, the major bodies of water—sea, rivers, lakes—location of cities and countries, location of famous landmarks, and the borders of surrounding countries existing in the period under study. As you study the New Testament—and, in particular, Paul's missionary journeys—you will need to become acquainted with the Mediterranean countries and cities that were active during the days of the Roman Empire. Throughout your study of biblical geography, you must continually ask this question: "What is the effect of the surrounding geography on what I am studying?" During this step, list all of the insights you can get on geography for the subject or book you are studying.

Proceed with Caution

Depending on the age of your group, particularly if it includes kids, maps can spell b-o-r-e-d-o-m. As the teacher, it's your job to cultivate the participants' interest in maps. Try to get group members interested by writing on the maps, tracing the path, filling in the details, illustrating what happened in each location, and more. They could also cut the map into a puzzle, adding a piece each week.

- **Step Four: Learn from history.** Strive toward gaining a working knowledge of the major historical events of the nation of Israel in the Old Testament. Learn the periods of history of the Hebrew nation, discover the origin and the history of famous cities, learn the divisions of Jesus' ministry, and be well versed on the history surrounding Paul's missionary travels. You might also want to know what major events were going on in the other parts of the world at that time, to have a proper perspective on what God was doing in the world. During this step, pause and ask yourself these questions: "What caused this particular event that I am studying?" "How did it affect the people involved?" "How did it affect the passage I am studying?" Be especially aware of events that illustrate God's sovereign control over the process of history. To complete this step, list all the various insights you get on history surrounding the subject or book you are studying.
- **Step Five: Get some culture.** In order to understand what went on in biblical times, you need to learn about the total lifestyle of the ancient people in the Bible. Here are some areas you could research while asking yourself, "How do all these things affect the message and the people about whom I am studying?" Some topics worth exploring include the art in the Bible, the language and literature of surrounding nations, religious ceremonies in Israel and among pagan neighbors, weapons and tools in use, family life, recreation, manners and customs in Scripture, and architectural styles in the Near East. To complete this step, list all the insights you can get from the way people lived in their cultures.
- **Step Six: Define the political context.** The majority of what happened to Israel in the Old Testament and in the Roman world of Jesus, Paul, and the apostles is related to the political environment of the times. Kings, emperors, rulers, and governments governed the people of the time. Israel, for example, spent much of its history under foreign rule and even in exile. These other nations and political systems were bound to have an effect on the way God's people lived. Recognize, however, that God is always in control of the political situation. Even King Nebuchadnezzar acknowledged this fact in Daniel 3:34–35. Rome, Greece, Persia, Babylon, Assyria, Philistia, and Egypt all played a major

part in the Bible. What were these nations like? How did they affect Israel or the New Testament church? Many of the prophets' messages can be understood only in light of their current political climate. To complete this step, write down all the insight you can from your research into the political conditions of the time period you are studying.

Potent Quotables

"It is better to be a poor but wise youth than to be an old and foolish king who refuses all advice." (Ecclesiastes 4:13, NLT)

Teaching Tips

No matter which kind of study method you use, keep in mind that it takes tremendous courage for most people to speak up in the group setting. When anyone in the group speaks, make that person glad he or she did. For right answers, respond with, "Good job!" For partially right answers, try, "You're on the right track. What else does verse 23 say about that?" For totally off-the-wall answers, try something like, "I'm pleased that you spoke up. This is a hard question." For dangerously wrong answers, try something like, "I can't agree with your conclusions because the Bible says ____, and that conclusion would hurt people by _____. What other conclusion would be more true to life?" Each time a person's answers are welcomed, that person stays involved with the study. If their contributions are ignored, ridiculed, or rejected, the members of the group will withdraw, learn less, and assume they're a failure at Christianity.

- **Step Seven: Summarize your research.** Now go back over Step Three through Step Six and, from the data you have gathered, summarize your research and answer the following two questions: How does this background information help you understand better what you are studying? What influence did any of these factors have on the subject (or book) that you are studying?
- **Step Eight: Write a personal application.** Although it may be difficult to create a personal application from this type of study, you should be able to get one from the original subject that you are studying. In fact, research into the background of your subject may enable you to find an application you need today, and the data can help you make that application personal and relevant.

Teaching the Book Background Method

Most of the people in the group that you teach will have some Bible background. They might have heard stories of Joseph and his "Technicolor Dreamcoat" and his rule over Egypt during a great famine. They might know about Moses, who grew up in Pharaoh's court and led his people out of Egypt in the great Exodus. Or, they might have heard about David the shepherd boy who became a king and built an empire. Or they might know about David's son, Solomon, and his glorious reign. They might have heard of Esther, who saved her people from destruction in the days of King Xerxes of Persia. They might know of Jesus, who came to show the world a new and better way to relate to God. They might know of the Apostle Paul, who charged across the Roman world with a message of good news but who endured beatings, stoning, and a shipwreck along the way. And almost everyone has heard the stories of Noah and Daniel and more.

We have heard all of this even if we didn't grow up in Sunday school or darken the door of a church or a synagogue. Films, videos, musicals, novels, dramas, and art images have told us the stories, in either fictionalized or faithful accounts.

Potent Quotables

"So don't you see that we don't owe this old do-it-yourself life one red cent? There's nothing in it for us, nothing at all. The best thing to do is give it a decent burial and get on with your new life. God's Spirit beckons. There are things to do and places to go!" (Romans 8:12, The Message)

And now we wonder how much of these stories may be true or plausible, or we might wonder what life was like in Bible times. We wonder how the people really lived. How did they dress? What did they eat? What kinds of houses did they live in? How did they make a living? What was their family life like? Can we discover anything about their government? What can be discovered about their religion? These and many other questions fill our minds and can be answered as we study the Bible background.

Your responsibility as the teacher and leader is to motivate your group to study the Bible background with your enthusiasm and energy. It's contagious.

The Least You Need to Know

- One of the primary rules of biblical interpretations states that since the Bible was written in the midst of history, it can be understood more fully only in light of that history. The Bible background is important.
- Archaeology and recent discoveries provide excellent insight into Bible history.
- This method of Bible study is totally dependent on reference resources.
- When you study the Bible background, the stuffy old facts about the Bible can take on new life.

Chapter 12

Getting an Overview

In This Chapter

- Surveying the Bible for valuable clues
- Cultivating important clues
- Charting biblical events
- Teaching the Overview Book Survey Method

The great reformer of the sixteenth century Martin Luther not only restored the Bible to the common people, but he also gave some practical suggestions for Bible study. He once said he studied the Bible like he gathered apples. First, he would shake the whole apple tree so that the ripest fruit would fall to the ground (study the Bible as a whole). Then he would climb that tree and shake each branch (study the whole book). Next he would move to the smaller branches and shake each one of the twigs (study of a chapter of a book). He would then shake each of the twigs (study of the paragraphs and sentences) and conclude by looking under each leaf (study of single words). That's the method of study we'll cover in this chapter.

From Survey to Synthesis

Because God gave his revelation in segments that we now call books, we should first study these books as a whole, then examine their parts carefully, and finally put our study together to see the whole again. For this chapter, we will be using this approach called survey, analysis, and synthesis.

> **Teaching Tips**
>
> Remind your group that the Bible was written in single units, and chapter and verse divisions were added many centuries later. For those who want to master the Bible, understanding the whole book leads to a far better understanding of the particulars, and understanding the meaning of the particulars leads to proper conclusions and greater mastery of the Word of God.

First you make an initial survey of the book to see it as a whole; this is your "telescopic view" study. Then you take the book apart chapter by chapter and do a detailed analysis of each one; you look at all the details through a microscope. Finally, you put it all together again in a synthetic study in which you summarize the book as a whole and produce *your own* outline. The process moves from the whole to the particulars and then back to the whole.

- **Survey.** Get a bird's-eye view of the book.
- **Analysis.** Study everything in each chapter in detail.
- **Synthesis.** Put it back together again and draw some conclusions.

This chapter examines the first point, which is the Book Survey Method.

Gaining an Overview

A book survey study involves gaining a sweeping overview of an entire book of the Bible. It is taking a "skyscraper look" or a "telescopic view" of a book by reading it through several times without stopping to consider the details. Then you ask a series of background and content questions so that you can draw a horizontal chart of its contents. This process helps you gain a general understanding of the writer's purpose, theme, structure, and content.

As the teacher, it becomes your challenge to make history, culture, and the entire background of the Bible come alive for the members of your group. As mentioned in Chapter 11, you can involve group members by making a game of learning the Bible. For instance, you can play a game in which members interview one another, one acting as the interviewer and the other pretending to be a person from the Bible. Assign parts ahead of the actual meeting, and arrange interview questions to match the story.

For example, with Mary, the mother of Jesus, your group could ask, "What did you and your cousin Elizabeth talk about when you discovered both of you were carrying special babies?" (Luke 1:39–45) and "What song did you write after learning you would be the mother of Jesus?" (Luke 1:46–56) The participants can dramatize the events, but make sure they quote from the Bible rather than speculate.

As you know, the Bible is really 66 different books compiled under 1 cover. Each of these books is unique and has an important message for us today. The Book Survey Method is a practical way to master the general contents of a single book.

Performing a book survey as the first part of an analysis and synthesis helps to reveal how each part of the book relates to the other parts. Many otherwise hard-to-understand verses become clear when seen in the larger context of the book in which they are found. Furthermore, locating where within a chapter a verse occurs helps us understand it and what God teaches through it.

A book survey also reveals the proper emphasis of each point in the book. It keeps the study of God's Word balanced, lessening the possibility that you'll overemphasize or minimize any one point in the book. It is interesting to note that most cults and heresies arise when people overemphasize some verse or doctrine and build their whole theology on a few verses taken out of context, ignoring most of the rest of God's revelation.

> **Teaching Tips**
>
> A good pace is a chapter a week. If a chapter is particularly long, you might decide to study the chapter in two studies. These steps will help you give good guidance to the group.

A number of the basic tools are necessary for this method of Bible study:

- A study Bible
- Several contemporary translations (These will enable you to see different renderings of the same material by able scholars.)
- A Bible dictionary and/or Bible encyclopedia
- A Bible handbook

In addition to these basic tools, you may want to consult Bible atlases, historical geographies, historical background books, and Bible surveys. Use these last tools only after you have done your own research. Later you may check yourself and your conclusions against what other reliable scholars have done. Some representative surveys and background books are listed here:

- *New Testament Survey*, by Merrill C. Tenney (Eerdmans, 1985)
- *The Old Testament Survey*, by Merrill C. Tenney (Eerdmans, 1985)
- *The Old Testament Speaks*, by Samuel J. Schultz (HarperCollins, 2000)
- *Old Testament Times*, by R. K. Harrison (Hendrickson Publishers, 2001)
- *Survey of the Bible*, by William Hendriksen (Baker, 1995)
- *What the Bible Is All About*, by Henrietta C. Mears (Regal, 2002)

Proceed with Caution

Don't be afraid to use reference materials. These books usually reflect years of study by men of God. However, don't completely rely on reference works because they're not infallible.

You must realize that these Bible surveys, like Bible commentaries, represent the opinions and theological positions of their authors. Read the descriptions about these books online or in the bookstore and select the ones that best meet your study needs. Remember to use them after you have done your own initial survey study.

Making Your Way Through the Overview Book Survey Method

To successfully perform a book survey, follow these six steps.

Step One: Read the Book

It may seem obvious that reading the book you're attempting to study is a necessary first step, but you'd be surprised at how many people spend all their time reading about the Bible rather than reading the actual text of the Scriptures. The only tools you will need for this first step are your study Bible and several recent translations. Do not read any Bible surveys, handbooks, or commentaries. Instead, follow these seven suggestions:

- **Read through the book in one sitting.** Except for the Psalms, the longest book in the Bible is Isaiah, and you should be able to read it in three to four hours. You can read most of the other books, particularly those in the New

Testament, in much less time. If you have to break up your reading, try to finish a book in no more than two sittings. (For example, read Isaiah 1–39 in one sitting of a few hours, and then read Isaiah 40–66 in another.) You will be amazed at what you begin to see in the Scriptures as you do this.

- **Read through the book in a recent translation.** This will enable you to better understand what you are reading because you will be doing your reading in contemporary language.
- **Read through the book rapidly, ignoring the chapter divisions.** Remember that the chapter divisions and verses were not in the original writing; they were added much later to enable you to find passages more easily. For now, you simply want to get the flow of the book and feel the pulse of the writer. Don't be concerned with the details at this stage; instead, read it quickly to get the main thrust.

> **Teaching Tips**
>
> The worst Bible-reading method is the one you use all the time—it gets stale. So find a new way to read Scripture to the group each week. Pick drama for dramatic passages such as parables. Match the method to the type of passage. The same goes for understanding and applying the Bible: Vary your methods from week to week.

- **Read through the book repeatedly.** Read over the passage as many times as you can, depending on the length of the book. For instance, you will not be able to read the Book of Isaiah as many times as the Book of Colossians because Isaiah is much longer than Colossians. Each time you read the book through, you'll notice something new and the overall picture will become clearer and clearer. The more times you read a book, the better you'll be able to understand it.
- **Read through the book without referring to commentaries or someone else's notes—or your own.** Otherwise, your mind will naturally fall into the notetaker's pattern and you'll be hindered from seeing new things. Only after finishing Step One should you begin to refer to other references.

> **Teaching Tips**
>
> Using the Bible during every study will encourage the members of your group to bring their own Bibles. As the individuals use their own Bibles, they locate passages, mark them, personalize them, and live them. Do provide some extra Bibles for those people who forgot, all the while encouraging students to bring their own and noticing when they do.

- **Read through the book prayerfully.** Ask God to speak to your heart and open your eyes, that you may see wonderful things in his Law. (Psalm 119:18)
- **Read through the book with a pen or pencil in hand.** As you begin reading the second or third time through, begin taking notes and making observations on what you are reading.

Step Two: Make Notes

As you read through the book during Step One, write down your impressions and important facts. Look for the following nine items:

- **Category.** Is the book history? Poetry? Prophecy? Law? A biography? A letter?
- **First impressions.** What is the first impression you get from the book? What do you think is the writer's purpose? What "feel" do you get from reading it?"
- **Key words.** What are some of the significant words the writer uses? What words are repeated the most? What word or words is the writer emphasizing?
- **Key verse.** What seems to be the key verse (if any)? What ideas or phrases are repeated that may show the writer's main thought? What is the writer's key statement?
- **Literary style.** Is the book a narrative? A drama? A personal letter? A discourse? Poetry? A combination of narration and poetry? Does the writer use figurative speech? Is he using a logical argument?
- **Major people.** Who are the principal personalities in the book? Which people are mentioned the most, and what parts do they play in the book?
- **Structure of the book.** Do you see any obvious divisions through the book? How is the book organized? Is it organized around people? Events? Places (geography)? Ideas? Time spans?
- **Main theme(s).** Write down what you believe the theme(s) is/are. What is the writer saying? What is his major emphasis?
- **Emotional tone.** Is the writer angry? Sad? Happy? Worried? Excited? Depressed? Calm? How do you think his hearers must have felt when they received this writing? How does it make you feel?

Just in Case

Teach your group how to mark their Bibles. If they prefer not to write in their Bibles, show them how to slip a card under the page and write on the card. Use three or four symbols, at most, and post the meaning of the symbols. Choose from samples like these:

O	Circle what you like
?	Question what puzzles you
X	What you need to remove from your life
>	Arrow actions you want to take
_	Underline actions you want to avoid
=	Equal commands you're already obeying in your life
!	Exclaim over what makes you glad about God

Step Three: Delve Into the Background

Find out the geographical and historical settings of the book. Into what background does the book fit? You can use the following questions to help you find some of the answers to these questions. Many of the answers can be found right in the book itself, so look there first. If you can't find the answers to your background questions in the text alone, then check outside references.

- To whom was the book written? Find out about the people's geographical and historical backgrounds.
- Where was the book written?
- When was the book written? (Date)
- Learn all you can about the writer. Who was he?
- Why was the book written? Investigate the circumstances related to the writing.
- What other background information sheds light on this book?
- What is the place of the book in the Bible? Is it a bridge between various periods of history?
- What geographic locations are mentioned in the book? Where are they? Draw a map if it will be helpful to you.

In addition to making a horizontal chart for the book's contents (see the following section), you can have the group make other types of charts. A chart can make a complex truth clear by showing differences and similarities. A chart could show divisions between right and wrong, helpful and destructive, Christian and non-Christian. Other possibilities for group charts are listed here:

- Qualities of the old life (life before Christ) vs. qualities of the new life (life with Christ)
- Reactions of the thieves on either side of the cross of Jesus
- Events that happened during each period in Bible history

Step Four: Make a Horizontal Chart of the Book's Contents

One of the helpful steps in doing a book survey is making a horizontal chart. A horizontal chart is a diagrammed layout of a book's contents on one or two sheets of paper. The value of making such a chart is that it enables you to picture the contents and divisions of a book. It gives you a new perspective of the book. The three parts to a simple horizontal chart are the major divisions of the book, chapter titles, and paragraph titles.

Why make a horizontal chart?

- It helps you summarize the main ideas and contents of a book.
- It enables you to see the contents of an entire book at a glance.
- It helps you discover the relationships between chapters and between paragraphs.
- It makes you aware of ideas that are repeated in several places in the book.
- It serves as a memory device to help you recall a chapter's content quickly.
- It enables you to think through a book and remember it.

To make a simple horizontal chart, you will need three tools:

- A Bible with paragraph divisions. Most recent versions have divided the text into paragraphs to enable you to see the units of thought. You have to know these in order to be able to make the chart.
- A blank sheet of paper, preferably 8½ by 11 in size. You should try to fit your chart on one sheet of paper so you can see the entire structure of the book at a glance. When you are

> **Potent Quotables**
>
> "You chart the path ahead of me and tell me where to stop and rest. Every moment you know where I am." (Psalm 139:3, NLT)

working on a long book (Isaiah, Genesis, Psalms, etc.), try to use as few sheets as possible. When you use more than one sheet, be sure to use the same scale so you can match the sheets together.

- A pencil (or pen) and a ruler.

Here's how to make a horizontal chart. Once you've got your tools together, follow these steps for each chart you make:

1. On a blank sheet of paper, make as many vertical columns as there are chapters in the book. For longer books, make the columns narrower and abbreviate what you write in them. For longer books, you may have to use two or more sheets of paper.
2. Read through the book again and find the major divisions of the book. Record these divisions in as few words as possible at the top of your chart.
3. Read through the book again and think of a title for each chapter (or group of chapters in a longer book). Record these at the top of each column directly below the major divisions. In his book *Independent Bible Study*, Irving Jensen suggests five characteristics of good chapter titles (Moody Press, 1963). Preferably use one word and not more than four. Use picturesque words that help you visualize the contents. Use words taken directly from the text, if possible. Use words that have not been used previously as chapter titles in your study of other books. Use words that tell you where you are in the book.
4. Read through the book once more, and do the same thing with all the paragraphs in your book. Try to relate the paragraph titles to the chapter title under which they fall.

As you become more proficient in this exercise, you may add things to your charts to personalize your study.

Another way to learn the different events in a particular book is to play a game called "Order the Events." Make a deck of cards with pictures (or names) of Bible events within the passage you are studying. Put one event on each card. Scramble the cards and challenge the individuals in your group to read the passage so they can put the events in order. Create a race between teams to make this exercise even more inviting.

Step Five: Outline the Book

After you have summarized the contents of the book on a horizontal chart, you are ready to make a simple tentative outline of it. In this type of Book Survey Method, you merely outline the high points of the book and show their relationship with one another. Here are some suggestions:

- Refer to your horizontal chart for ideas. Often your chart will show the obvious natural organization of the book's contents.
- Outline from the major to the minor. Look for major divisions of the book first, then the subdivisions (which could be the chapters themselves), and finally the important points that fall under the subdivisions (which could be the paragraphs). In longer books, you may need to have further subpoints under these.
- Watch your paragraph divisions for clues. Since the paragraph is the basic unit of thought in writing, you can use the paragraph divisions as a guide in designing the outline of the chapter. Write down a summary statement of each paragraph's content; then use those statements as the major points of your outline.
- After you have done your own outlining, compare yours with as many other outlines as you can. Look into the reference books available to you and compare your work with other writers. Don't be concerned if your outline doesn't match these exactly, for often there are many ways to outline a book. You will discover that even the scholars disagree with each other.

Step Six: Apply Your Results

While the main purpose of the book survey is to get you acquainted with the general contents of a book, you should not forget to make a personal application of some insights you discovered while surveying the book. Select one thing the Lord spoke to you about from your survey, and write a personal, practical, possible, and measurable application on that truth.

Based on the Bible passage you are studying, guide your group to declare a life motto. Here are some examples:

- Ephesians 4:29: "Compliments, not cuts" or "Use loving words, not sarcasm."
- 1 Thessalonians 4:29: "Jesus is my steering wheel, not a spare tire."
- Psalm 23: "God will get me through anything."

Teaching the Overview Book Method

Through teaching the Overview Book Survey Method to the members of your group, you give each individual some big-picture handles for a major portion of the Bible (an entire book). Remember to pace yourself and the group through the entire experience at about a chapter a week. Otherwise, you will not take the time to totally absorb the truth in the passage, and you will simply be racing to complete something instead of enjoying the journey along the way.

The Least You Need to Know

- The Overview Book Survey Method helps each person gain a sweeping overview of a single Bible book and celebrates the unique message of each book.
- Read through the book in different ways, and read different translations of the Bible to gain a deeper picture of the book.
- Set a goal for the group to go through one chapter per week; if the chapter is long, then break it into two weeks. Don't rush through the material, but learn everything you can from each chapter.
- As you read the book, write down your impressions and facts about the book. It will help you remember it better and also help each individual contribute to the group meetings.

Chapter 13

Getting in Deep with In-Depth Study

In This Chapter

- Examining a chapter, word by word
- Seven simple steps for analyzing a chapter of the Bible
- Teaching the Chapter Analysis Study Method

While it is common to study a single chapter in the Bible, the entire system of chapters is a human invention designed to make it easier to locate a particular passage. The ancient Jews divided the Old Testament into certain sections for use in the synagogue service. During a later period, in the ninth century A.D., the Jews divided the sections into verses. About the middle of the thirteenth century, Cardinal Hugo introduced our modern system of chapters for all the books of the Bible. Chapters are short units in the Bible that are ideal for a small group or individuals to study. In the following pages, we examine the specifics about how to study a single chapter from the Bible.

From Summary to Conclusion

When you study a single chapter of the Bible, you gain a thorough understanding of the material because you explore each paragraph, sentence, and word in an intensely detailed and systematic manner. There are three parts to this method: a chapter summary, a verse-by-verse analysis, and a chapter conclusion. These parts may be done on a blank piece of paper.

When Chapter Analysis is combined with the methods of Book Survey (Chapter 12) and Book Synthesis (Chapter 14), it allows you to understand the Bible in the way in which it was written: in whole books. This is also a method in which you use limited outside reference books, so you can learn the Scriptures on your own.

Dawson Trotman, the founder and first president of The Navigators, an interdenominational nonprofit ministry, believed this method was the major means for Christians to take into their minds and hearts the Word of God. Hundreds of men and women in the early days of the organization were trained to perform chapter analysis and received a biblical education comparable to that available in Bible colleges and institutes. Since that time, a number of excellent books have been published that expand this method in detail. If this method especially interests you, then I suggest you locate some of these resources:

- *Personal Bible Study*, by William Lincoln (Bethany Fellowship, 1975)
- *The Navigator Bible Studies Handbook*, by The Navigators (NavPress, 1995)
- *Methodical Bible Study*, by Robert A. Traina (Zondervan Publishing House, 2002)
- *The Joy of Discovery*, by Oletta Wald (Augsburg Press, 1975)

Proceed with Caution

Read the passage several times as you prepare a chapter summary. While you may want to supplement your reading from one or more recent Bible translations or paraphrases, be sure to use a standard version of the Bible, without embellishment or paraphrasing for your basic study.

Seven Simple Steps for Analyzing a Chapter of the Bible

This method involves an introduction (chapter summary), which is Step One. Then it explains the verse-by-verse analysis in Step Two through Step Five and finishes with a chapter conclusion in Step Six and Step Seven.

Step One: Write a Chapter Summary

First, read the chapter many times. Through this reading process, you'll be making general observations about the chapter as a whole. After you've read it through several times, describe the general contents in one of the following ways. Don't try to interpret what you see at this time, but aim to become familiar with the chapter. Here are three ways to summarize the chapter:

- **Paraphrase it.** The simplest way to summarize the chapter is to rephrase the contents in your own words. Write the summary so you could read it to another person and convey the big picture. To see some examples of this type of paraphrase, check out some recent paraphrased translations.
- **Outline it.** Another simple way to summarize is through an outline that follows the paragraph divisions of the chapter. Give a title to each paragraph, and then place some subpoints under each paragraph.
- **Rewrite it without the modifying phrases and clauses.** Use the subjects, verbs, and objects in your summary. This method is a great way to summarize some of Paul's writings, where run-on sentences (especially in the King James Version) are difficult to understand because of their complexity.

Proceed with Caution

When writing your chapter summary, be sure to observe what is being said—not why. Don't attempt to analyze when writing your passage description. Don't overlook the obvious in your description.

Potent Quotables

"I will study your commandments
and reflect on your ways.
I will delight in your principles
and not forget your word."
(Psalm 119:15–16, NLT)

After you have completed your chapter summary, give a title to the chapter, using either your title from the book survey or a new one that occurred to you during this study.

Step Two: List Your Observations

This step begins the verse-by-verse analysis of the chapter. You start with the activity of observation. In this step, you examine every sentence and word in detail, and write down everything you see. You are trying to answer the question "What does it say?"

It's important to write down what you read and observe as you read. Professor Louis Agassiz, a nineteenth-century professor of zoology at Harvard who taught his students the art of observation, used to say "A pencil is the best eye." We need to write down what we see, and we will begin to see more facts.

> **Teaching Tips**
>
> Be sure your group understands this maxim: "If you are looking for something, you are more likely to find it." While the statement seems obvious, the more intentional you are about searching the text, the more facts you will glean from the chapter.

Also, be careful not to rush through the passage too quickly. Slow down so that you have the time and space to understand, learn, and incorporate what you read. Finally, don't give up too soon. The longer we squeeze a lemon, the more juice we will get out of it—up to a point. But unlike lemons, the Bible never goes dry. We can study a text a hundred times and never exhaust the riches in the passage. So we shouldn't give up too soon; instead, we should keep on looking—the longer, the better.

It's important to ask questions as you read. As the beginning of this book discussed, the secret of good Bible study is learning to ask the right questions. The only limit to the number of questions you can ask of a text of Scripture is determined by your willingness to stick with it. As you continue to develop Bible study skills, the type and number of questions you ask will improve, and you will be able to observe more and more. The key to good observations, then, is a combination of using patience and diligence, asking many questions, and writing down everything you observe.

The following ideas are a few things you can look for in your observation step of Bible study. Don't let this long list discourage you. You shouldn't try to do each one of the suggested items. It will take time for you to get into the habit of seeing more and more things in the text. As you practice observing more, it will increase your alertness. So remember: Look, search, observe, and then write down your findings.

- Ask the six vital observation questions: Who? What? When? Where? Why? How?
- Look for key words.
- Look for repeated phrases and words.
- Look for questions being asked.
- Look for answers being given.
- Look for commands.
- Look for warnings.
- Look for comparisons—things that are alike.
- Look for contrasts—things that are different.

- Look for illustrations.
- Look for the causes and effects, and reasons for doing things.
- Look for promises and their conditions to fulfillment.
- Look for progression from the general to the specific.
- Look for progression from the specific to the general.
- Look for steps of progression in a narrative or biography.
- Look for lists of things.
- Look for results.
- Look for advice, admonition, and attitudes.
- Look for the tone of the passage—emotional atmosphere.
- Look for connectives, articles, and prepositions.
- Look for explanations.
- Look for Old Testament quotes in the New Testament.
- Look for the literary form.
- Look for paradoxes.
- Look for emphasis through the use of space—proportion.
- Look for planned exaggerations or hyperboles.
- Look at the grammatical construction of each sentence.
- Look for the use of current events of the times.
- Look for the force of the verbs.
- Look for anything unusual or unexpected.

Just in Case

If there are commands in your chapter, encourage your group to take this additional step: Write a short version of every imperative. You'll find two types of admonitions: Time-bound commands, usually found in a historical narrative, require immediate follow-through in a particular situation. For example, Jesus told the paralytic to "get up, take your mat and go home." (Mark 2:11, NIV) The other type is timeless commands, which apply to the contemporary reader as well as the author's original audience. What Peter said to first-century believers is also God's directive for us: "But just as he who called you is holy, so be holy in all you do." (1 Peter 1:15, NLT)

Step Three: Ask Interpretive Questions

After you observe all that you can about the passage, you're ready to begin to interpret what you've read by asking interpretive questions and then trying to find the answers to them. In this exercise, you will discover the biblical writer's purpose and message by discovering the meaning of his ideas.

Usually, interpretive questions include asking what or why. Some examples of these are as follows:

- Why did the writer say this?
- What is the meaning of ______________________________?
- What is the significance of ______________________________?
- What is the implication of ______________________________?
- Why is this important?

You should be able to think of many other interpretive questions. Never think that any question is too silly or too dumb to ask. Always write down every question on your study papers, even though you may not find the answer to it. Possibly later, when studying another chapter, you may be able to answer it; if so, come back to this chapter's section and fill in the answer. Remember that the more questions you ask, the more you will draw out of the text.

> **CAUTION**
>
> **Proceed with Caution**
>
> Different people have different interpretations. Transferring a message from one person's mind to a different mental receptacle is sometimes a precarious process. Incorrectly interpreting someone else's words can be humorous, but when it comes to Bible study and teaching, accurate interpretation is essential. What you are after is meaning, not just factual information.

As you write down your questions about the meaning of the text, it is a good idea to write down any difficulties you have in understanding what is being said. Two common types of difficulties are personal difficulties, or questions you would like answered in the future or items for future study, and possible difficulties, which are matters that don't bother you at this time but that might be good to study so that you can help others who are bothered by them.

Teaching the Chapter Analysis Study Method

Many people like to perform in-depth Bible study on a particular chapter of the Bible. This type of study works well with the short epistles in the New Testament, such as Ephesians, Colossians, and Philippians.

With the in-depth nature of this method, don't try to rush through a chapter together each session. If a single chapter takes three or four weeks, make the group feel free to take this time. The key is thorough understanding and the opportunity for the various members to talk about their individual study and how the Scriptures apply to their everyday lives. The journey of studying together is much more valuable than completing a particular portion of the Bible in the prescribed time period.

The Least You Need to Know

- The Chapter Study Method is a detailed study, summarizing the contents, doing a verse-by-verse analysis, and writing a conclusion.
- This method involves using a Bible and a blank piece of paper, which means almost no equipment or reference books.
- Good observation skills are key to this method: Look, search, and observe—then write down your findings.
- The more questions you ask about a text, the more you will draw out of the text.

Chapter 14

Teach the Bible In-Depth, One Book at a Time

In This Chapter

- Pull the information about a single book together into one place for the deeper meaning
- Use study tools to foster comprehension
- Take six steps to complete the Comprehensive Study Method
- Teach the Comprehensive Study Method

Like classical music building to a crescendo, this chapter puts the final touches to this symphony of Bible study methods. In Chapter 12, you learned how to gain an overview of a book of the Bible, while in Chapter 13, you discovered how to analyze an entire book, chapter by chapter, using the Chapter Study Method. In this chapter, you'll gain an understanding of how to study a book of the Bible comprehensively.

Synthesis: The Goal of the Comprehensive Study Method

The Comprehensive Study Method of Bible study involves studying a book as a whole unit of thought by reading it straight through many times and summarizing its contents on the basis of the Chapter Study Method and the analysis of each of its chapters. As Merril C. Tenney wrote in *Galatians: The Charter of Christian Liberty* (Eerdmans, 1989), "The word *synthetic* is derived from the Greek preposition *syn*, which means together, and the verbal root *the*, which means to put, so that the resultant meaning is 'a taking apart'" When you perform a synthesis of a chapter, you'll learn to ignore the details and look at the whole picture.

Teaching Tips

One way to help your students feel smart and capable is to provide them resources with which to find answers. Guide them to open to the right Bible passage before you ask a question or assign the learning strategy about it. Here's an example of how to give an answer source: "Look in 1 Timothy 6:1–10 to write three guidelines for how a Christian should use money."

The Comprehensive Study Method is a natural conclusion to an in-depth study of a single book of the Bible. Used in combination with the previous two methods, this study enables you to see the book as a whole again after having looked at its parts in detail. You "put the book back together" so that you can see all the details of the book in the proper perspective. You accomplish this feat by rereading the book, producing a final outline, finding a descriptive title for it, summarizing your overall conclusions about the book, and, finally, writing an application.

Potent Quotables

"At once Jesus realized that power had gone out from him. He turned around in the crowd and asked, 'Who touched my clothes?'

'You see the people crowding against you,' his disciples answered, 'and yet you can ask, "Who touched me?"'

"But Jesus kept looking around to see who had done it. Then the woman, knowing what had happened to her, came and fell at his feet and, trembling with fear, told him the whole truth. He said to her, 'Daughter, your faith has healed you. Go in peace and be freed from your suffering.'" (Mark 5:30–34, NIV)

Gathering Your Tools

Many of the basic reference tools were discussed in previous chapters. Most of these basic tools will also be helpful with this method of study. These helpful tools include the following:

- A Bible handbook.
- A Bible dictionary or Bible encyclopedia.
- Several different contemporary Bible translations. These different translations enable you to see different versions of the same material from various qualified scholars.
- A study Bible.

Besides these basic tools, you may also want to consult Bible atlases, historical geographies, historical background books, and Bible surveys. Use these last tools only after you have done your own research. Later you may check yourself and your conclusions against what other reliable scholars have done in these reference books. Some representative surveys and background books are listed here:

- *What the Bible Is All About* by Henrietta C. Mears (Regal, 1997)
- *Survey of the Bible* by William Hendriksen (Baker, 1995)
- *Old Testament Times* by R. K. Harrison (Hendrickson Publishers, 2001)
- *The Old Testament Speaks* by Samuel J. Schultz (HarperCollins, 2000)
- *New Testament Survey* by Merrill C. Tenney (Eerdmans, 1985)

CAUTION

Proceed with Caution

Don't ignore success! Even when the members of your group know that they are right, they'll discredit the answer if you don't welcome it. In one class, one person answered that the end to Peter's timidity was the indwelling of the Holy Spirit. Another person then said that Peter stopped being timid about sharing Jesus when the Holy Spirit came. Both of these answers were correct. But the teacher said, "Uh-huh" to the first response and an enthusiastic, "You are exactly right!" to the second. This teacher had grown so used to the second person answering that she didn't even hear when the first one was correct. And the first person wondered why the second copied her answer and got credit. Deliberately highlight the wisdom in each person's answer to avoid this destructive teaching mistake.

As you examine and use these books, recognize that, like Bible commentaries, they represent the opinions and theological positions of their authors. Try to select one or two books that best suit you, and use them only after you have done your initial survey study and formed your own opinions.

Six Simple Steps

The Comprehensive Study Method includes six steps. Before you get started, make sure that you and each of your students completes the forms for the Overview Book Method (Chapter 12) and the In-Depth Chapter Study Method (Chapter 13). Keep this material handy so that you can easily refer to them often as you go through this study.

Teaching Tips

Consider the teaching example of Jesus and start with simple questions. When Jesus talked with his disciples after the resurrection, he began by asking about their feelings: "Why are you troubled?" (Luke 24:38) He then showed them the answer to their question: his hands and feet. (Luke 24:39) He then asked another easy question: "Do you have something to eat?" (Luke 24:41) He ended by explaining deep spiritual truths. (Luke 24:44–49) Imagine the disciples relaxing and opening their minds to spiritual truth as Jesus talked with them as recorded in Luke 24:36–49. Invite Jesus to guide you to teach in a similar fashion.

Step One: Reread the Book

Your first task is to spend time reading the Scriptures. Because your goal is to really read and understand the Bible text itself, the only tools that you need are your study Bible and several different Bible translations. Avoid reading any Bible commentaries, handbooks, or surveys at this point. Here are some other tips to help make this step an easy one to take:

- Read through the book rapidly, ignoring the chapter divisions. Remember, these chapter divisions weren't in the original writings, but were added much later. For now, just try to follow the flow of the book and feel the pulse of the writer. Read it quickly to get the main thrust.

- Read through the book in a recent translation. A modern translation will use familiar language, helping you to better understand the text.

- Read through the book in one sitting. Except for a long book like Psalms, most books can be read in three or four hours or less, particularly the books of the

New Testament. If you have to break up your reading, try to finish the book in no more than two sessions. You will be surprised at what you begin to see in the Bible if you read long portions in one sitting.

- Read through the book again and again, as many times as you can. Each time you do, you'll notice some new aspects, and you'll find the overall theme becoming more clear. The more you read a book, the greater an understanding you'll have of it. Be persistent.
- Read through the book prayerfully. While reading the passages, ask God to open your eyes and speak to your heart so that you can see and feel the wonderful things in the Scriptures.
- Read through the book without referring to commentaries or notes. Select a Bible with no marks or notes in it, to avoid being distracted and thereby fail to gain new insight.
- Keep a pen or pencil in hand as you read. When you begin to read the book a second or third time, start taking notes and observations on what you are reading.

Potent Quotables

"Observe the requirements of the Lord your God and follow all his ways. Keep each of the laws, commands, regulations, and stipulations written in the law of Moses so that you will be successful in all you do and wherever you go." (1 Kings 2:3, NLT)

Step Two: Devise an Outline

Compare the horizontal chart and tentative outline that you prepared in your book survey with the passage summaries that you did in your in-depth chapter studies. Using your comparison of these results, combined with your recent multiple readings, create a detailed final outline of the book.

Step Three: Create a Descriptive Book Title

After considering what you've learned not only from your horizontal chart, book survey, and detailed final outline, but also from your chapter titles, come up with a descriptive title for the book you have just studied. Create an original title that describes in a few words what the book is all about.

Step Four: Summarize Your Insights

Review and compare the concluding thoughts in each of your chapter analysis studies, and summarize what you believe are the major themes of the book. Again, do not refer to commentaries at this point, for these should be your own insights into God's Word. These insights could also include additional observations gained from your new readings.

Teaching Tips

Give specific instructions to your students. Rather than saying "Write the passage in your own words," be more specific: "Write the verse line by line, leaving a blank line in between each line. Then, on the blank line, note situations that could happen today that are like the Bible event." When the members of your group know how to study the Bible step by step, they increase their chances of more fully understanding the text.

Step Five: Devise a Personal Application

Review all of the personal applications that you made in your book survey and in-depth chapter analysis studies, and the possible applications that you listed for each chapter. If you haven't fulfilled some of them yet, write down those still left and make specific plans to carry them out as soon as possible. If you've completed your goals, choose another possible application from the chapter studies or one from your overview of the book study, and write it down here.

Step Six: Share the Results of Your Study

Bible study should be more than food for your soul and an increase in your understanding of the Bible. The results of Bible study, including your applications, need to be shared with others. You can do this in two ways:

First, throughout this book, I've emphasized the dynamic of the group and the importance of talking through these studies together. Sharing what you've learned with others will help you gain strength through your understanding of the Bible and will help others in your group do the same.

Second, in addition to sharing with the group as a whole, you may find it inspiring to talk about what you've learned and are learning with another person one on one. Find a "Timothy" to mentor. Share what you are learning from your Bible study with him or her, explain the applications you've been working on, and let the person know how he or she can profit from studying the Bible. The more you give of yourself to another, the more you'll learn yourself.

Teaching the Comprehensive Study Method

More complicated than any other method covered in this book, the Comprehensive Study Method is not the first one for you to attempt to teach your group. You'll need to build on what you learn from other methods to successfully share this with others. Think of yourself as an engineer, who doesn't instantly build a complex bridge or building, but instead begins simply and then increases the structure's complexity. As you build the foundation by working through the other methods, you will be ready to lead your group into this final Comprehensive Study Method. By doing so, you help the group connect the dots and put together the bigger picture from the Scriptures.

Another aspect of teaching that you should consider is a common teacher experience: "My group members talk just fine until I ask a question about the Bible. Then no one will say a word, and I end up doing all the talking. Why won't the members of my group talk about the Bible?" Making small talk is easy because the individuals in your group will have had lots of practice in this area.

Make talking about the Bible just as easy by giving Bible-talking practice. Help the members of your group feel safe and smart so that they can discover how to be spiritual. First, refuse to answer any of the questions you pose to the class. After all, you've been thinking about it ever since you started preparing. The members of your group need a little time to think about it. Let silence prompt them to speak. If they don't get the answer after a bit, rephrase the question. Show them the verse, then the line, and then the word until they get it. Give them practice looking in their own Bibles to voice their own answers.

Once you've asked a person a question, never move on to someone else. That person needs the Bible encounter of finding the answer. He or she can do it because the Bible's answers are available to everyone. If another person tries to answer for that person, tease the one who responds with, "Wow! How did you make your answer come out of her mouth? Great ventriloquism! Now make it come out of your mouth." When that person voices the answer, he gains confidence in reading and understanding the Bible.

When the person answers incorrectly, point out the part of the answer that was right, and then prompt the person on the rest of the answer: "Paul was not one of the original 12 disciples, but he was a disciple in the way every Christian is a disciple. So you were partly right. Try looking in the last few verses of the chapter."

Finally, enforce the "no slam" rule so that no one can put down another person. Everyone in the group needs to know that nobody will make fun of someone else for talking. Help this happen by forbidding any cutting remarks: "In this group, we listen to each other and value each other. I will not allow insults or sarcasm." If you're the heavy about this rule but also make certain that you follow it, too, the other members of the group learn the treasuring habit from you. We Christians can give each other a bit of heaven right here—a place where we can experience the treasuring love of Jesus from people who genuinely want to hear what we have to say.

The Least You Need to Know

- The Comprehensive Study Method is the culmination of the previous two chapters and the most complex of the various methods.
- This method involves looking at a book from the Bible as a single unit of thought and summarizing its contents based on the groundwork from previous study.
- The six-step process is built on experience derived from previous methods and helps the group see the big picture of the selected book for study.

Part 4 Practical Lessons and Examples: Where the Rubber Meets the Road

Let's say your pastor or director of Christian education calls you at the last minute. Someone in the church is ill or has another obligation and can't teach. "Can you do it?" the pastor pleads into the telephone with the desperation of someone who has called five other people and been turned down flat. "No problem," you say. "I'd be glad to do it." Or maybe you regularly teach, but you simply don't have time to fully prepare. In either case (or any other), turn to this part of the book. For each of the 12 major Bible study methods explained in the earlier chapters of the book, this part includes an Old Testament example and a New Testament example, complete with some starter questions and other biblical information.

After you've read and taught the material using a particular method for teaching the Bible, turn to this part for a practical and detailed example about the method. The hands-on and easily applicable nature of this section will help you be more effective in teaching the Bible and will increase your confidence level.

Chapter 15

The Devotional Method: Sample Lessons

In This Chapter

- Strengthen your relationship to God
- Learn to meditate, apply, and memorize
- Using the Devotional Method for the Old Testament and the New Testament
- Teaching ideas

If a person is devoted, he or she has a deep and abiding love for someone else. By using the Devotional Method, you and the members of your group will be able to express and build your abiding, loving relationship with God the heavenly Father. This devotional attitude will be strengthened by taking the time to meditate and consider a short passage from the Bible.

Devotional Method Basics

God uses the Bible to capture the attention of man and teach him spiritual truth. Following the Devotional Method, you and the members of your group select a short passage from the Bible and then meditate on it until the Holy Spirit shows you how to apply the truth from the section to your life. Then you write out a short application. The Devotional Method is one of the easiest and simplest means of studying the Bible.

Before we get started, I want to explain a little more about meditation, which dominates the third step in this method. The psalmist wrote, "Oh, how I love your law! I meditate on it all day long." (Psalms 119:97, NIV) And we read in Psalms 1:1–2 (NIV), "Blessed is the man … [whose] delight is in the law of the Lord, and on his law he meditates day and night." When many of us hear the word *meditation*, we think of quiet reflection about God. But does that constitute biblical meditation? If we were to peek around the corner and catch the Old Testament believer in the act of meditation, what would we see?

The Old Testament Jewish meditator cried out to Yahweh (Psalms 64:1). In both of these passages, the Hebrew term *siyach* is used. *Siyach* is one of two words that we find translated as "meditate" in our English Bibles. In fact, both Hebrew words for "meditate" in the Old Testament (*siyach* and *hawgaw*) carry the idea of vocalization. The word *siyach* is defined as "to ponder," but it can also mean "to converse aloud." The primary meaning of *hawgaw* (Joshua 1:8; Psalms 1:2, 19:14, 77:12, 143:5) is to make a low sound, such as the moaning of a dove (Isaiah 38:14) or the growling of a lion. (Isaiah 31:4) The English equivalent is "to mutter." Biblical meditation was almost always a noisy affair.

> **Teaching Tips**
>
> If you feel that your teaching methods aren't working, talk to other teachers; they can give you tried-and-true tips. Focus on the members of your group, and let them do most of the doing, talking, creating, and reporting. Have a few options; if an activity flops, you'll have an alternative plan.

Pray for Insight

The first step in the Devotional Method is to pause and pray for insight from God. In these examples, I include a sample prayer, although there is nothing extraordinary about it. Although in the eyes of some people prayer is only for the priest or someone specially trained, prayer is simply talking with God about the matters in your heart. Jesus gave us the example of the prayer called The Lord's Prayer; he also showed us his commitment to communicating with God, whether early in the morning or in quiet times in the evening.

Motivate Your Group

Many people don't enter a Bible study openly motivated to learn, but they will grow motivated as you take the time to show them how to encounter and live the Bible. The Bible says, "Whoever believes in him will not be disappointed." (Romans 9:33, GNB) Keeping this in mind, focus on four elements of good motivation: Guide the members of your group into meaningful Bible study by relating it to their lives. Show the individuals how moving toward the Bible answers their questions and gives them the happiness they seek. People learn better when some part of them is moving to shape righteousness or to take their place in a learning game—especially on a sleepy Sunday morning or during a nighttime Bible study after a long day at work. Finally, because individuals remember what they themselves say, give opportunity for the individuals to use their mouths.

Devotional Lesson #1

In the following pages, I've provided a devotional study. Imagine that you are doing this study on your own but with my help. I'm going to fill out each area of the study, but everyone will complete the study differently with his or her own prayers, insight, and, in particular, his or her own personal applications. God is working in each of our lives differently and even the same passages of the Bible will speak to you in a unique way depending on what point you are in your life. In the meditation section, you will draw different points than what I've drawn. In these examples, I've given you a visual idea of how to fill out each of these sections for the devotional study.

Immediately following two distinct devotional studies, I include a blank form. You can take this blank form and replicate it in a notebook, in a computer file, or by photocopying it, then fill in the blanks by hand. This system was created with the greatest flexibility so each person can adapt it to his or her lifestyle and needs.

Date: ________________________ *Passage:* Judges 6:1–18 (NLT)

> Again the Israelites did what was evil in the Lord's sight. So the Lord handed them over to the Midianites for seven years. The Midianites were so cruel that the Israelites fled to the mountains, where they made hiding places for themselves in caves and dens. Whenever the Israelites planted their crops, marauders from Midian, Amalek, and the people of the east would attack Israel, camping in the land and destroying crops as far away as Gaza. They left the Israelites with nothing to eat, taking all the sheep, oxen, and donkeys. These enemy hordes, coming with their cattle and tents as thick as locusts, arrived on droves of camels too numerous to count. And they stayed until the land was stripped bare. So

Israel was reduced to starvation by the Midianites. Then the Israelites cried out to the Lord for help.

When they cried out to the Lord because of Midian, the Lord sent a prophet to the Israelites. He said, "This is what the Lord, the God of Israel, says: I brought you up out of slavery in Egypt and rescued you from the Egyptians and from all who oppressed you. I drove out your enemies and gave you their land. I told you, 'I am the Lord your God. You must not worship the gods of the Amorites, in whose land you now live.' But you have not listened to me."

Then the angel of the Lord came and sat beneath the oak tree at Ophrah, which belonged to Joash of the clan of Abiezer. Gideon, son of Joash, had been threshing wheat at the bottom of a winepress to hide the grain from the Midianites. The angel of the Lord appeared to him and said, "Mighty hero, the Lord is with you!"

"Sir," Gideon replied, "if the Lord is with us, why has all this happened to us? And where are all the miracles our ancestors told us about? Didn't they say, 'The Lord brought us up out of Egypt'? But now the Lord has abandoned us and handed us over to the Midianites."

Then the Lord turned to him and said, "Go with the strength you have and rescue Israel from the Midianites. I am sending you!"

"But Lord," Gideon replied, "how can I rescue Israel? My clan is the weakest in the whole tribe of Manasseh, and I am the least in my entire family!"

The Lord said to him, "I will be with you. And you will destroy the Midianites as if you were fighting against one man."

Gideon replied, "If you are truly going to help me, show me a sign to prove that it is really the Lord speaking to me. Don't go away until I come back and bring my offering to you."

The Lord answered, "I will stay here until you return."

Prayer

Lord, open my eyes to receive your insight and wisdom from this story. I want to learn from the Bible what you want me to learn and apply in my life. Thank you, God, for your care about the details of my life. Amen.

Meditation

This passage is on the call of Gideon. The Israelite people were not receiving any guidance from God. Gideon was surprised to see an angel of the Lord. When you meditate on the passage, first you read it several times then you draw basic principles from the message or story in the passage. Each individual in your study group will have different wording and different insight from the passage. I've written some principles that I drew from this section as I meditated on the passage. Therefore, consider meditating on the following ideas:

- When God wants to accomplish something, he looks for people to use.
- God often uses the most unexpected people.
- God can show his strength best through our weaknesses.
- God's power in us is the answer to our inadequacies.
- Sin to confess/attitude to change: Lord, forgive me for not being willing to be used by you. I've felt that you couldn't use me because of my weaknesses. I've used my inadequacy as an excuse for laziness. Help me remember that trusting in myself will cause failure, but relying on your strength in me will bring victory. Use my weaknesses to bring glory to yourself.

Application

I've been afraid to step out and ask my family to study the Bible together on a regular basis. I've made up excuses and tried to salve my own conscience about not being able to spend the time or being inadequate in my studies. I know that God wants me to have regular teaching time in the Scriptures with my family, so I'm going to talk with my spouse and accept the responsibility of regularly teaching the Bible to my family.

Potent Quotables

"The eyes of the Lord watch over those who do right; his ears are open to their cries for help." (Psalm 34:15, NLT)

Memorization

Remember what God told Gideon in verse 16: "I will be with you."

Draw Insight from Your Students

Although the preceding text includes an example of a devotional lesson, in the classroom it's important that you not lecture or speak from these notes. Instead, use these thoughts as a way to draw insight from the individuals in your group.

1. Select someone in the group to open the time in prayer.
2. Ask someone else to read aloud the Scripture passage for the week (Judges 6:1–18), or as another idea, read around the room, with each person reading a single verse.
3. Ask if someone can name one lesson or truth from this passage. Continue to use this question until a number of truths have been brought out from the passage.
4. As you've examined this passage, what attitude has been brought to the surface that you need to change? Again, allow several people to bring out their attitudes from this passage.
5. Discuss the application and what members did to apply the passage to their own lives. Look for several people to participate in this section.
6. Finally, ask what memory verse members can pull from today's passage.

Devotional Study Lesson #2

Date: ______________________ *Passage:* Luke 12:22–26

> Then turning to his disciples, Jesus said, "So I tell you, don't worry about everyday life—whether you have enough food to eat or clothes to wear. For life consists of far more than food and clothing. Look at the ravens. They don't need to plant or harvest or put food in barns because God feeds them. And you are far more valuable to him than any birds! Can all your worries add a single moment to your life? Of course not! And if worry can't do little things like that, what's the use of worrying over bigger things?" (Luke 12:22–26, NLT)

Prayer

Lord, you are the source of wisdom and strength. As I consider your words in the Bible, open my mind and guide my thoughts. Thank you for your ever-present concern for me and your guidance in my life. Amen.

Teaching Tips

Maybe you feel like you aren't creative enough to try some of the methods in this book. The only truly creative person is God himself. He works through each of us to impart his creativity to others. See creativity as a type of courage—courage to try something new to further learning for the members of your group. Try one method at a time, to get comfortable with it. Step by step, you can do it. Why? Because God is your guide.

Meditation

Let's personalize the passage and paraphrase it this way:

I shouldn't worry so much. God will take care of all my needs. Since God gave me my life, surely I can trust him to sustain it. I can learn from the example of the birds in the air. These birds don't worry about the future. God takes care of them on a daily basis. And if God takes care of the birds, of course he will take care of me! Besides, worrying never does me any good. It never really changes the situation. So what's the use of worrying? None!

Command to obey: Don't worry. (verse 22)

Promise to claim: God will take care of me! (verse 24)

Application

I need to apply this lesson in the area of our family finances.

I plan to take my application one month at a time. For the next month, every time the devil tempts me to worry about our bills, I'll resist the thought by quoting Luke 12:24 out loud.

Teaching Tips

Ask the class "How can you avoid worry?" Yet Jesus commands us not to worry. Only faith can free us from the anxiety caused by greed and covetousness. It is good to work and plan responsibly. It is bad to dwell on all the ways our planning could go wrong. Worry is pointless because it can't fill any of our needs; worry is foolish because the Creator of the universe loves us and knows what we need. He promises to meet all our real needs, but not necessarily all our desires. Emphasize the necessity of learning faith more than worry.

Memorization

"Consider the ravens: They do not sow or reap, they have no storeroom or barn, yet God feeds them. And how much more valuable you are than birds!" (Luke 12:24, NIV)

Teaching the New Testament Lesson

Although the previous text includes an example of a devotional lesson, it's important that you not lecture or speak from these New Testament notes when you're in the classroom. Instead, study this chapter and then work with what you learn to derive insight from the individuals in your group. Here are the steps you can take:

1. Select someone in the group to begin your time as a group in prayer. Ask God to give you insight into the Scriptures.
2. Ask someone else to read aloud the Scripture passage for the week (Luke 12: 22–26) or, as another idea, read around the room, with each person reading a single verse.
3. Can someone name one lesson or truth from this passage? What about a command to obey or a promise to claim? Continue to use this question until a number of truths have been brought out from the passage.
4. As you've examined this passage, what attitude has been brought to the surface that you need to change? Again, allow several people to bring out their attitudes from this passage.
5. Ask the group members, "What did you apply to your own life from studying these words of Jesus Christ?" Look for several people to participate in this section.
6. Finally, what memory verse can you pull from today's passage?

> **Teaching Tips**
>
> Are you struggling to find preparation time to be able to teach the Bible? Set aside a regular time during the week, and keep it just like you would any other appointment. Adjust the time until you find a set time that you can keep weekly: before work, after work, while waiting for a child to finish a practice or a lesson, during lunch break, or on the bus.

This blank study form allows you take over the devotional Bible study. You select the passage, create the prayer, find the points for meditation, etc. You can use this form over and over to complete different devotional studies.

Devotional Study Form

Date: ______________________ *Passage:* ______________________

1. Prayer: ______________________
2. Meditation: ______________________
3. Application: ______________________
4. Memorization: ______________________

The Least You Need to Know

- The Devotional Method of teaching the Bible is one of the easiest. It involves choosing a short passage of Scripture and then reading it and asking God to show you some truth for your own life.
- This chapter contains a detailed Old Testament example of how to complete the Devotional Method. Some specific ideas also were included for teaching this passage.
- A detailed New Testament example of the Devotional Method of Bible study is included in this chapter. Besides the actual Bible study, some specific teaching aids are included so that the passage can be taught with little preparation time.

Chapter 16

The Chapter Summary Method: Two Lessons

In This Chapter

- Reviewing the Chapter Summary Method
- Preparing an Old Testament lesson
- Teaching ideas for the Old Testament lesson
- Preparing a New Testament lesson
- Teaching ideas for the New Testament lesson

Someone once said, "The purpose of Bible study is transformation, not information." That maxim expresses God's desire for us as we study the Bible. The Apostle Paul taught Timothy that "the goal of our instruction is love from a pure heart and a good conscience and a sincere faith." (1 Timothy 1:5, NASB) In the same way, James wrote, "Do not merely listen to the word, and so deceive yourselves. Do what it says." (James 1:22, NIV) Do note that neither author emphasized the accumulation of knowledge or doctrine as an end in itself. Bible study is a two-step process: to learn the material and then apply it to everyday life.

Remember, when the Bible was originally written, it was a series of scrolls with no verses or chapter divisions. In 1228 A.D., Bishop Stephen Langston added the chapter divisions because he wanted to make the various sections of the Bible more accessible to the readers. Occasionally, you will notice that these divisions are arbitrary and interrupt the flow of a writer's message. Usually, however, these chapters are good breaking points and are helpful for Bible study.

The Bible has almost 1,200 chapter divisions. If you studied a chapter a day, it would take you a little over three years to complete the entire Bible. I don't recommend that you use the Chapter Summary Method all the time because it would become boring and tedious. Instead, select random chapters of Scripture and use the summary method on these passages for variety.

The Chapter Summary Method Basics

The Chapter Summary Method helps the individual gain a general understanding of the contents of a chapter of the Bible by reading it at least five times, creating a title or a caption for the theme of the chapter, asking a series of content questions, and then summarizing the central thoughts of the passage.

This method has several advantages. First, it's easy to learn. It also doesn't take much time or require any outside reference books or aids. Finally, it's a good type of study method to use when you are engaged in a rapid reading survey through the Bible.

Potent Quotables

Well, how much more do I need to say? It would take too long to recount the stories of the faith of Gideon, Barak, Samson, Jephthah, David, Samuel, and all the prophets. By faith, these people overthrew kingdoms, ruled with justice, and received what God had promised them. They shut the mouths of lions, quenched the flames of fire, and escaped death by the edge of the sword. Their weakness was turned to strength. They became strong in battle and put whole armies to flight. (Hebrews 11:32–34, NLT)

Preparing an Old Testament Lesson: Daniel 3

For this lesson, read Daniel 3, "The Fiery Furnace and Obedience," five times.

___ *(Check here when you're done)*

Caption (Title)

The first thing you should do is create the title for the chapter. It can capture the main theme or summarize the story or simply call attention to the main elements of the story. In this particular lesson, I've called it "The Fiery Furnace and Obedience," which captures the main event and the main lesson in one single phrase.

"The Fiery Furnace and Obedience"

Contents

This chapter contains one story about idol worship that you can divide into the following sections:

- **Verses 1–18:** King Nebuchadnezzar sets up a gold statue.
- **Verses 19–27:** Shadrach, Meshach, and Abednego are thrown into the fiery furnace.
- **Verses 28–30:** Shadrach, Meshach, and Abednego come out unharmed from the fire and are promoted in Babylon.

Teaching Tips

Some members of your group may wonder how big a cubit is, since it's a measurement often mentioned in the Bible. A cubit in Israel was approximately 18 inches; in Babylon, it was about 20 inches. Using these figures to calculate, we know that Nebuchadnezzar's image was 90 to 100 feet tall. The image most likely served as a symbol of the rule of King Nebuchadnezzar. Since the statue and its king could not be separated from the gods, the king commanded everyone to bow down and worship before the image.

Chief People

Now it's time to read through the chapter and identify the major characters in it. The following list is one I came up with while reading Daniel 3.

- King Nebuchadnezzar
- Shadrach
- Meshach
- Abednego

Choice Verse

For this step, select a key or choice verse in the passage. I've selected Daniel 3:28 here.

Daniel 3:28 (NLT): "Then Nebuchadnezzar said, 'Praise be to the God of Shadrach, Meshach, and Abednego, who has sent his angel and rescued his servants! They trusted in him and defied the king's command, and were willing to give up their lives rather than serve or worship any god except their own God.'"

> **Teaching Tips**
>
> What did the blazing furnace look like? It was not a small oven for cooking or heating a house, but a huge industrial furnace that could have been used for baking bricks or smelting metals. The temperatures were hot enough to assure that no one could survive. The roaring flames could be seen leaping from its top opening, and a fiery blast killed the soldiers who went up to the large opening. (verse 22)

Crucial Word(s)

This step involves selecting the crucial words or phrases you find throughout the chapter. The ones below are the ones I identified in Daniel 3.

Refuses to obey (verses 6, 11, 15)

God will rescue (verses 17, 28, 29)

Challenges (Difficulties I Need to Study)

Each chapter of the Bible that you study will raise challenges or difficulties that will require additional study. For the Daniel 3 passage, I found several of these challenges and listed them below.

Where is the prophet Daniel in this story?

What did the blazing furnace look like?

Cross-References

The chapters of the Bible are interconnected, and in this section I list several cross-references or other references in the Bible that connect to Daniel 3.

Exodus 20:3–5

Hebrews 11:34

Psalms 91:9–12

Christ Seen

Jesus Christ, or how God came to mankind in the form of Jesus, is a key focus of the entire Bible. Throughout the Bible, the evidence of Jesus is seen even in the Old Testament. It's true for this chapter, Daniel 3, in that many scholars believe that Jesus appeared in the fiery furnace. If there is a reference to Christ, then the teacher and/or the student would write it into this section of each chapter study.

In Daniel 3:25, King Nebuchadnezzar looks inside the fiery furnace and sees not three men, but four men. The fourth man was supernatural, but no one knows for certain his identity. Some commentators believe it's an Old Testament appearance of Jesus Christ, while others contend that it's an angel. In either case, God sent a heavenly visitor to accompany these faithful men during their time of great trial.

CAUTION

Proceed with Caution

When it comes to studying Daniel 3, consider the excuses that Shadrach, Meshach, and Abednego didn't use:

1. We will fall down but not actually worship the idol.
2. We don't become idol worshippers, but will worship it this one time and then ask God for forgiveness.
3. The king has absolute power, and we must obey him. God will understand.
4. The king appointed us; we owe this to him.

Each excuse is a rationalization. To worship the image violates God's command in Exodus 20:3. It also erases their testimony for God forever. Take time in your group to discuss excuses that individuals use to not stand up for God.

Central Lesson(s)

Within any single chapter of the Bible, there is a central lesson. In this step, the student and teacher capture the central lesson. As with other steps in the study, each individual completes the study on his or her own, then comes together to discuss it in a group context. Everyone will have different ideas about the central lessons. I've included some of these central lessons from Daniel 3 in the following lists.

Insights:

- There is great strength in the friendship of others.
- It's important to stand with others who have similar convictions.
- Obedience to God's law is more important than worshipping an idol.
- God can be trusted even when we can't predict the outcome.

Characteristics of Shadrach, Meshach, Abednego:

- They never allowed friendship to usurp God's place in their lives. (verse 18)
- They trusted God to rescue them from the king's power. (verse 17)
- They shared a friendship that stood the tests of hardship, success, wealth, and possible death. (verses 12 and 30)
- They spoke about God without fear. (verse 16)

> **Potent Quotables**
>
> "Look!" Nebuchadnezzar shouted. "I see four men, unbound, walking around in the fire. They aren't even hurt by the flames! And the fourth looks like a divine being!" (Daniel 3:25, NLT)

Making a Personal Application

Each individual will create his or her own personal application from Daniel 3. A sample personal application follows.

Although these days are uncertain about my job and future, I can follow the example of Shadrach, Meshach, and Abednego. I will continue to trust God and be unwilling to compromise my convictions, even in the face of death or loss.

Ideas for Teaching the Old Testament Lesson

After you complete your personal preparation on Daniel 3, return to the Bible text of the chapter and prepare a series of questions for your group. First, you might ask someone to retell the story of Daniel 3 in his or her own words.

Ask volunteers to answer questions about the various parts of the chapter. Questions might include the following:

- What did you name the caption for Daniel 3?
- How did you divide the contents?
- Who were the chief people in the chapter?

- Which verse did you select as the choice verse? Why was it the choice verse?
- Which were the crucial words in this chapter?
- Are there areas of difficulty that you need to study at a later date?
- What are some of the significant cross-references for this chapter?
- Where was Christ seen in this passage?
- What were the central lessons from the chapter?
- What personal application did you draw from Daniel 3?

You will likely create more questions than the ones listed, but these will start you on the right course of action.

As you work through the lessons of Daniel, also help your group learn these basic methods of Bible study preparation, which will work for any of the methods included in this book.

Read the passage first, and jot down what God says to you through that passage. Your God-given insight is valuable.

Examine the Bible passage by using Bible commentaries and other resources.

Ask Jesus to show you how he would communicate this Bible passage and assess the needs of your group members. How would he answer your members' questions? How would he meet the needs they have expressed recently? Seek methods that make application of the Bible passage obvious.

Decide which method you will use in the study process.

You open and close with a specific verse or point. What one Bible truth do you want your class to remember? Repeat it during the session, let your methods demonstrate it, and emphasize it at the end.

Bathe all of these steps in prayer, and request the Holy Spirit's guidance. As John 16:5–15 explains, the Holy Spirit is the one who convicts, guides, and makes Bible truth clear.

Prepare a New Testament Lesson

For this lesson, let's choose Luke 15. Your first task with any chapter is to read it five times.

___ *(Check here when you're done)*

Caption

You create the title for the chapter. It can capture the main theme or summarize the story or simply call attention to the main elements of the story. In this particular lesson, I've called it "Lost and Found," which captures the main event and the main lesson in one single phrase.

"Lost and Found"

Contents

In this section, you list the main contents of the chapter in a summary form. I've captured this summary of the contents for Luke 15 here.

This chapter contains three parables:

- **Verses 3–7:** The lost sheep
- **Verses 8–10:** The lost coin
- **Verses 11–32:** The lost son

Just in Case

If sheep were so valuable in Bible times, as discussed in verses 3–6 of Luke 15, why did the shepherd leave the 99 sheep and search for the lost sheep? The shepherd knew that the 99 would be safe in the sheepfold, whereas the lost sheep was in danger. Because each sheep was of high value, the shepherd searched diligently for the lost one. God's love for each individual is so great that he seeks out each one and rejoices when he or she is "found." Jesus associated with sinners because he wanted to bring the lost sheep—people considered beyond hope–the good news of God's kingdom.

Chief People

In this step of the study, list the key or chief people in the chapter. Everyone will likely have the same or similar list but in different order. Here's my list from Luke 15:

- The shepherd with the lost sheep
- The woman with the lost coin
- The father with the lost son

Choice Verse

Each chapter in the Bible has a central verse or choice verse. In this section of the study, every person selects what he or she perceives as the key verse. I've selected Luke 15:7 and included it here.

Luke 15:7: "I tell you that in the same way, there will be more rejoicing in heaven over 1 sinner who repents than over 99 righteous persons who do not need to repent." (NIV)

Crucial Word(s)

To complete this step, write down the keywords in the chapter. I've included the key or crucial words in Luke 15:

Lost: verses 4, 5, 9, 24, 32

Found: verses 5–6, 9, 24, 32

Challenges

As you study the chapter, does it raise issues or other questions which require further study? Write down this information in this section called "Challenges." I've listed a question from Luke 15 as an example:

What does the verse "99 righteous persons who do not need to repent" mean?

Cross-References

Because of the interrelationship among chapters of the Bible, it's important to list verses in other parts of the Bible (outside of Luke 15) that relate to this chapter.

- Luke 15:4–6
- Matthew 18:11–14
- John 10:10–14
- 1 Peter 2:25
- Isaiah 53:6
- Psalms 119:176

Teaching Tips

What was the value of each coin described in verses 8–10 of Luke 15? A drachma was worth about an average day's wages. Palestinian women received 10 silver coins as a wedding gift. Their monetary value was like that of a wedding ring, and losing one would be extremely distressing.

Christ Seen

Jesus Christ, or how God came to mankind in the form of Jesus, is a key focus of the entire Bible. Throughout the Bible, the evidence of Jesus is seen in the Old and New Testament. It's true for this chapter, Luke 15, because in the parables, Jesus often referred to himself. If there is a reference to Christ, then the teacher and/or the student should write it into this step of the chapter study.

First parable: Jesus, the good shepherd, searching for lost sheep

Second parable: The Holy Spirit, our rightful owner, finding and restoring us

Third parable: God the Father waiting to welcome us home

Central Lesson(s)

Every chapter of the Bible contains a central lesson. This section captures this information and insight about Luke 15.

Insights:

The son went away saying, "Give me" (verse 12). He returned saying, "Make me" (verse 19).

God cares for sinners and anxiously waits for them to return home.

Characteristics of the immature brother:

Anger: verse 28

Childishness: verse 28

Jealousy: verses 29–30

Wrong perspective: verses 29–30

Grumbling: verses 29–30

Teaching Tips

Why did Jesus tell three parables about something lost? Jesus told the three parables after the Pharisees and teachers of the law complained about how Jesus welcomed sinners and ate with them. The three parables ends with the complaint of the elder son—like the Pharisees, who had no idea why Jesus would want to associate himself with sinners. These three parables are a glorious picture of the heavenly Father and his angels welcoming home returning souls. When we grow discouraged over our sinfulness, this chapter is a good one to read.

Personal Application

Every person who studies Luke 15 (or any other chapter in the Bible) will have his or her own personal application. I give an example of a personal application from this chapter here. Your application will be different.

In each of the three parables, a concrete effort was made to recover what was lost. Many of my friends are lost without Christ. I need to develop specific witnessing plans for reaching them with the good news. I will start by sharing my faith with my friend _____ this weekend.

I need to express more joy when I hear of people who have accepted Christ.

Just in Case

Once a month, during the application portion of your Bible study, guide the participants to write an unsigned piece about what God has taught them that month and how they have lived it; even if you collect just two sentences from each person, this communicates God's ongoing work. Suggest that they include line drawings.

Teaching a New Testament Lesson

After your personal preparation on Luke 15, return to the Bible text of the chapter and prepare a series of questions for your group. As for the Old Testament lesson, a good place to start is by asking someone to retell the story of Luke 15 in his or her own words.

Then ask a volunteer to answer questions about his or her study of the chapter. Ask the following:

- What did you name the caption for Luke 15?
- How did you divide the contents?
- Who were the chief people in the chapter?
- Which verse did you select as the choice verse? Why was it the choice verse?
- Which were the crucial words in this chapter?
- Are there areas of difficulty that you need to study at a later date?
- What are some of the significant cross-references for this chapter?
- Where was Christ seen in this passage? What were the central lessons from the chapter?
- What personal application did you draw from Luke 15?

You will likely create more questions than the ones listed, but they will start you on the right course of action.

Another idea to try in your group is called affirmation by secret compliment. Give all participants notebook paper and direct them to write their names in the big space at the top. Then, leaving their papers on their chairs, direct them to move one chair to the left, write on the bottom line of that paper a specific thing that they like about the person whose name is at the top, and fold their compliment up one line so no one can read it. Direct them to move again to the left, write on the next line up a specific compliment about the person named at the top of the paper, and again fold the paper. Repeat until everyone has a compliment or the papers are completely folded.

Base this exercise on a specific Bible passage, inviting the participants to draw upon it. For example, while studying the Ten Commandments, individuals would write how they see the other person obeying a specific commandment. Or, while studying Deborah, they would write how they see this person leading others, recognizing that everyone leads with some action or attitude.

Chapter Summary Form

This section includes a blank form to be used with any future chapter summary. It gives you the basic elements of the study and you can photocopy the page and write in it, or create your own notebook or computer file to keep the information.

Chapter: ____________________

Read five times.

___ *(Check here when you're done)*

1. Caption (title): ____________________
2. Contents: ____________________
3. Chief people: ____________________
4. Choice verse: ____________________
5. Crucial word(s): ____________________
6. Challenges (difficulties I need to study): ____________________

   ____
7. Cross-references: ____________________
8. Christ seen: ____________________

9. Central lesson(s): ____

____

10. Conclusion (personal application): ____

____

Proceed with Caution

Whether we like it or not, the individuals in our group may become easily bored, and you should keep that in mind. This boredom is frequently blamed on our quick-paced, highly visual society. It could be that people are bored in Bible study because they feel that it doesn't address true questions they have about life. As the teacher, show your participants where to look in the Bible for answers, and continually relate the Scriptures to everyday life. This is the essence of life-application Bible study methods.

The Least You Need to Know

- The Chapter Summary Method of Bible study is uncomplicated, yet it is a way to learn in-depth the contents of a single chapter from the Bible.
- This chapter contains an Old Testament detailed example of how to complete the Chapter Summary Method, along with some teaching aids.
- This chapter includes a New Testament detailed example of how to accomplish the Chapter Summary Method, plus some teaching aids.

Chapter 17

The Bible Character Quality Method: Two Sample Lessons

In This Chapter

- Reviewing the Bible Character Quality Method
- Preparing a lesson about boldness and gaining insight into teaching this character quality to others
- The character quality of servanthood, and how it brings students closer to understanding the Bible
- Character qualities worth studying

It has often been said that when push comes to shove, the issue often boils down to character. The Bible is filled with characters and stories. As you teach the Bible, one of the key elements to examine is character. What traits help you and the members of your group grow to become more like Jesus Christ? What can you do to increase your good character qualities and decrease your negative traits? Through this Bible study method, you and your group take a step toward embodying these good characteristics. You begin to study the Scriptures and learn what the Bible says about character.

Reviewing the Bible Character Quality Method

The Bible Character Quality Method is a nine-step method:

1. First, name the character quality for study.
2. Then specify the opposite quality.
3. Create a simple word study.
4. Locate some cross-references related to the characteristic.
5. Find at least one Bible character who showed this character quality in his life.
6. Locate a memory verse.
7. Select a situation or relationship to work on to apply this characteristic in your daily life.
8. Plan a specific project related to the characteristic.
9. Finally, write out a personal illustration of how you've been able to work on this character quality.

Proceed with Caution

Be sure to change around the seating order. Take out all of the chairs to help your group move around freely and actively participate, or arrange the chairs in small groups of three or four.

Teaching Tips

Mark 6:20 (NIV) says, "… because Herod feared John and protected him, knowing him to be a righteous and holy man. When Herod heard John, he was greatly puzzled; yet he liked to listen to him." King Herod feared John because of John's boldness in reproving sin. What lesson can you and the members of your group learn about boldness from John the Baptist's example?

Learning About Boldness

In the next few pages, you will see my study about boldness. I've included my responses to each of the sections for a Character Quality Study. Your answers and the answers of each individual in your study group will be different.

- **Character quality.** Boldness. "An exhibition of courage and fearlessness; bravery; willingness to move ahead confidently in the face of danger."
- **Opposite quality.** Timidity, fearfulness. "To shrink back from a difficult or dangerous circumstance; to be hesitant."

Simple Word Study

One aspect of the character quality study is to study the specific words in the original languages from the Old Testament and the New Testament. The example of boldness is in the study that follows.

Old Testament word: *Batah* means "to be confident." For example, Proverbs 28:1 states that "The righteous are as *bold* as a lion."

New Testament words: *Tharreo* means "to be confident, bold, or daring." Take this example from Hebrews 13:6: "So that we may *boldly* say, 'The Lord is my Helper, and I will not fear what man shall do unto me.'" (KJV)

Parresiazomai means "to speak boldly or freely." Example: Acts 19:8, "He went into the synagogue and *spoke boldly* for the space of three months, disputing and persuading the things concerning the kingdom of God." (KJV)

Reference tools used:

- *Young's Analytical Concordance of the Bible* (Hendrickson Publishers, Inc., 1984)
- *Vine's Expository Dictionary of New Testament Words* (Thomas Nelson, 1985)

Just in Case

Acts 4:13 in the Greek language of the New Testament literally says that Peter and John were uninstructed or unlettered. The boldness of the apostles was all the more remarkable because they lacked formal education. The outstanding thing that the high priest and those who were with him could remember about these men was "that they had been with Jesus." This was their credential for extraordinary power. Take time with your group to celebrate the boldness of these apostles, and ask God to give you this type of boldness in your own witness for Christ.

Cross-Reference Insights

When examined, the various references to Boldness in the Bible lead to a number of insights about this character quality. These various references or cross-references provide a number of insights:

- Christ spoke boldly in the face of opposition. (John 7:26)
- Our confidence and boldness comes from knowing that the Lord will help us in difficult situations. (Hebrews 13:6)
- Peter and John were bold because they had been with Jesus. (Acts 4:13)

Potent Quotables

"For when your faith is tested, your endurance has a chance to grow. So let it grow, for when your endurance is fully developed, you will be strong in character and ready for anything." (James 1:3–4, NIV)

- When the Holy Spirit fills your life, you will be able to speak the Word of God boldly. The first Christians prayed for boldness in witnessing, and God answered their prayer by filling them with the Holy Spirit. (Acts 4:29–31)
- When Christ's love is in us, we will be bold because there is no fear in love. Perfect love casts out all fear. (1 John 4:17–18)

Simple Biographical Study

Another step in the Character Quality study is to select a Bible figure who characterizes the particular quality which you are studying. In this case, I selected the Apostle Paul as an example of this quality.

The Apostle Paul is a major example of boldness. His entire life seemed to be characterized by this quality. As a young Christian in Damascus, he witnessed boldly for Christ (Acts 9:27). Everywhere he went, he shared his faith boldly in spite of opposition and persecution:

- In Jerusalem. (Acts 9:28–29)
- In Pisidian Antioch. (Acts 13:46)
- In Iconium. (Acts 14:3)
- In Ephesus. (Acts 19:8)
- In Thessalonica. (1 Thessalonians 2:2)
- He wrote bold letters to the churches. (Romans 15:15)
- He asked people to pray that he would continually preach and teach with boldness. (Ephesians 6:19–20)
- His Christian testimony while in prison caused others to speak boldly for Christ. (Philippians 1:14)
- He even faced death boldly: "For I live in eager expectation and hope that I will never do anything that causes me shame, but that I will always be bold for Christ, as I have been in the past, and that my life will always honor Christ, whether I live or I die." (Philippians 1:20, NLT)

Teaching Tips

Have your group turn to 1 John 5:13–21, and read together the epilogue of this epistle. John reassures the believers that because of their assurance of eternal life in Christ, they can act in boldness to pray to God and, in particular, to pray for a member of their community who has strayed from the faith. Use this illustration from Scripture as an opportunity for people to share their own personal prayer concerns and to take the time to pray together for boldness.

Memory Verse(s)

From the various verses that you have been studying about this character quality, select one verse to capture this theme and memorize. I selected Hebrews 13:6 related to this boldness character quality.

"So we say with confidence, 'The Lord is my helper; I will not be afraid. What can man do to me?'" (Hebrews 13:6, NIV)

Working the Quality

In this section, each person will begin to apply the quality to a situation in their life. I have written some examples in the area of boldness.

I have been afraid to witness to my friend, Max, who works with me at the office.

My Project

In this section called "My Project," each person selects a concrete application or project and puts the character quality into practice. My example for boldness follows.

First, I will ask my wife to pray with me about overcoming my humility in witnessing to Max. Then, each day this week, I will pause before going in to the office and ask the Holy Spirit to fill my life and give me boldness to witness to Max. (Acts 4:31)

Personal Illustration

This section allows the individual to capture the results of their "project." How does the character quality apply in everyday life? My personal example with boldness follows.

Monday and Tuesday of this week, I prayed for boldness to witness to Max, but the opportunity just didn't arise. Tuesday night, I decided that I needed to be more earnest in my prayers, so I asked my wife to pray with me specifically for a chance to share my faith with Max on Wednesday.

Wednesday morning, I paused at the office door before going in and I prayed silently that Max would sense that I "had been with Jesus," like Peter and John (Acts 4:13). Then I went in and placed my Bible on top of my desk, hoping Max would recognize it.

During the coffee break, Max came over to talk with me. He noticed my Bible and said, "Is that a Bible?"

I answered, "It sure is. Have you ever read it?"

"Not lately," he said.

I said, "Well I've been reading it a lot lately, and I've discovered some neat things in it." I then shared a brief testimony of what God was doing in my life. Max seemed mildly interested; at least he wasn't turned off. It's a start, and I thank God for giving me the boldness to go this far.

Teaching the Boldness Lesson

The series of questions that follows assumes that everyone in the group has filled out the Character Quality study on their own. With each person doing the preparation for the study time, everyone will be prepared to talk through the various questions. These are some questions to get you moving in the right direction; you will have others to add to the list.

Ask the group to talk about the idea of boldness. Ask them to name some bold people and the qualities that they admire about boldness. Ask them to consider what the opposite of boldness is.

Spend some time talking about fears and what is standing in the way of boldness. Look at the definitions of boldness from the Greek or Hebrew. What additional insight into the word do you gain from learning about these definitions?

Consider the various ways boldness is used throughout the Bible. Look up some cross-references. Name some of the people in the Bible who exhibit this character quality.

Take a few minutes to consider the life of the Apostle Paul. How and when did he show boldness? What effect did Paul's witness have on others around him?

Discuss what memory verse on boldness the individuals selected. It probably will be a different verse for each person.

In what situation or relationship does God want you to have boldness? Give several people an opportunity to answer this question and talk about it.

Ask about the various "projects" the individuals made to work on this character quality of boldness. How did they decide to apply this character quality to everyday life?

Finally, ask several people to talk about their personal illustration of how boldness is starting to be more evident in their lives.

An alternative exercise is to have your group consider the many valuable character qualities in the 31-chapter Book of Proverbs. With short, pithy statements, the book is a catalog of God's perspective on daily life. You'll find maxims on everything from keeping a lid on your temper to the side effects of drinking too much. Proverbs also comments extensively on relationships, mentioning more than 180 different kinds of people.

Here's a systematic approach to study through the entire book, chapter by chapter; it is an additional method to anything else in this book. Let's examine nine keywords to help you observe the text from different points of view:

Keyword 1: Communication. Ask God to increase your powers of observation and show you verses that relate to your life.

Keyword 2: Home. Read the chapter and ask God to link the contents with situations around your home.

Keyword 3: Attitudes. An attitude is a feeling or internal reaction toward a person or circumstance. Read the text and determine whether your attitude compliments or censures the other person.

Keyword 4: Relationships. What is your connection between the chapter and your relationships outside the home?

Keyword 5: Actions. In each chapter, try to pinpoint one behavior that God wants you to implement or curb.

Keyword 6: Consequences. Many passages in Proverbs describe the positive or negative consequences of a particular action. Think of a behavior in your life and the consequences.

Keyword 7: Tongue. More than 100 verses in Proverbs talk about the tongue. Identify these verses to help you understand God's philosophy of conversation.

Keyword 8: Expression. What are you conveying to others? As you study Proverbs, pick out a truth to express to someone else.

Keyword 9: Remembrance. Which of the previous words left the biggest impression? Return and meditate on this verse.

The initial letters of the nine keywords in the study spell CHARACTER.

A Lesson of Servanthood

Here are some verses on servanthood. Have the members of your group each read some of these passages, then talk about what they learn: Job 1:8 and 2:3; Psalms 27:9, 31:16, and 34:22; Isaiah 22:20–25, 37:35, 41:8–9, 42:1–4, 42:18–22, 43:10, 44:1, 44:21, 45:4, 48:20, 49:1–7, 50:4–11, 52:13–53:12, 54:17, and 65:13–16; Jeremiah 43:10 and 46:28; Daniel 9:11 and 9:17–19; Joel 2:29; Haggai 2:23; Zechariah 3:8; Matthew 20:20–28 and 23:11; Mark 9:33–37 and 10:35–45; Luke 1:38, 1:48, and 22:26–27; John 15:14–15; Acts 26:16; Romans 1:1; 2 Corinthians 4:5, 6:4, and 11:23; Galatians 1:10; Ephesians 3:7 and 6:21; Philippians 1:1; Colossians 1:7, 1:23, 1:25, 3:24, 4:7, and 4:12; 2 Timothy 2:24–25; and Jude 1.

Defining and Contrasting Servanthood

One definition of servanthood is "a person in the state of serving others." Its opposite quality is laziness, or "someone in the state of being without energy and who is inactive."

Simple Word Study

This section examines the original words related to servanthood in the Old Testament and the New Testament. They are simple word studies to examine the words and definitions. I've included my examples of the word servanthood here.

Old Testament word: *ebed*, which literally means "slave."

One example is in Exodus 20:10: "But the seventh day is a day of rest dedicated to the Lord your God. On that day, no one in your household may do any kind of work. This includes you, your sons and daughters, your male and female *servants*, your livestock, and any foreigners living among you."

Teaching Tips

Leaders that we can trust display a persistent commitment to servanthood, which is also displayed in hard work, in suffering, in deep concern for God's people, and in evidence that God is at work despite human weakness. How do the members of your group see servanthood exhibited in today's leadership?

A similar New Testament word is *douis*, which means "slave." Bear in mind that the notion of slave often lies behind the translation of "servant." It is most often used in the Gospels, especially in the parables of Jesus. For Jesus, the concept of servant becomes a way of expressing humankind's relationship to God. God is the Lord to whom the Christian owes unreserved service—for example, "No one can *serve* two masters." (Matthew 6:24)

Reference tools used: *HarperCollins Bible Dictionary.*

Cross-Reference Insights

In this section, the individual examines various references throughout the Bible for servanthood. These references or cross-references provide some insight about the Biblical meaning of this character quality. My insights related to servanthood are captured below. Note that your insights and the insights of every individual in your group will be distinct and unique.

In the Old Testament, the righteous person (Psalms 119) and the patriarchs Abraham, Isaac, and Jacob (Exodus 32:13) were called servants of the Lord.

Jesus presents himself as a servant when he washes his disciples' feet at the Last Supper. (John 13:1–20) Jesus told his disciples that he came "not to be served, but to serve." (Mark 10:45) Jesus encouraged his disciples to be servants of each other. (Mark 10:44 and John 13:14) The concept of servanthood is embodied in Jesus Christ, the servant.

The Apostle Paul most frequently used the term "servant of Jesus Christ." (Romans 1:1, Galatians 1:10, and Philippians 1:1)

Simple Biographical Study

What Biblical individual captures the essence of servanthood? I've selected James for this study. Others will select other Biblical characters.

James, the half-brother of Jesus and one of the disciples, shows us an example of servanthood. Known as James the Just (Matthew 13:55), he begins his epistle with the phrase "James, a bondservant of God and of the Lord Jesus Christ." (James 1:1) He doesn't mention his family relationship to Jesus in the epistle, but he claims his authority based on his servanthood to the Lord Jesus Christ.

Memory Verse(s)

I selected a single Bible verse which captures the essence of servanthood in the New Testament. This verse is one to memorize. Other people will select different verses.

"Sitting down, Jesus called the twelve and said, "If anyone wants to be first, he must be the very last, and the servant of all." (Mark 9:35, NLT)

Teaching Tips

Consider with your group one of the ways Jesus illustrated servanthood. He set a little child from the home (perhaps Peter's child) among the disciples. Then Jesus told the disciples to be the "servant of all"—this included giving attention to a child, the least significant person in Jewish as well as Greco-Roman society, which idealized the mature adult. To welcome—that is, to serve or show kindness to—one of these little children, who represented the lowliest disciple (Mark 9:42) in Jesus' name (on his behalf) is equivalent to welcoming Jesus himself. This gives dignity to the task of serving others.

Applying Servanthood

In the next section, each person gives their personal application from the study about servanthood. To give you an example, I've written my personal application about this character quality. Each person will have his or her own application from the study and time in your group session to talk about the variety of applications from a single character study. Here's my application:

In my workplace, I need to serve others whenever I can and in an inconspicuous way, but to the best of my ability.

My Project

This method also includes a specific project which you create to apply the character quality. Each person will have a unique project. Here's my application for an example about servanthood:

I want to consciously serve some of my co-workers. When they need anything, I will make an effort to do it as soon as possible over the course of the next week.

Personal Illustration

This final step of the method involves finding personal illustrations about how the character quality of servanthood applies in everyday life. I've listed several examples of servanthood in my own life. Your illustrations will be completely different than mine but it will give you some examples of what you could do in this area:

Because of my role, almost no one expects me to make coffee at the office. I've consciously decided that when I walk past the coffee pot and see that it's empty, I will stop for a minute and make coffee.

Also, I've tried to make a point to check in with my colleagues and see how they are doing, be an encouragement, and help them in specific ways.

If I walk past the mailroom and see the mail for our department or that someone in my area has left something printed, I will take it back to the appropriate person.

In my servanthood, I'm not seeking to be recognized or for anyone to know about these acts of kindness. Instead, I'm trying to follow the example of Jesus Christ and use that information in everyday life in my workplace.

Potent Quotables

"Obviously, I'm not trying to be a people pleaser! No, I am trying to please God. If I were still trying to please people, I would not be Christ's servant." (Galatians 1:10, NLT)

Teaching the Servanthood Lesson

The following series of questions assumes that everyone in the group has filled out the Character Quality study on their own. With each person doing the preparation for the study time, they all will be prepared to talk through the various questions that follow. These are questions to get you moving in the right direction; you will have others to add to the list.

Ask the group to talk about the idea of servanthood. Name some people who exhibit this quality of servanthood? Also, what qualities do you admire about servanthood?

- What is the opposite quality of servanthood?
- Spend some time talking about laziness and what is standing in the way of service to others.
- Look at the definitions of *servant* from the Greek or Hebrew. What additional insight into the word do you gain from learning about these definitions?
- Consider the various ways boldness is used throughout the Bible. Look up some cross-references. Name some of the people in the Bible who exhibit this character quality.
- Take a few minutes to consider the life of James, the half-brother of Jesus. How and when did he show servanthood?

- Discuss the memory verse on servanthood that the individuals selected. This will be a different verse for each person.
- In what situation or relationship does God want you to serve others? Give several people an opportunity to answer this question and talk about it.
- Ask about the various "projects" the individuals made to work on this character quality of servanthood. How did they decide to apply this character quality to everyday life?
- Finally, ask several people to talk about their personal illustration of how service to others is starting to be more evident in their lives.

Bible Character Quality Method Form

The following paragraphs include a blank form for the Character Quality Method. You can use this form over and over to complete different character studies. I suggest that you photocopy the form or write it into a notebook along with your studies, or create a word-processing document on your computer and keep your Bible study notes in that manner.

1. Character quality: ________________________________
2. Opposite quality: ________________________________
3. Simple word study: ________________________________
4. Cross-reference insights: ________________________________
5. Simple biographical study: ________________________________
6. Memory verse(s): ________________________________
7. A situation or relationship (in which God wants to work on this quality in my life):
   ____
   ____
8. My project: ________________________________
9. Personal illustration: ________________________________

The Least You Need to Know

- The Bible Character Quality Method examines a specific trait—positive or negative—that occurs repeatedly in the Bible with a specific project or personal application.
- Boldness is one of the character qualities shown in this chapter with a specific example, along with some possible questions for teaching the lesson to others.
- Servanthood is another character quality shown through example in this chapter, with some potential questions for teaching the lesson to others.

Chapter 18

Two Sample Lessons on the Bible Theme Method of Teaching the Bible

In This Chapter

- Study the themes you discover as you study the Scriptures—and your own, too
- Consider the theme of praising the Lord in the Psalms
- How did Jesus define the word *disciple?* You'll see in this chapter

The Bible has a number of themes that run throughout the text of Scripture. Some entire versions of the Bible are designed to highlight various themes. The Rainbow Bible is one of the most well known and comes in four different versions. This Bible traces 12 different themes—such as God, discipleship, love, and family—throughout the entire Bible. Each theme uses a different color, and every verse in the Bible is tagged with one or all of the colors of the rainbow.

You don't need a Rainbow Bible for this particular Bible study method. Instead, with some simple questions, you and the members of your group can trace Bible themes yourselves.

The Bible Theme Method: The Basics

The Bible Theme Method involves six simple steps and requires you to approach a theme with a set of no more than five predetermined questions. Then you trace the theme throughout the Bible or in a single book, asking only these questions and then summarizing your conclusions and writing down a personal application.

The first step is to select a theme for study and then list all of the verses that you plan to study. Next, you determine a list of five questions or fewer that you will ask about these verses. For each reference, you ask these questions. Finally, you draw some conclusions from the study and write a personal application.

Do make sure that your theme is specific and that you limit the number of questions you ask. Otherwise, if the selected theme has hundreds of references or you have more than about five questions, it will take many hours to complete the study, and you and the members of your group will grow discouraged by the process. If you identify tightly specified themes and limit your questions, however, you'll find this method to be an ideal way to investigate the Scriptures.

> **Potent Quotables**
>
> "While they were living in Nazareth, John the Baptist began preaching out in the Judean wilderness. His constant theme was, 'Turn from your sins … turn to God … for the Kingdom of Heaven is coming soon.'" (Matthew 3:1–2, Living Bible)

Also, remember that the key to any Bible study method is to emphasize application. As you look at Bible themes in this chapter, you should make a point to always look for ways to return the conversation to how the Bible is relevant for everyday life and how to apply the lesson to everyday life. The Bible will do you and your group little good if you don't practice what you learn in daily life.

Praising the Lord in the Psalms: A Lesson

Theme: Praising the Lord in the Psalms

List of references:

- **Psalms 7:17:** "I will give thanks to the Lord because of his righteousness and will sing praise to the name of the Lord most high." (NIV)

- **Psalms 27:6:** "Then I will hold my head high, above my enemies who surround me. At his tabernacle I will offer sacrifices with shouts of joy, singing and praising the Lord with music." (NLT)
- **Psalms 33:1:** "Let the godly sing with joy to the Lord, for it is fitting to praise him." (NLT)
- **Psalms 43:3–4:** Send forth your light and your truth, let them guide me; let them bring me to your holy mountain to the place where you dwell. Then will I go to the altar of God, to God, my joy and my delight. I will praise you with the harp, O God, my God." (NIV)
- **Psalms 145:1:** "I will exalt you, my God the king; I will praise your name for ever and ever." (NIV)
- **Psalms 149:3–5:** Praise his name with dancing, accompanied by tambourine and harp. For the Lord delights in his people; he crowns the humble with salvation. Let the faithful rejoice in this honor. Let them sing for joy as they lie on their beds." (NLT)

Teaching Tips

As a group, re-examine Psalm 145. Here some of the keys to understanding this Psalm: Verse 1, David praises God for his fame; verse 8, for his goodness; verse 11, for his kingdom; verse 14, for his providence; verse 17, for his justice, holiness, and saving mercy. This incomparable song of praise is the last of the acrostic or alphabetical Psalms. David apparently composed each verse beginning with a consecutive letter of the Hebrew alphabet toward the close of his life.

Some people in your group might ask why so many Psalms are organized into different "books." Scholars believe that these several collections were made at times of high religious life: the first probably near the close of David's life, the second in the days of Solomon, the third by the singers of Jehoshaphat (2 Chronicles 20:19), the fourth by the men of Hezekiah (2 Chronicles 29, 30, and 31), and the fifth in the days of Ezra. The Mosaic ritual makes no provision for the service of song in the worship of God. David first taught the church to sing the praises of the Lord.

Asking and Answering

The following questions are ones you could generate if you were creating this study on the Psalms. I've written some possible questions and their answers.

Questions to Be Asked	Answers to Questions					
	Psalms 7:17	**Psalms 27:6**	**Psalms 33:1**	**Psalms 43:3**	**Psalms 145:1**	**Psalms 149:3–5**
1. Why should I praise the Lord?	Because of his righteousness.	Because even when I am surrounded by my enemies, the Lord is present.	Because it is appropriate or fitting.	Because God's light and truth guide us.		The Lord delights in his people and crowns the humble with salvation.
2. How can I praise the Lord?	Through singing.	Through singing and music.	Singing with joy.	With the harp and with a willingness to go to God.	Lift up the name of God, the king.	Through dancing accompanied with tambourine and harp.
3. When should I praise the Lord?		At all times—good and troubled.		As God guides us into light and truth.	Praise the Lord for ever and ever.	
4. What are some results of praising the Lord?	I give thanks to his name.	Because I can hold my head high even when surrounded by enemies.		God gives us joy and delight.		Salvation for the humble and joy as they lie in their beds.
5. Where should I praise the Lord?		At his tabernacle.		At the altar of God.		Any place—even on your bed.

Teaching Tips

Human praise of God is one of Scripture's major themes. *Praise* comes from a Latin word meaning "value" or "price." Thus, to give praise to God is to proclaim his merit or worth. Many terms are used to express this in the Bible, including *glory, "blessing, thanksgiving,* and *hallelujah,* with the last one being a transliteration of the Hebrew for "praise the Lord." The Hebrew title of the book of Psalms ("Praises") comes from the same root as *hallelujah.*

Conclusions

Characteristics I discovered:

- God's righteousness deserves my praise.
- God is present even when I am surrounded by enemies.
- God's light and truth guide me.
- God delights in the praise of his people.

Results I discovered:

- I can give thanks to God's name.
- I can hold my head high when surrounded by enemies because of God's presence.
- God guides me into light and truth.
- God gives salvation to the humble.
- God gives joy to me as I lie on my bed and sleep.
- God delights in my praise.

Application

- Based on Psalms 149:3–5, praise is a powerful force that God honors and blesses, yet so often it's easier for me to complain and not use this spiritual resource. I will make a conscious effort to spend time every day on the way to work praising God.
- Based on Psalms 43:3–4, I have not been actively attending church on a regular basis, but I know that God sends forth light and truth in his houses of worship. I will attend church more often and will worship and praise God.

Teaching the Praising Lesson

Praise is a simple way to give God our thanksgiving. Talk with the group members about how they praise God. What are some of the ways they praise God? With song? In meditation? How do they express praise and joy to God? What are some of the results?

Prepare a Lesson: Jesus' Definition of a Disciple

The Greek word means *disciple* means "pupil" or "learner." In its most intense sense, discipleship suggests a total commitment to stay close to and to obey the person chosen as one's teacher. In this section, you'll see how to prepare a lesson about how Jesus defined disciple.

The Gospels clearly show that the word *disciple* can refer to others besides the twelve. The verb *follow* became something of a technical term that Jesus used to call his disciples, who were then called "followers." (Mark 4:10) These "followers" included a larger company of people from whom Jesus selected the twelve. (Mark 3:7–19 and Luke 6:13–17) This larger group of disciples/followers included men and women (Luke 8:1–3, 23:49) from all walks of life. (Even the twelve included a variety: fishermen, a tax collector, a Zealot.) Jesus was no doubt especially popular among the socially outcast and religiously despised, but people of wealth and of theological training also followed. (Luke 8:1–3, 19:1–10; and John 3:1–3, 12:42, and 19:38–39)

Teaching Tips

Discuss how God is glorified by the Christian's fruitfulness. (John 15:5–8) But as in all things, that which glorifies God benefits the disciple. Note the benefits you and I experience when we stay close to Jesus. We produce "much fruit" and thus find a sense of satisfaction in fulfilling our destiny. (verse 5) We gain power in prayer, asking "whatever you wish." (verse 7) We demonstrate our discipleship, showing the reality of our link with Jesus. (verse 8)

List of References

If you were completing this study, you wcould find references that relate to being a disciple and list them in this section. I've filled out the verses as an example.

Questions to Be Asked			**Answers to Questions**			
	Matthew 10:24–25	**Luke 14:26–28**	**Luke 14:33**	**John 8:31–32**	**John 13:34–35**	**John 15:8**
1. What are the characteristics of a disciple?	A disciple will be like Christ (his Master)	A disciple gives supreme love to Christ and bears his cross and follows Christ.	A disciple gives all to follow Christ.	A disciple continually abides in Christ's Word.	A disciple love for others.	A disciple bears fruit.
2. What are the results of being a disciple?	He should expect to be treated as Christ was by the world.			He knows the truth and is set free.	Others will know that he belongs to Christ.	His bearing fruit brings glory to God.

Conclusions

Characteristics I discovered:

A disciple …

- Is like Christ.
- Gives supreme love to Christ.
- Bears his cross and follows Christ.
- Gives up all to follow Christ.
- Continually abides in Christ's Word.
- Loves others.
- Bears fruit.

Results I discovered:

- He should expect persecution.
- He knows the truth and is set free.
- He brings glory to God.
- Others notice that he belongs to Christ.

Teaching Tips

Talk about these aspects of discipleship with your group: If the closest relationships of a disciple's life conflict with the claims of Jesus Christ, then our Lord requires instant obedience to himself. Discipleship means personal, passionate devotion to a person—our Lord Jesus Christ. There is a vast difference between devotion to a person and devotion to principles or to a cause. Our Lord never proclaimed a cause; he proclaimed personal devotion to himself. To be a disciple is to be a devoted bondservant motivated by love for the Lord Jesus.

Application

Because this study is on discipleship, how will you apply it into your life? Each person's application of this study will be different. As an example, here's my personal application from this study.

Based on John 8:31–32: I will establish a regular, daily quiet time in the Word, starting tomorrow morning.

Based on John 13:34–35: I will demonstrate love for the person in my Bible study group who irritates me by asking his family to come to dinner this next week.

Teaching the Discipleship Lesson

During your time with the group, explore what each individual gained from the study of Jesus' definition of discipleship. Which portions of Scripture stood out, and what did the person individually gain from it? Read the various verses in different translations, and discuss what additional information and perspective the group gains from this experience. For this particular lesson, be sure to use the teaching points as discussion starters on the various aspects of discipleship and what it takes to follow Jesus consistently and daily.

The Bible Theme Method Form

As with the other chapters, this method includes a blank form which you can photocopy and use for other Bible Theme Method studies.

Theme: ______________________________

List of references:

- ______________________________
- ______________________________
- ______________________________
- ______________________________
- ______________________________
- ______________________________
- ______________________________

Questions to Be Asked	Answers to Questions					
	Scripture	Scripture	Scripture	Scripture	Scripture	Scripture
1.						
2.						
3.						
4.						
5.						

Conclusions

Characteristics I discovered:

- ______________________________
- ______________________________
- ______________________________
- ______________________________
- ______________________________
- ______________________________
- ______________________________

Results I discovered:

- ______________________________
- ______________________________
- ______________________________
- ______________________________
- ______________________________
- ______________________________
- ______________________________

Applications:

- ______________________________
- ______________________________
- ______________________________
- ______________________________
- ______________________________
- ______________________________
- ______________________________

The Least You Need to Know

- The Old Testament lesson example in this chapter relates to praise in the Psalms. In these days of negative talk and discouragement, use praise of God in the Psalms as a way to raise hope and encouragement of the members of your group.
- Jesus' definition of a disciple is the second lesson in this chapter and comes from the New Testament. You can use this lesson to explore with your group what it takes to follow Jesus. Through these two practical lessons, you will easily have examples to lead others in the Bible Theme Method.
- The Bible Theme Method is an excellent way to learn more specifics about a concept throughout the Bible.
- A blank form for the Bible Theme Method is included in this chapter for you to fill in your own studies.

Chapter 19

Sample Lessons: The Biographical and Topical Teaching Methods

In This Chapter

- Study the people who populate the Bible
- The loves of Joseph from the Old Testament and Stephen from the New Testament
- Teach the Bible more effectively with the Biographical Teaching Method
- Help student gain appreciation of the Bible through the Topical Teaching Method
- Two practical lessons using the Topical Teaching Method

Two of the key ways of studying the Bible focus on people (the Biographical Teaching Method) and on specific topics (the Topical Teaching Method). This chapter includes two examples of each type of Bible study, along with the teaching tools you'll need to use these methods in a group setting.

The Basics of the Biographical Method

Before looking at two detailed examples of the Biographical Method, let's review the process of studying the life of an individual from the Bible. The Biographical Method involves a 10-step study process to dig into the lives of people in the Bible:

1. First, select the Bible person for study.
2. Make a list of all the Bible references about that person.
3. Write down your first impression (from your first reading).
4. Make a chronological outline (from your second reading).
5. Get some insights into the person (from the third reading).
6. Identify some character qualities (from the fourth reading).
7. Show how other Bible truths are illustrated in this person's life.
8. Summarize the main lesson or lessons.
9. Write out a personal application.
10. Finally, make your study transferable to others.

Potent Quotables

"But you are not like that, for you are a chosen people. You are a kingdom of priests, God's holy nation, his very own possession. This is so you can show others the goodness of God, for he called you out of the darkness into his wonderful light." (1 Peter 2:9, NLT)

Prepare a Name

The first step in any biographical study is to select the person to study. In this case, I've selected the name for you:

Joseph

Scripture References

Where do you find the particular Bible character that you are studying in the Scriptures? You list the general reference and then some particular references in this section. I've completed the study and listed the ones for Joseph.

Genesis 30–50

Some particular references:

Genesis 37:5–9

Genesis 39

Genesis 41

Genesis 43

Genesis 45

Genesis 50

Just in Case

Some members of your group may identify with Joseph and his hardships. He was betrayed and deserted by his family, exposed to sexual temptation, and punished for doing the right thing. Joseph endured long imprisonment and was forgotten by those he helped. As you read about the life of Joseph, make sure the group notes his response to these hardships. He acknowledged God's presence and had a positive response to each setback. He knew that with God's help, any situation could be used for good, even when others intended it for evil. Talk about Joseph's attitude.

First Impressions and Observations

In this section, each person captures their initial impressions about the selected character. I've written this information about Joseph.

Joseph was overconfident as a young man. He gained this confidence because he was his father's favorite son and knew God's design on his life. Joseph's self-confidence was molded by pain combined with a personal relationship with God that allowed him to survive and prosper where most would have failed. He added wisdom to his confidence and won the hearts of everyone he met. He led the nation of Egypt and preserved the Jewish people.

Proceed with Caution

Some members of your group may question whether they would ever be jealous enough of someone else to kill that person. Before they say, "Of course not," ask them to consider the story of Joseph. His ten brothers were willing to kill their younger brother over a robe and some reported dreams. Their deep jealousy grew into an ugly rage that completely blinded them about what was right. Jealousy can go unrecognized because our reasons for it seem to make sense; yet, unchecked, it can lead to serious sins. Talk about these feelings with the group.

Outline of Joseph's Life

In this section, each individual creates a brief outline of the person's life. I've completed this step for Joseph's life.

I. His early life

A. The son of Jacob and Rachel (Genesis 30:22–24)

B. The favorite child of his father (Genesis 37:3)

C. Because of father's partiality, hated by his brothers (Genesis 37:3–11)

D. Dreams about the future (Genesis 37:5–10)

E. Sold into Egypt (Genesis 37:1–28)

II. His life in a foreign land (Genesis 39:1–50:26)

III. Joseph's seven steps to honor

A. Godly influence (Genesis 39:2–3)

B. Business honesty (Genesis 39:5–6)

C. Resistance to temptation (Genesis 39:7–9)

D. Divine favor (Genesis 39:21)

E. God-guided circumstances (Genesis 40:5–8)

F. Honoring God (Genesis 41:16)

G. Divine revelations (Genesis 41:25–36)

IV. His Christlike spirit shown

A. In forgiving his brothers' sin (Genesis 45:15)

B. In his final devotion to God (Genesis 46:29)

C. In returning good for evil (Genesis 50:19–21)

> **Potent Quotables**
>
> "As they discussed who should be appointed for the job, Pharaoh said, 'Who could do it better than Joseph? For he is a man who is obviously filled with the spirit of God.'" (Genesis 41:38, NLT)

General Insights (Answers to Questions)

This next section includes a series of questions and the answers with the Bible references related to the life of Joseph. Each person doing this biographical study will create different answers, but I've included my answers for a detailed example of this process.

A. How was Joseph shown to be favored above his brothers?

- Joseph was born to his father in Jacob's old age. (Genesis 37:3)
- Joseph wore a beautiful robe from his father. Almost everyone wore some type of robe, but Joseph's robe was the type reserved for royalty. (Genesis 37:3)
- Joseph had dreams about his ruling over his brothers, which only fueled their anger. (Genesis 37:6–11)

B. How did Joseph's brothers deceive their father?

- After selling Joseph into slavery into Egypt, the brothers told their father that Joseph was dead. (Genesis 37:31–35)

C. When Joseph avoided Potiphar's wife, how did she respond to his resistance?

- Joseph refused her sexual advances, so she falsely accused him of raping her. (Genesis 39:6–18)

D. How did God protect Joseph while in prison?

- The Lord granted Joseph favor with the chief of the prison, so he was soon over the other prisoners and the entire jail. (Genesis 39:19–23)

E. Why was Joseph elevated to the second-in-command in Egypt?

- Joseph interpreted a dream for the Pharaoh's cupbearer and chief baker. The dream was true for both, but the cupbearer returned to Pharaoh. Then when the Pharaoh had a dream, the cupbearer told Pharaoh about Joseph. (Genesis 40 and 41)

F. How did Joseph save the Jewish people in the long term because he ruled Egypt?

- Because of the years of famine, Joseph brought Jacob, his brothers, and their family and possessions to the land of Goshen. Joseph kept the Jewish people alive through this move. (Genesis 45–47)

Character Qualities Identified: Genesis

Because you've studied the various Bible passages about Joseph, in this section you stand back and create a detailed list of the various character qualities which you have identified. Again I've completed my view of these qualities and the appropriate Scriptures as an example.

- Confident (Genesis 37:5–11)
- Known for his personal integrity (Genesis 39:4, 23)
- Spiritually sensitive (Genesis 39:2–3 and 41:25–32)

- Intent on doing his best when he knew the situation was the worst (Genesis 39:22–23)
- Focus to carry out the task he was given (Genesis 41:46–49 and 53–57)
- Ability to use power and influence compassionately for reconciliation (Genesis 45:3–15 and 50:20)

Teaching Tips

As you talk with the group about Joseph, make sure you keep the larger perspective in mind about the Jewish people. God used Joseph's faithfulness to preserve the children of Jacob (Israel) in order to fulfill his promise to Abraham (Genesis 45:5–8). In the same way, God intends to use Christians in positions great and small to accomplish his purposes. Therefore, it is crucial that we honor God through our work. Like Joseph, we need to be people of whom there can be no doubt—we are those "in whom is the Spirit of God." (Genesis 41:38)

Bible Truths Illustrated in Joseph's Life

The next step in the Biographical Method is to write out Bible truths from the previous research. I've written my view of these truths about Joseph.

Joseph maintained his faith in God throughout the worst possible situations, such as prison. (Genesis 39:22–23)

God wants us to be faithful with the tasks the Lord has given us. (Genesis 41:46–49 and 53–57)

Power and influence can be used with compassion and for reconciliation. (Genesis 45:3–15 and 50:20)

Summary of Lessons

This step captures the summary of the lesson which you have learned about Joseph. Each person doing the study will likely have a different answer. My insight into Joseph's life is written here as an example of this process.

Joseph is an example of continually doing your best even when the situation is the worst. Unjustly thrown into prison, Joseph could have easily been bitter toward God. Instead, he continued doing what God designed him to do: He exercised authority, even in prison.

Influence and power often go to people's heads, but instead of using his power and influence for revenge against his brothers or Potiphar's wife, Joseph was compassionate and forgiving and used his power for reconciliation.

Personal Application

The personal application here is my personal application from studying the life of Joseph. Each person in your group (including yourself) will have a different personal application from this study.

In situations at work and at home, I need to be careful of how I use my power and influence. Instead of using it for revenge or to get back at the other person, I need to use that influence for reconciliation and compassion, following the example of Joseph.

Potent Quotables

"But Joseph told them, 'Don't be afraid of me. Am I God, to judge and punish you? As far as I am concerned, God turned into good what you meant for evil. He brought me to the high position I have today so I could save the lives of many people. No, don't be afraid. Indeed, I myself will take care of you and your families.'" (Genesis 50:19–21, NLT)

Transferable Concepts

Now that you've studied the life of Joseph, how do these concepts transfer into the lives of other people who cross your life (family, neighbor, co-workers, friends)? One of the steps for this method is to talk about what you are learning from studying the Bible with others. My transferable concept follows as an example.

The concepts in this study that are transferable include the following:

- Personal integrity can be maintained in difficult circumstances. Like Joseph, I can understand that a moral compromise is offensive not only to my family, but also to God. I can remain committed to what is right.
- Doing right to people, even when they have wronged you and you could easily seek revenge, is necessary. It's the Christlike action never to use power or influence for revenge, but instead to use it for good, as Joseph did.
- Consistency and faithfulness for the tasks that I am given are important. Joseph recognized the necessity of consistently accomplishing the work that God gave him.

> **Potent Quotables**
>
> "And as they stoned him, Stephen prayed, 'Lord Jesus, receive my spirit.' And he fell to his knees, shouting, 'Lord, don't charge them with this sin!' And with that, he died." (Acts 7:59–60, NLT)

Sharing the Study

Rather than just create the concepts and not have definite plans to tell them to another person, this study method calls for you to make a specific plan about who you will talk to about what you have learned. I have written my personal example as an illustration.

I will share what I've learned with the following people: my wife, Mary, and Harry, one of my co-workers.

Ideas for Teaching the Lesson on the Life of Joseph

Use the life of Joseph to talk with each member of your group. Discuss the various stages of his life, and collect characteristics from the group. For example, as a young man, Joseph was extremely confident. What are the positive qualities of confidence and the potential pitfalls or negative qualities?

Walk the members of the group through the various steps of this study method, and have the members volunteer their ideas and thoughts about each step.

Prepare a Lesson About the Life of Stephen

This section begins the second detailed example of the Biographical Teaching Method. Because the last example was from the Old Testament, I selected a Bible figure from the New Testament. As in the last example, I will include each step of the biographical method along with my answers to this study.

Scripture References

This section lists the specific Bible verses in the New Testament which relate to Stephen. I've filled in the verses.

- Acts 6:3–8:2
- Acts 11:19
- Acts 22:20

First Impressions and Observations

At this point, each person has read the Bible verses related to the person from the Bible so they can write some impressions and observations. I've recorded my response to this section about Stephen.

Stephen was an early Christian who was well known among the early church for following Jesus faithfully, was a powerful preacher and witness, and was willing to die for his faith.

Outline of His Life

This section outlines the life of Stephen with as much information and detail as the Bible reveals about his life. I've written my outline as an example.

A. Chosen by the early church as a leader

1. To help resolve a conflict (Acts 6:5)
2. On the basis of certain godly characteristics (Acts 6:3, 5, 8)

B. Had a wide ministry

1. Waited on tables (Acts 6:2, 5)
2. Performed miracles (Acts 6:8)

C. Was persecuted

1. Opposed by Jews from "overseas" (Acts 6:9)
2. Falsely accused (Acts 6:11)
3. Arrested and brought before the Sanhedrin (Acts 6:12)
    a. False witnesses testified against him.
    b. He defended himself with a masterful review of Old Testament Scripture. (Acts 7:2–53)
    c. He testified to Jesus. (Acts 7:55–56)
    d. He was killed by an angry mob. (Acts 7:57–60)

D. He had a ministry after his death; persecution caused the church to spread. (Acts 8:2–4 and 11:19)

Just in Case

Members of your group may wonder why Stephen was stoned outside of the city gate. Jewish law did not allow an execution within the walls of Jerusalem, so the religious leaders took Stephen outside the city walls. Jewish custom was that the first witness would push the condemned person's face forward into a pit about 12 feet deep. If the person survived the fall, he was turned over and large boulders were thrown down on him. The situation may have been a little different with Stephen because of the haste of the executioners. The text says that Stephen was kneeling.

General Insights (Answers to Questions)

For this part of the biographical study on Stephen, each person asks some basic questions about his life and also includes their written answers to these questions with the Bible references when appropriate. As another example of how to complete this step, I've included my answers.

A. Why was he chosen to be a leader?

1. He was full of the Holy Spirit and wisdom. (Acts 6:3)
2. He was full of faith and the Spirit. (Acts 6:5)
3. He was full of God's grace and power. (Acts 6:8)
4. He knew the Scriptures. (Acts 7:2–53)

B. What was his response to false accusations?

1. He "held his tongue" and remained silent, and answered only when he was directed to speak by the high priest.

C. Are there any parallels with Jesus?

1. Yes: He was falsely accused, demonstrated love and concern for his accusers, and died an "undeserved" death.

D. What was his attitude toward his executioners?

1. He was forgiving, even to the point of praying that God would forgive them for their sin of murder.

E. What were the long-term results of his life, ministry, and death?

1. Stephen advanced God's long-term plan for the spread of the Good News about Jesus Christ. His death caused the disciples to scatter and take the Gospel to other parts of Judea, Samaria, and regions beyond Palestine in fulfillment of Acts 1:8, which is part of the Great Commission. Jesus told his disciples when

he left the earth that they would spread his name across the earth. Also, Stephen's death helped bring Paul to the Lord.

Teaching Tips

When teaching the life of Stephen, make sure you emphasize the power of forgiveness. The church father Augustine wrote that the church owes Paul to Stephen's prayer. Saul, who later became Paul, never forgot the way Stephen died—he also did not conceal that he was in full agreement with the killing. God promises in Romans 8:28 that all things work together for good. Even though Paul was struggling against the work of the early church and the church was experiencing persecution, this struggle eventually led Paul, the man who wrote half of the New Testament, to eternal life.

Character Qualities Identified: The Book of Acts

In the following section, I've included some character qualities from Stephen and the appropriate Bible passages. Every person doing this study will have their own insights and words for this study. I've included mine as an example.

- Spirit-filled (Acts 6:3, 5, 10)
- Wise (Acts 6:3 and 10)
- Faithful (Acts 6:5)
- Available to God (Acts 6:8)
- Persistent (Acts 6:10)
- Holy (Acts 6:15)
- Knowledgeable (Acts 7)
- Bold (Acts 7:5–53)
- Brave (Acts 7:51–53)
- Forgiving (Acts 7:60)
- Respected by others (Acts 8:2)
- A witness to Jesus (Acts 22:20)

Bible Truths Illustrated in the Life of Stephen

For this step, each person summarizes the Bible truth from the person they are studying (Stephen). I've included my Bible truths.

- The presence and comfort of the Holy Spirit in the trials of life (Acts 7:54–55 and Hebrews 13:5-6)
- False accusations and persecution will come into our lives. (Acts 6:11ff)
- God's grace is sufficient when we walk with him. (Acts 6:10, 1 Corinthians 1:27–31, 2 Corinthians 12:9)

Summary of Lessons Learned from His Life

In this section, the individual provides the lesson that they have learned about the Bible character (Stephen). I include my personal lessons learned as an example.

The outstanding characteristic of Stephen was his commitment to the Lord and his willingness to do anything for him, including give up his life. This commitment is demonstrated by the fact that he was a man who walked with God (he was "full of the Holy Spirit, wisdom, faith, God's grace, and power"). He had great testimony before others in the church. He witnessed to people both in life and in death. Furthermore, he was a man of the Word. He really knew his Bible, the Old Testament. He must have spent hours studying the scrolls and the parchments.

Teaching Tips

Make it clear to the group that Stephen saw the glory of God and Jesus, the messiah standing at God's right hand. His words were similar to those that Jesus spoke before the high council. (Matthew 26:64, Mark 14:62, Luke 22:69) Stephen's vision supported Jesus' claim and angered the Jewish leaders who had condemned Jesus to death for blasphemy. They would not tolerate Stephen's words, so they dragged Stephen out and killed him. People might not kill us for talking about Christ, but they might let us know if they don't want to hear the truth and might try to silence us.

Personal Application

For this step in the biographical study, every person will have their own personal application. Here is my application as an example.

I need to become a person like Stephen—a person of the Word who knows Jesus Christ intimately and who is able to answer others with Scripture when they ask questions. As a result of this study, I will commit myself to having a daily quiet time for at least 15 minutes to get to know Christ better. I will also commit myself to memorizing two Scripture verses each week so that I can answer people who ask me questions.

Transferable Concepts

As I consider the life of Stephen, what concepts are something to pass along to others in my life? I've listed a few but every person completing this study will have something different, which is the material that will be discussed in the group setting.

- The need to take a personal walk with Jesus Christ. The only way we can become men and women of faith and wisdom like Stephen is to have a daily quiet time with the Lord. Stephen had a dynamic walk with Jesus Christ.
- The need to be in the Word of God on a regular basis—Bible study and Scripture memory. If I am to know my Bible as Stephen did, I need to spend quality time in it and be able to teach others how to do so as well. This book is one means to help me. I need to teach these methods to others.
- The need to have courage in times of adversity and persecution. I need to pray that God will give me boldness with others.

Teaching Tips

As you work with the various questions from members of your group, let the Bible do what God designed it to do: prompt the members to understand him, live for him, and love his people. Let the Bible show them how to solve a friendship struggle or manage a challenge at work or home. Let the Bible answer their important questions, like "Why doesn't God talk out loud?" and "How do I please him?"

Sharing the Study

In this final step, the person completing the study writes a specific person or two that he or she plans to talk about the lessons from they have personally gained from the study. As an example from this study of the life of Stephen, I list my response.

Choose people with whom you want to share what you've learned through this method. I chose James Saylor and Sam Morris (by mail).

Teaching the Lesson on the Life of Stephen

One of the keys to teaching this biographical study to your group will be to understand that each person is going to answer the questions differently and use different words. Return to each section of the study and prepare some questions in advance of your meeting.

Make sure you ask questions to draw the information from the others in your group. It's not your responsibility as the teacher to instruct and lecture to the various members. Instead, you want to gently guide the discussion about the life of Stephen.

Blank Form for the Biographical Teaching Method

In the following section, I've included a blank form for the Biographical Teaching Method. You could photocopy this form for the various members of your group, or copy the information into a notebook or a computer file. Use whichever method is the most convenient for you to get the information to the members of your group.

1. Name: ______________________________
2. Scripture references: ______________________________
3. First impressions and observations: ______________________________
____
4. Outline of the person's life: ______________________________
____
5. General insights (answers to questions): ______________________________
____
6. Character qualities identified: ______________________________
____
7. Bible truths illustrated in the person's life: ______________________________
____
8. Summary of lessons learned from the person's life: ______________________________
____
9. Personal application: ______________________________
____
10. Transferable concepts (ways I can share this with others): ______________________________
____
11. People to share the study with: ______________________________
____

Potent Quotables

"Remember how the Lord your God led you through the wilderness for 40 years, humbling you and testing you to prove your character, and to find out whether or not you would really obey his commands." (Deuteronomy 8:2, NLT)

Reviewing the Topical Teaching Method

There are numerous topics in the Bible for study. Before we examine two examples of the Topical Method of Bible study, let's review the essential ingredients in any topical study.

The Topical Teaching Method has six steps:

1. First, compile a list of words.
2. Then collect Bible references.
3. Consider each reference individually.
4. Compare and group the references.
5. Condense your study into an outline.
6. Finally, conclude the study by summarizing your study and applying the topic to your personal life.

In this case, we're going to take the specific example of this method with the promises for the future in Jesus.

Compile a List of Words

The first step for a topical study is to compile a list of words. I've included my version of this study.

- Promises
- Future

Collect Bible References

Each person will have different Bible verses for this step but the ones I will be studying for the example are as follows.

- Matthew 26:64
- Luke 21:27
- Acts 1:11
- Hebrews 9:28
- Mathew 24:27
- Luke 12:40
- 1 Thessalonians 5:2
- Revelation 16:15
- Philippians 4:5
- Hebrews 10:37

- James 5:8
- Revelation 3:11
- Revelation 22:20
- Matthew 16:27
- Matthew 25:31-32
- 1 Corinthians 4:5
- 2 Timothy 4:1
- Jude 14–15
- Matthew 24:44
- Luke 19:13
- 1 Corinthians 1:7
- 1 Thessalonians 5:23
- 1 Timothy 6:14
- Titus 2:13
- 1 John 2:28
- Luke 12:37
- John 14:3
- Philippians 3:20–21
- Colossians 3:4
- 1 Peter 5:4
- 1 John 3:2

Teaching Tips

As you ask questions and listen to the members of your group, make sure you exhibit enthusiasm for their responses. Remember, what you say right after someone contributes is crucial. Make sure you speak a couple of sentences that dignify your members' discoveries and build them up as individuals. Your affirmation will build their confidence in their study skills and convince them that God's spirit can unveil biblical truth for them.

Comparison Chart

What is a Comparison chart? It is different from the Compare and Group references.

Compare and Group References

References	Cross-References	Observations and Insights
Matthew 26:64	Mark 14:62	In the future, Jesus will sit at God's right hand.
Luke 21:27		Jesus will return with power and great glory.
Acts 1:11		Jesus will return from heaven.
Hebrews 9:28	2 Peter 3:10	Jesus will return.
Matthew 24:27		Jesus will return suddenly.

References	Cross-References	Observations and Insights
Matthew 24:36		Only God knows when Jesus will return.
Luke 12:40		Be ready all the time because Jesus will return unexpectedly.
1 Thessalonians 5:2	Revelation 3:3	Jesus will return like a thief in the night.
Revelation 16:15		Always be prepared.

Condensed Outline

For this next step, you draw some summary statements about the topic along with your Bible references. I'm including my example here.

I. Jesus promised to return in the future.

  A. Matthew 26:64

  B. Luke 21:27

  C. Acts 1:11

  D. Hebrews 9:28

II. Only God knows when Jesus will return.

  A. Matthew 24:27

  B. Matthew 24:36

  C. Luke 12:40

  D. 1 Thessalonians 5:2

  E. Revelation 16:15

III. Jesus promised that his return would be near.

  A. Philippians 4:5

  B. Hebrews 10:37

  C. James 5:8

  D. Revelation 3:11

  E. Revelation 22:20

IV. Jesus promised that his return would have purpose and reward.

A. Matthew 16:27

B. Matthew 25:31–32

C. 1 Corinthians 4:5

D. 2 Timothy 4:1

E. Jude 14–15

V. Jesus told us to be ready.

A. Matthew 24:44

VI. Jesus told us to be good stewards of our time.

A. Luke 19:13

VII. Jesus told us to wait patiently.

A. 1 Corinthians 1:7

VIII. Jesus told us to have charity as we wait.

A. 1 Corinthians 4:5

IX. Jesus told us to live blamelessly.

A. 1 Thessalonians 5:23

X. Jesus told us to live in perfect obedience.

A. 1 Timothy 6:14

XI. Jesus told us to live in joyful expectation.

A. Titus 2:13

XII. Jesus told us to constantly abide in him.

A. 1 John 2:28

XIII. Jesus said that we would be rewarded with honor, lifetime fellowship, and appearance like his, complete with glory and a fadeless crown.

A. Luke 12:37

B. John 14:3

C. Philippians 3:20–21

D. Colossians 3:4

Potent Quotables

"There will be special favor for those who are ready and waiting for his return. I tell you, he himself will seat them, put on an apron, and serve them as they sit and eat!" (Luke 12:37, NLT)

E. 1 Peter 5:4

F. 1 John 3:2

Summary and Application

In this section, I've included my personal application as an example for this study. Every person who completes this topical study will have their own application.

As I have worked through this study on the promise of a future with Jesus, God has impressed me again with the moment-by-moment expectancy that we are to have as believers in Jesus. I am to live as today may be my last day on earth and my first day in eternity. I've lost that sort of gleam and constant reminder that Jesus will soon return. Philippians 3:20 is a great reminder of this urgency and that my citizenship is in heaven, not on Earth.

Projects

I will memorize Philippians 3:20 and focus on eternal life with Jesus and that Jesus may return any moment. In the stress of daily life here, that promise verse will help keep everything in its proper perspective.

I will return to memorizing Scripture and reviewing it on a constant basis to keep more in touch with the spiritual side of my life.

Teaching the Lesson of Promises for the Future with Jesus

Take time in class to read through some of the collected Bible verses (vary the number, depending on the length of the class time). Ask the class members what steps they take in their everyday life to remember the possibility that Jesus Christ might return and his return might be immediate. What steps do they take in their daily life to recall and celebrate the return of Jesus? Ask the group if anyone is willing to talk about a personal application (if they are willing—no pressure).

Just in Case

If you find yourself using the same responses to students' comments, try to be more specific with your verbal praise. Repeat some of their own words as you respond to them and use these words as encouragement. This also shows you're actively listening when members contribute.

Prepare a Lesson About the Faithful Man

In the next few pages, we're going to cover the second example of a topical study using the Topical Teaching Method. I've selected the topic "faithful man" which is used throughout the Bible.

Topic: The faithful man (2 Timothy 2:2 is a key verse but it is used throughout the Bible)

Compile a List of Words

While this step in the study implies that more than one word will be studied, it can also be narrowed to a single word. In this example, I've narrowed the topic to a single word for study: *faithful.*

Collect Bible References

The phrase "faithful man" appears throughout the Bible and the various members of your group will create different lists of Bible references. The next step in the method is to create or collect a list of Bible references. My list for this topic follows, but your list will be different.

- Numbers 12:7
- 1 Samuel 2:35
- 1 Samuel 22:14
- Nehemiah 7:2
- Nehemiah 13:13
- Isaiah 8:2
- Daniel 6:4
- Psalms 12:1
- Proverbs 20:6
- Proverbs 28:20
- Matthew 24:45
- Luke 16:10–13
- Luke 19:17
- 1 Corinthians 1:9
- 1 Corinthians 4:1–2 and 16–17
- 1 Corinthians 10:13
- Ephesians 6:21
- Colossians 1:7
- Colossians 4:7 and 9
- 1 Timothy 1:12
- 2 Timothy 2:2
- 1 Peter 5:12
- 1 John 1:9

Potent Quotables

"I gave the responsibility of governing Jerusalem to my brother Hanani, along with Hananiah, the commander of the fortress, for he was a faithful man who feared God more than most." (Nehemiah 7:2, NLT)

References	Cross-References	Observations and Insights
Numbers 12:7	Deuteronomy 34:5	Moses was called faithful by God.
1 Samuel 2:35	1 Kings 1:8	It was prophesied that Samuel would be a faithful man. A faithful man is obedient to God's will.
1 Samuel 22:14	1 Samuel 19:4	David was called a faithful man by Ahimelech.
Nehemiah 7:2	Matthew 24:45	Hanani was called a faithful man by Nehemiah. A faithful man was given leadership roles.
Nehemiah 9:7–8		The Lord considered Abraham faithful.
Nehemiah 13:13		Nehemiah's treasurers were considered faithful by Nehemiah, so he gave them responsibility.
Isaiah 8:2		Uriah and Zechariah were faithful witnesses in the sight of the Lord.
Daniel 6:4	John 19:4	The Persian princes could not accuse Daniel of any wrongdoing because he was a faithful man.
Psalm 12:1	Proverbs 20:6 Philippians 2:19–20	Faithful men are few in number and are hard to find.
Proverbs 20:6	Philippians 2:19–22	There are not many faithful men in the world. A faithful man lives a blameless testimony before the world.
Proverbs 28:20		A faithful man abounds with blessing.
		A faithful man has his values right, in contrast with a man who is eager to get rich.

continues

continued

References	Cross-References	Observations and Insights
Matthew 24:45	Nehemiah 7:2	A faithful man is given leadership roles.
Matthew 25:21, 23	Luke 19:17	A faithful servant will be rewarded with greater responsibilities in heaven and will experience the Lord's joy over his faithfulness.
Luke 16:10–13		This passage shows four ways to test a man's faithfulness: 1. Test him in small things before giving him big things. 2. Test him in nonspiritual matters before giving him spiritual truth. 3. Test him in how he values what isn't his. 4. Test his commitment to God.
Luke 19:17	Matthew 25:21, 23	A faithful servant is rewarded with greater responsibility.
1 Corinthians 1:9	1 Corinthians 10:13 1 John 1:9	God is faithful.
1 Corinthians 4:1–2		A faithful man demonstrates wise stewardship.
1 Corinthians 4:16–17	Ephesians 6:21 Colossians 1:7	Timothy was called a faithful man by Paul.
	Colossians 4:7, 9	A faithful man's disciple shows confidence in him by sending him in his place.
1 Corinthians 10:13	1 Corinthians 1:9 1 John 1:9	God is faithful.
Ephesians 6:21	Colossians 4:7	Tychicus was called a faithful minister by Paul.
Colossians 1:7		Epaphras was a faithful minister of Jesus Christ.
Colossians 4:7	Ephesians 6:21	Tychicus was sent by Paul to the Colossians because he was a reliable, faithful man.
Colossians 4:9		Onesimus was considered faithful by Paul.

References	Cross-References	Observations and Insights
1 Timothy 1:12		God considered Paul faithful. A faithful man will be given a ministry.
2 Timothy 2:2		A faithful man is entrusted with spiritual truth. A faithful man passes on to others what he has learned.
1 Peter 5:12		Silas was called faithful by Peter.

Condensed Outline

The next step in this study is to create an outline which captures the main points learned in the previous step. As with the previous steps, each person will write their own version of this study. My study for this topic follows.

I. Faithfulness is a godly quality.

A. 1 Corinthians 1:9

B. 1 Corinthians 10:13

C. 1 John 1:9

II. Faithful men are hard to find.

A. Psalms 12:1

B. Proverbs 20:6

C. Philippians 2:19–20

III. Biblical examples of faithful men.

A. Old Testament examples

1. Abraham: Nehemiah 9:7–8
2. Moses: Numbers 12:7
3. Samuel: 1 Samuel 2:35
4. David: 1 Samuel 22:14
5. Hanani: Nehemiah 7:2
6. Nehemiah's treasurers: Nehemiah 13:13

7. Uriah and Zechariah: Isaiah 8:2

8. Daniel: Daniel 6:4

B. New Testament examples.

1. Timothy: 1 Corinthians 4:17

2. Tychicus: Ephesians 6:21

3. Epaphras: Colossians 1:7

4. Onesimus: Colossians 4:9

5. Paul: 1 Timothy 1:12

6. Silas: 1 Peter 5:12

C. Insights.

1. Many men called faithful in the New Testament received training from Paul.

2. Paul himself was a faithful man. He was an example to those he trained.

IV. Characteristics of a faithful man.

A. He cares for others' interests, not his own. (Proverbs 20:6 and Philippians 2:19–22)

B. He has his values right. He is not anxious to get rich. (Proverbs 28:20)

C. He lives a blameless testimony before the world. (Daniel 6:4)

D. He is obedient to God's will. (1 Samuel 2:35)

E. He demonstrates wise stewardship. (1 Corinthians 4:1–2)

F. He passes on to others what he has learned. (2 Timothy 2:2)

V. Ways to test a man's faithfulness. (Luke 16:10–13)

A. Test him in small responsibilities before giving him large ones. (verse 10)

B. Test him in nonspiritual matters before giving him spiritual truth. (verse 11)

C. Test him in how he values what isn't his, before giving him his own. Observe how he serves faithfully in someone else's ministry before sending him out on his own. (verse 12)

D. Test him in his commitment to God. (verse 13)

VI. The benefits of being a faithful man.

A. He is given leadership roles. (Nehemiah 7:2 and Matthew 24:45)

B. He will abound with blessing. (Proverbs 28:20)

C. He will be rewarded with greater responsibilities in heaven and will experience the Lord's joy over his faithfulness. (Matthew 25:21, 23; Luke 19:17)

D. He is entrusted with spiritual truth. (2 Timothy 2:2)

E. His disciple shows confidence in him by sending him in his place. (1 Corinthians 4:16–17, Philippians 2:19–24, Ephesians 6:21)

Potent Quotables

"Lots of people claim to be loyal and loving, but where on earth can you find one?" (Proverbs 20:6, The Message)

Summary and Application

The final step in the Topical Teaching Method is for the individual to write a personal application or consider how the study has affected them. The application should be personal and particularly in the "project" section that follows you will see that the application is measurable and concrete. Here is my example of a personal application.

As I have worked through this study on the faithful man, God has impressed on me the need to be more faithful in two specific areas. First, I need to be more faithful in my prayer life. I need to be more disciplined in setting aside a daily period for prayer. The other area in which I need to be more faithful is in my finances. Luke 16:10 is a verse that I needed. It teaches that if I am not faithful in handling my money, God will not trust me with true riches of spiritual blessings.

Projects

- I plan to memorize the passage on the tests of a man's faithfulness by next week: Luke 16:10–13.
- I will set up a family budget with my wife this weekend. We will start keeping better records of how we spend our money and will ask God to guide us in our spending, saving, and giving.
- I will begin spending 20 minutes each morning before breakfast to review my prayer list and pray.

Teaching the Lesson on the Faithful Man

Take a few minutes to read several of the Bible references collected in the second step of this method. What is the primary focus of these verses when you read them together? Encourage the members of the group to talk about their impressions from listening to Scripture.

Talk with your small group about the topic of faithfulness. As they worked through the study on faithfulness, what stirred their hearts and impressed them the most about this topic? What did they find for a personal application? (Ask if they are willing to talk about it—no pressure, because it might be private.)

Potent Quotables

"But there will come a glorious day, says the Lord, when the whole topic of conversation will be that God is bringing his people home from a nation in the north, and from many other lands where he had scattered them. You will look back no longer to the time when I rescued you from your slavery in Egypt. That mighty miracle will scarcely be mentioned anymore. Yes, I will bring you back again, says the Lord, to this same land I gave your fathers." (Jeremiah 16:14–15, The Living Bible)

Blank Form for the Topical Teaching Method

The next few pages include a blank topical teaching form which can be used for individuals or as a model to be copied in a notebook or for your students to use on a computer as they create their own topics to study in your small group.

Topic: ______________________________

1. Compile a list of words: ______________________________
2. Collect Bible references: ______________________________
3. Comparison chart: ______________________________
4. Comparison chart and group references: ______________________________

   ____
5. Condensed outline: ______________________________
6. Conclusion (summary and application): ______________________________

   ____

The Least You Need to Know

- The Biographical Teaching Method will open the Bible to the truth about the lives of people as you focus on a single person.
- Specific studies on the lives of Joseph and Stephen are detailed in this chapter as a practical example of how to complete the biographical type of study.
- The Topical Teaching Method focuses on a particular topic; this chapter includes two examples of this method.
- "The future in Jesus" and "the faithful man" as detailed topical studies are included in this chapter.

Chapter 20

Sample Lessons: The Word Study and Verse-by-Verse Teaching Methods

In This Chapter

- Use the Word Study Method to examine one of the smallest units in the Bible: the "word"
- Dig into the words *repent* and *peace*
- Delve into the Bible using the Verse-by-Verse Method

Jesus Christ was always interested in the little details of life. He exhorted his disciples to be faithful in the little matters of life. He brought the children to him and blessed them when his disciples wanted to push them away. And he told his disciples that if they had faith as small as a mustard seed, they could command the mountain to be tossed into the sea.

This chapter provides practical Bible lessons for two of the smallest studies in this book: word studies and verse-by-verse studies. The small aspects of Bible study can become a large blessing in your life.

The Word Study Method: The Basics

Understanding many of the great doctrines in the Bible requires understanding a single word. Our word studies must be based on the original-language words, not on the English words. The context of the word also indicates the ultimate meaning of the Bible word that you are studying.

The Word Study Method involves eight basic steps:

1. Choose your word.
2. Find its English definition.
3. Compare various Bible translations of this word.
4. Write down the definition of the original word.
5. Using a concordance, check how and where the word appears in the Bible.
6. Find the root meaning and the origin of the word.
7. Discover the word's usage in the Bible.
8. Write out an application from your word study.

A suggested list of words for possible study is included in Appendix E.

Teaching Tips

Words are powerful and have the potential to help or to inflict pain. This truth is evident as you study words. The Apostle James wrote about the tongue in James 3:5 and how it is small but can inflict enormous damage. Take a few moments at the end of the discussion to pause and pray for God to constantly guide the words that you each speak.

The first two steps of this lesson include choosing the word to study—here we've chosen *repent*—and then defining that word. *Repent* means "to feel such remorse or regret for past conduct as to change one's mind regarding it."

Step Three: Compare Translations: Luke 13:3

For this portion of the study, you need to select a single verse which uses the word (Luke 13:3), then find the verse in various Bible translations and compare how the word is used. As is true for other studies, every person in your group will have access to different translations and select different verses as the key verse to compare. The variety of answers has the potential to provide some interesting group discussion. In the following section, I've done this work for the word *repent* in Luke 13:3.

- "Repent": NIV, NASB, KJV, Amplified
- "Turn from your sins": Good News Bible
- "Leave your evil ways and turn to God": Living Bible

Step Four: Define the Original Word

To complete this step in the study, write the words in the original language along with their meaning. For the word *repent*, I've written the Greek word and definition here.

- *metanoeo* (Greek): "to change one's mind"
- *metamelomai* (Greek): "to regret or show remorse"

Just in Case

Words are fascinating. The members of your group might like to know that *Logos* and *Rhema* are the two primary Greek words meaning "word." They are used interchangeably and variously, along with the Old Testament *dabar*. The New Testament can use these words to apply to Jesus' message, the message about Jesus, and Jesus himself.

Step Five: Find Occurrences of the Word

After understanding the definition of the word, you next search the Bible to find where it is used. For the word "repent," I've listed the various places it occurs in the New Testament as an example for you when you do a word study.

Two different Greek words are translated *repent* in the New Testament.

Repent (verb)	Repentance (noun)
A. Metanoeo	
34 times	24 times
5 times in Matthew	3 times in Matthew
2 times in Mark	2 times in Mark
9 times in Luke	5 times in Luke
5 times in Acts	6 times in Acts

continues

continued

Repent (verb)	Repentance (noun)
1 time in 2 Corinthians	1 time in Romans
12 times in Revelation	2 times in 2 Corinthians
	1 time in 2 Timothy
	3 times in Hebrews
	1 time in 2 Peter
B. Metamelomia	
"Repent" (verb—6 times)	
3 times in Matthew	
2 times in 2 Corinthians	
1 time in Hebrews	

It is interesting to note that the word is never used in the Gospel of John, but it is used in Revelation 12 times. The author Luke used it the most (Luke and Acts). Repentance is not emphasized much in the Epistles because they were written to Christians.

Step Six: Identify the Root Meaning and Origin of the Word

Using some of the reference books which were mentioned in the first chapter of this book, research the root meaning of the word you've chosen to study (in this case, *repent*) and identify its origin.

Metanoeo literally means "to perceive afterward." It is made up of two Greek words: *meta*, which means "after" (implying change), and *noeo*, which means "to perceive" (*nous* is Greek for "the mind").

Potent Quotables

"And I tell you this, that you must give an account on judgment day of every idle word you speak. The words you say now reflect your fate then; either you will be justified by them or you will be condemned." (Matthew 12:36–37, NLT)

From this, we understand that one aspect of the word *repent* is "to change one's mind or purpose." In the New Testament, this change is always for the better, and it denotes a genuine, complete change of heart and life.

Repent implies not only a turning away (negative) from sin, but also a turning to (positive) that which is right and goodly. It means more than just feeling sorry for wrong you've done. It also means to completely change your mind about the sin and go a different way.

Metamelomai, on the other hand, comes from the words *meta* ("after") and *melo* ("to care for"). It means to regret or to express remorse for something you wish you hadn't done. It means to have painful anxiety (sorrow) over a past deed. However, the meaning behind this form of the word does not signify genuine repentance. Instead, it means to regret something you did, but not admit or understand that the deed was sinful or evil (as in, "I'm sorry I got caught, but I'm not sorry I did it" or "I'm not sure I wouldn't do it again"). The best illustration of this type of regret is the kind experienced by Judas. He regretted betraying Jesus (*metamelomai*—Matthew 27:3), but he never genuinely repented of it (*metamoeo*).

Just in Case

How did Jesus define repentance? Jesus differed from his predecessors in his proclamation of repentance. He related it closely to the arrival of the kingdom of God (Mark 1:14–15) and specifically associated it with one's acceptance of him. Those who were unrepentant were those who rejected him (Luke 10:8–15 and 11: 30–32); those who received him were the truly repentant. In his name, repentance and forgiveness were to be proclaimed to all nations. (Luke 24:47)

Step Seven: How Was the Word Used?

First, identify where in other writings the word you're studying can be found, and then note how it is used. For instance, *metanoeo* was not used much in classical Greek literature. When the word was used, it did not mean the radical change of a man's life as a whole like it does in the New Testament.

You can also find it throughout the Bible, as in these examples:

- Repentance in the Old Testament is seen most clearly in Ezekiel 18 and 33:10–20 (*naham*).
- "Repent" was the basic message of John the Baptist (Matthew 3:2), Jesus (Matthew 4:17), the 12 disciples (Mark 6:12), and Peter at Pentecost (Acts 2:38).
- It is commanded by God for everyone. (Acts 17:30 and 2 Peter 3:9)
- It is part of saving faith. (Luke 13:5 and Acts 3:19)
- It produces joy in heaven. (Luke 15:7, 10)
- It is proven by our actions. (Acts 26:20)
- Jesus used the word 17 times in the Gospels and 8 times in Revelation.

- What causes us to repent? God's goodness to us (Romans 2:4), Godly sorrow for our sins (2 Corinthians 7:9–10), and God's grace (2 Timothy 2:25).
- It is a foundational truth of the Christian life. (Hebrews 6:1)

Also, examine the word within the context of the passage. In this case, take a look at 2 Corinthians 7:9–10. This verse shows the difference between genuine repentance (*metanoeo*) and mere regret (*metamelomai*). Real godly sorrow brings about genuine repentance. This brings about a change of life, not just regret.

Potent Quotables

"Therefore, let us leave the elementary teachings about Christ and go on to maturity, not laying again the foundation of repentance from acts that lead to death, and of faith in God, instruction about baptisms, the laying on of hands, the resurrection of the dead, and eternal judgment. And God permitting, we will do so." (Hebrews 6:1–3, NIV)

Step Eight: Apply the Lesson

The final step in the Word Study Method is to create a personal application or apply the lesson to your own life. As in other chapters, every person who completes this study on "repent" will make a different personal application. This fact alone is something you can depend on for the group discussion time and will be fascinating to see distinctly it is applied. My personal application for this study on repentance follows.

"Or do you show contempt for the riches of his kindness, tolerance and patience, not realizing that God's kindness leads you toward repentance?" (Romans 2:4, NIV)

As the individual thinks about "repent," is there something to repent in his or her own life. Is there a sin to confess or an attitude to change (both call for repentance)?

Sin to confess/attitude to change:

Ever since the incident in the office last spring with Harry, I have held a personal grudge in my heart. This grudge has strained our relationship. The Lord has convicted me about this in the past, but I have put off making restitution. I know I have sinned. I want to repent of this sin now. Tomorrow afternoon I will visit Harry and ask his forgiveness. I want to straighten out this matter.

Teaching the Repent Lesson

Discuss these ideas with the group:

- What did they learn about repent and repentance through this word study?
- What surprised them about what they learned?
- What will they take away from the study and remember for a long time?
- Ask several members to tell about their application from the study.

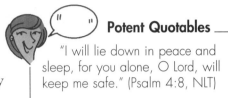

> **Potent Quotables**
>
> "I will lie down in peace and sleep, for you alone, O Lord, will keep me safe." (Psalm 4:8, NLT)

Word Study Method Lesson 2: Peace

As you know, the first two steps involve choosing a word (*peace*) and defining it. The English word *peace* is used as both a noun and transitive verb. Its English definition is "s state of tranquility or quiet." In a spiritual sense, peace is a sense of well-being and fulfillment that comes from God and is dependent on his presence.

Step Three: Compare Translations: Isaiah 26:3

In this step, select a single verse that contains the word you are studying (peace in Isaiah 26:3), then compare the verse in different Bible translations. Different people in your small group will use different translations and it will again result in some lively potential discussion in your group time together. My research findings on Isaiah 26:3 and the word *peace* is as follows.

- "Perfect peace": NIV, NLT, NKJV, Living Bible, KJV
- "true peace": International Children's Bible
- "fortifiest peace": Young's Literal Translation
- "completely whole": The Message

Step Four: Find the Original Word and Its Short Definition

In this step, look for the Hebrew word for "peace" and write it into this section. My research for this study follows.

The Hebrew root *slm* and its derivatives, the most familiar being the noun *shalom*, "the concept of spiritual peace," at its basic meaning is "wholeness" or "well-being."

The Greek word *eirene* corresponds to the Hebrew *shalom*, expressing the idea of peace, well-being, restoration, reconciliation with God, and salvation in the fullest sense.

Teaching Tips

Work with group members to define a peacemaker. Then consider this biblical definition: those who actively work to bring about peace and reconciliation where there is hatred and enmity. God blesses peacemakers and declares them to be his children. (Matthew 5:9) Those who work for peace share in Christ's ministry of bringing peace and reconciliation. (2 Corinthians 5:18–19, Ephesians 2:14–15, Colossians 1:20)

Step Five: Locate Occurrences in the Bible

Throughout the Bible, the word *peace* occurs 250 times: 159 times in the Old Testament and 91 times in the New Testament.

Eirene

- 4 times in Matthew
- 2 times in Mark
- 13 times in Luke
- 6 times in John
- 6 times in Acts
- 60 times in the Epistles

The word *peace* is used as a noun (*peacemaker*), as an intransitive verb (*peace*), and an adjective (*peaceful*).

The law, the prophets, and the writings of the Old Testament each bear testimony that such peace is the gift of God, for God alone can give peace in all its fullness. (Leviticus 26:6; 1 Chronicles 12:18 and 22:9; 1 Kings 2:33; Isaiah 26:12 and 52:7; Ezekiel 34:25 and 37:26; Zechariah 6:13; Malachi 2:5–6; Job 22:21 and 25:2; Psalms 4:8, 29:11, 37:37, 85:8, 122:6–8, and 147:14; and Proverbs 3:17) Spiritual peace may be equated with salvation. (Isaiah 52:7 and Nahum 1:15) Its absence may be equated with judgment. (Jeremiah 12:12, 14:19, 16:5, and 25:37; Lamentations 3:17; and Ezekiel 7:15) It is available to all who trust in God (Isaiah 26:3) and love his law. (Psalms 119:165—note that in verses 166–168, this love is clearly understood to mean obedience) This peace is clearly identified with a righteous life, apart from which no one is able to find true peace. (Isaiah 32:17, 48:22, and 57:1–2) Thus, peace and righteousness are often linked in the Old Testament (Psalms 72:7 and 85:10, and Isaiah 9:7, 32:17, 48:18, and 60:17), as are peace and justice (Isaiah 59:8). To be at peace is to be upright (Malachi 2:6), to be faithful (2 Samuel 20:19), to be an upholder of the truth (Esther 9:30 and Zechariah 8:19), and to practice justice (Isaiah 59:8 and Zechariah 8:16). Throughout the Old Testament, spiritual peace is realized in relationships. It is realized when people are rightly related to each other and to God.

In the New Testament, God is "the God of peace." (Romans 15:33, Philippians 4:9, 1 Thessalonians 5:23, and Hebrews 13:20) The Gospel is "the good news of peace" (Ephesians 6:15 and Acts 10:36) because it announces the reconciliation of believers to God and to one another (Ephesians 2:12–18). God has made this peace a reality in Jesus Christ, who is "our peace." We are justified through him (Romans 5:1), reconciled through the blood of his cross (Colossians 1:20), and made one in him (Ephesians 2:14). In him, we discover that ultimate peace that only God can give. (John 14:27) This peace is experienced as an inner spiritual peace by the individual believer. (Philippians 4:7, Colossians 3:15, and Romans 15:13) It is associated with receptiveness to God's salvation (Matthew 10:13), freedom from distress and fear (John 14:27 and 16:33), security (1 Thessalonians 5:9–10), mercy (Galatians 6:16 and 1 Timothy 1:2), joy (Romans 14:17 and 15:13), grace (Philippians 1:2 and Revelation 1:4), love (2 Corinthians 13:11 and Jude 2), life (Romans 8:6), and righteousness (Romans 14:17, Hebrews 12:11, and James 3:18). Such peace is a fruit of the Spirit (Galatians 5:22) that forms part of the "whole armor of God" (Ephesians 6:11 and 13), enabling the Christian to withstand the attacks of the forces of evil.

It is interesting to note that the New Testament gives more attention to the understanding of spiritual peace as an inner experience of the individual believer than does the Old Testament. In both the Old Testament and the New Testament, spiritual peace is realized in being rightly related to God and to one another.

Step Six: Identify the Root Meaning and Origin

In the Old Testament, the Hebrew word for peace is *shalom*, which means "completeness, soundness, welfare, and peace." *Shalom* is used throughout the Old Testament in other ways in which the word translated as peace can also be used in the context of words like *close*, *ease*, *favorable*, *friend*, *friendly terms*, *friends*, *greet*, *greet*, *greeted*, *health*, *how, Peace, peace, peaceably, peaceful, peacefully, perfect peace, prosperity, rose, safe, safely, safety, secure, state, trusted, welfare, well, well-being, who were at peace,* and *wholly.*

In the New Testament, the Greek word for peace is *eireôneô*, which probably derives from the primary verb *ânñù eiroô* (to *join*); *peace* (literally or figuratively); by implication, *prosperity:* one, peace, quietness, and rest.

Step Seven: How Was the Word Used?

Throughout the Bible, you'll find the word used in these ways:

- God is the author of peace (*shalom*).
- Psalm 147:14: "He grants peace to your borders and satisfies you with the finest of wheat." (NIV)
- 1 Corinthians 14:33 "For God is not a God of disorder, but of peace, as in all the other churches." (NLT)
- God bestows peace on those individuals who …
    - Obey him: "I will give you peace in the land, and you will be able to sleep without fear. I will remove the wild animals from your land and protect you from your enemies." (Leviticus 26:6, NLT)
    - Please him. "I will bless the Lord who guides me; even at night my heart instructs me." (Psalms 16:7, NLT)

In the context of the New Testament, Christians who would have peace should …

- Seek peace. (1 Peter 3:11)
- [T]urn from evil and do good; he must seek peace and pursue it. (1 Peter 3:11, NIV)
- Follow peace. (2 Timothy 2:22)
- Flee the evil desires of youth, and pursue righteousness, faith, love, and peace, along with those who call on the Lord out of a pure heart. (2 Timothy 2:22, NIV)
- Live in peace. Aim for perfection, listen to my appeal, be of one mind, live in peace. And the God of love and peace will be with you. (2 Corinthians 13:11, NIV)
- Live in peace with each other. "Salt is good for seasoning. But if it loses its flavor, how do you make it salty again? You must have the qualities of salt among yourselves and live in peace with each other." (Mark 9:50, NLT)

- Endeavor to have peace with all men. "Do your part to live in peace with everyone, as much as possible. (Romans 12:18, NLT)

When I look at the word *peace* in the context of Isaiah 26:3, I see that this verse points out the path to consistent peace with mankind and with God—keeping my mind centered on God. As I stay focused on God, his peace fills my life.

> **Teaching Tips**
>
> A Bible study must be systematic and consistent. Jesus explained the Bible systematically (Luke 24:27), and the Berean Jews evaluated the Gospel that they heard by its consistency with Scripture (Acts 17:11). R. A. Torrey, the great Bible teacher of another generation who lived in the late nineteenth and early twentieth century, advised: "Have a good system of Bible study and follow it. System counts in everything, but it counts more in study than in anything else, and it counts more in Bible study than in any other form of study."

Step Eight: Apply the Lesson

The final step in this word study on peace is to personally apply the lesson for the person doing the study. Each person in your study group will create a different and unique personal application. As an example, I've written my personal application from this study.

"He will keep in perfect peace all those who trust in him, whose thoughts turn often to the Lord!" (Isaiah 26:3, Living Bible)

Sin to confess/attitude to change: Anxiety often fills my days in the face of deadlines and projects to complete. Yet God desires for me to keep focused on him and to have his peace throughout my day and life. I've not achieved this level of peace. My mind is the greatest gift God has given me, and it ought to be devoted entirely to him. I seek to bring "every thought into captivity to the obedience of Christ." (2 Corinthians 10:5) This will be one of my greatest assets of my faith when a time of trial comes because then my faith and the Spirit of God work together.

Teaching the Word *Peace* Lesson

Now that you have either completed the word study on *peace* or used the bulk of what I've put together and led your small group, I'll give you an idea of how to use this study in the group context. In addition, each person should develop his or her own ideas and questions for use in teaching as a part of their preparation time for teaching.

In the usual course of life events, our days are not filled with peace. Take time in your small group to work through the meanings of peace in Hebrew and Greek. What new insight did they personally gain from their word study on *peace?* As they studied the word, which Scriptures, in particular, spoke to their current need or situation? What types of personal application did they write as they worked through this word study on peace? Encourage honest dialogue about how to find peace in today's world.

Just in Case

Make sure the members of your group understand that Bible study must not depend on what others have said about the Scriptures, but must involve the individual studying the Bible itself. Libraries of books have been written about the Bible, but there is only one Bible, so go to the source. As you and the members of your group study, compare Scripture with Scripture. One portion of it sheds light on another, enriching your Bible study experience and answering your questions.

Blank Form for the Word Study Method

Now that you've seen two word studies as practical examples, in the following section, I include a blank form for use with the Word Study Method. You can use this form to guide the members of your group in additional word studies. Either this form can be photocopied or you can have people copy it into a notebook (to make sure they follow all the steps) or they can generate a form on the computer and use it each time.

1. English word: ______________________________
2. English definition: ______________________________
3. Comparison of translations: ______________________________
4. Original word and short definition: ______________________________

   ____
5. Occurrences in the Bible: ______________________________
6. Root meaning and origin (use reference books): ______________________________

   ____

7. How the word was used:

   A. In other writings: ______

   B. Throughout the Bible: ______

   C. In the context of the passage: ______

8. Application: ______

A Brief Review of the Verse-by-Verse Method

The Verse-by-Verse Method is useful when you or the members of your group don't have the time for in-depth study. This method takes a verse-by-verse analysis of a passage and involves five different steps. You can use this method without reference tools or using just a few works, such as a study Bible, an exhaustive concordance, and a Bible dictionary.

You'll follow five simple steps for each verse that you study:

1. Write out a personal paraphrase.
2. List some questions, answers, and observations that occur to you as you read the verse.
3. Find some cross-references for each verse.
4. Record any insights that you get from each verse.
5. Write down a brief personal application for each verse.

Teaching Tips

Encourage the members of your group to follow the psalmist's example when he wrote "I thought on my ways, and turned my feet unto Thy testimonies. I made haste, and delayed not to keep Thy commandments." (Psalms 119: 59–60, KJV) The Scriptures are the means by which God can work in our lives, but they must be personally applied to our lives throughout the study.

1 Timothy 1:1–3

When you use the verse-by-verse analysis form, use a wide piece of paper and place the two forms side by side.

Teaching Tips

Keep reminding the individuals in your group that every personal Bible study must be simple enough to easily pass on. Teaching someone else how to study the Bible for himself is far better than telling this person what you have received from your own study, although this process is helpful as well.

Verses	Personal Paraphrase	Questions and Answers	Cross-References	Insights	Possible Personal Applications
1:1 This letter is from Paul, an apostle of Christ Jesus, appointed by the command of God our Savior and by Christ Jesus our hope.	Paul, one sent forth as Christ's representative, by the commandment of God, the One who saves us, and Christ Jesus our hope;	Q: What does the word "apostle" mean? A: The Greek word *apostolos* comes from the verb *apostello*, "send forth."	Apostle: 2 Cor. 1:1 God my Savior Luke 1:47 Titus 1:3 Christ our hope: Colossians 1:27	1. The name Paul came from the Latin name *Paulus*, which means "little." 2. The name Timothy means "he who honors God." 3. Paul did not need to tell Timothy that he was an apostle so perhaps this letter was intended to be read by others as well.	I must begin to see myself in the role of Christ's ambassador who has been authorized and sent out with a divine message. The authority of my witness will only be as effective as my awareness of my mission.

Verses	Personal Paraphrase	Questions and Answers	Cross-References	Insights	Possible Personal Applications
1:2 It is written to Timothy, my true child in the faith. May God our Father and Christ Jesus our Lord give you grace, mercy, and peace.	to Timothy my first child in the Christian faith. May love, mercy, and peace from God the Father and Christ Jesus our Lord be yours.	Q: God the Father rather than Christ is called Savior. Q: Does the name Timothy have any special meaning? A: Timothy means "he who honors God."	My child: 2 Timothy 1:2	1. Messiah in Hebbrew means *Christo* in Greek, which means Christ in English. Christ means "the anointed one of God." 2. Jesus means "Jehovah Saves!" It comes from the word Joshua.	May my name become synonymous with a life that is honoring to God, like Timothy's.

Verses	Personal Paraphrase	Questions and Answers	Cross-References	Insights	Possible Personal Applications
1:3 When I left for Macedonia, I urged you to stay there in Ephesus and stop those who are teaching wrong doctrine.	As I urged you upon my departure for Macedonia, keep staying in Ephesus, so you can instruct certain men not to teach non-Christian doctrines.	Q: What doctrines were being taught by these men? A: Not doctrines of false religions, but a false teaching posing as inspired Christian doctrine. Q: What was Timothy's ministry in Ephesus?	False teaching: 1 Timothy 6:3	1. Paul criticized the Christians in Corinth for their weakness in dealing with false doctrine. (2 Cor. 11:4) Since Timothy was with Paul in Corinth for a long time, he received good training, which he would need in Ephesus.	I will work hard to become knowledgeable of Christian doctrine so I can differentiate between true and false teaching. Christian Science, Mormonism, and Jehovah's Witness are some of the ones that need my attention in this regard.
			2 Cor. 11:4	2. Timothy went to Ephesus with Paul, then later after Paul's first Roman imprisonment, he was there again. This is when he was urged to stay.	

As you teach any of these Bible study methods, emphasize to the individuals in your group that good Bible study methods alone can't guarantee a changed life. The Bible can be understood fully only with the aid of the Holy Spirit. Unless they develop a growing personal relationship with God, the academic study of the Scriptures will produce little change.

Just in Case

Some individuals in your group may be struggling with their personal Bible study. Remind them that refusing to deal with sin in their life breaks fellowship with God. The secret to restored fellowship with God is a cleansed life. John tells us what we need to do: "If we confess our sins, he is faithful and just and will forgive us our sins and purify us from all unrighteousness." (1 John 1:9) Before beginning any Bible study, stop and confess to God any known sins.

Teaching Ideas 1 Timothy 1:1–3

Return to each aspect of this study: the personal paraphrase, the questions and answers, the cross-references, and the insights and personal applications. For each section, ask the members of your group to talk about their study. What does the passage say? What does it mean? What does it mean for you? These three simple questions are often all that is needed to stir an active discussion about the verses.

Teaching Tips

As you teach any of the Bible studies, pray for illumination and encourage the individuals in your group to also pray for insight. Understanding Scripture can come only through the illuminating ministry of the Holy Spirit. Encourage the group to follow the example of the psalmist who prayed, "Praise be to you, O Lord; teach me your decrees .... Open my eyes that I may see wonderful things in your law .... Let me understand the teaching of your precepts; then I will meditate on your wonders .... Direct me in the path of your commands, for there I will find delight." (Psalms 119:12, 18, 27, and 35)

Prepare a Lesson About Psalms 46:1–3

As you teach your group, make sure you constantly depend on the Holy Spirit. It's easy to depend on your own energy, but one of the ministries of the Holy Spirit is to teach Christians the truths from the Bible. Jesus promised, "But when the Father sends the Counselor as my representative—and by the Counselor I mean the Holy Spirit—he will teach you everything and will remind you of everything I myself have told you." (John 14:26, NLT)

Verses	Personal Paraphrase	Questions and Answers	Cross-References	Insights	Possible Personal Applications
46:1 God is our refuge and strength, always ready to help in times of trouble.	God is my shelter and where I turn for power and energy. He is always eager to help in trouble.	Q: What is a refuge? A: The NASB says "abundantly available for help."	Deut. 4:7 Ps. 9:9, 14:4, 62:7–8, 145:18 Ps. 18:7, 23:4, 82:5	God is our impenetrable defense and our fortress, our sure defense. Whether facing ordinary weapons or natural disasters, God is our protector.	In times of fear, I know God's presence can comfort me. Sometimes, my imagination works in the shadows and I need to turn to God in prayer for His peace.
46:2 So we will not fear, even if earthquakes come and the mountains crumble into the sea.	Because of God's presence, I will not fear even if the earth shakes or the mountains crumble into the sea.	Q: Are the words earthquake and mountains literal or figurative? A: It could be either way. Some fear earthquakes or anything of total destruction.			

Verses	Personal Paraphrase	Questions and Answers	Cross-References	Insights	Possible Personal Applications
46:3 Let the oceans roar and foam. Let the mountains tremble as the waters surge!	Before the rush and roar of the sea or the shaking mountains.	Q: The concept of verse 2 was repeated in this verse. Does this technique have a name and is it a common technique? A: The Psalms are Hebrew poetry and use this method of repeating for emphasis; they are called couplets.	Ps. 93:3 Isa. 17:13 Jer. 5:22 Eze. 1:24	Whether real or imagined, upheaval is ever-present.	Whether I am facing a crisis that is real or imagined, I can be reassured of God's care and strength.

Just in Case

Jesus pointed out that a prerequisite to knowing the truth is willingness to obey the truth. He said in John 7:17, "If anyone chooses to do God's will, he will find out whether my teaching comes from God or whether I speak on my own." (NIV) The person who is willing to obey will receive God's instruction.

Teaching Ideas Psalm 46:1–3

As your group meets to study these verses, talk about their fears. What types of fears can they verbalize, and are they real or imagined? Are they natural or spiritual? What helps them turn to God and the Scriptures in the midst of these fears? How do they meditate on the Scriptures and allow God's strength to calm their fears and provide peace? Use these questions to stir discussion and follow-up questions.

The Least You Need to Know

- Although a word study might seem simple on the surface, it can provide deep insight into the Scriptures and have relevant personal application.
- Verse-by-verse study is a fascinating way to gain depth in a few verses in the Bible.
- Through two detailed studies, such as 1 Timothy 1:1–3 and Psalms 46:1–3, you can dig into the Scriptures with a practical illustration of the Verse-by-Verse Method.

Blank Form for the Verse-by-Verse Method

Cross-References	Insights	Possible Personal Applications

Chapter 21

The Background Method: Two Sample Lessons

In This Chapter

- Understanding the Bible's background
- Accomplishing the Bible Background Method
- Teaching ideas for you to pass along in your small group
- A practical example of the Bible Background Method in a New Testament setting

Some of the Bible is a challenge to understand without understanding the Bible background for a particular passage. You can read the words, but they won't make as much sense without learning the background. In this chapter, you'll find two practical examples of the Bible Background Method.

The Bible Background Method: The Basics

The Bible Background Method involves eight simple steps:

1. Select a subject that you want to study or a particular book from the Bible.
2. List your various reference tools.
3. Consider any insights from geography.
4. Consider insights from history.
5. Discover some insights from culture.
6. Research and learn some insights from the political environment.
7. Summarize your research.
8. Write out a personal application.

Just in Case

Some members of your group may wane in their interest in Bible study. Remind them that serious Bible study is work. There are no magic books that give you all the answers without effort on your part. The point is not to become a master of the Bible, but to be a serious student of the Scriptures.

Judah from 612 to 586 B.C. (Time of Habakkuk): A Lesson

The first step in the Bible Background Method is to select a subject or a book of the Bible. For the study from the Old Testament, I selected to study Judah from 612 to 586 B.C. or during the lifetime of the prophet Habakkuk. This background study will teach us about what was going on during Habakkuk's life.

Step Two: Gather Reference Tools

With a particular subject in mind like Judah, the next step is to pull your Bible reference tools together to learn the background. For this study, I suggest (and used) these tools:

- *Talk Thru the Bible*, by Bruce Wilkinson and Kenneth Boa (Thomas Nelson, 1990)
- *Nelson's New Illustrated Bible Manners & Customs*, by Howard F. Vos (Nelson Reference, 1999)

Step Three: Explore the Geography

For this next portion, every person begins to learn about the geography of the Near East in general and Palestine in particular. There are many geographical features found there, such as mountains, hills, various landmarks, and bodies of water. As you study, ask the question, "What is the effect of the surrounding geography on what I am studying?" You will need to use the reference books to locate the information. Get comfortable with the index in the back of the books and reading to find this insight. My answers on Judah will serve as a practical example of how to complete this step in the method.

Although for part of its history, Judah controlled Edom and the land far south to the Gulf of Aqaba branch of the Red Sea, most of the time its territory consisted of a slice of land wedged between the Dead Sea and the coastal plain or the land of the Philistines. So the Judean heartland stretched some 40 to 50 miles east and west. Extending from a little north of Jerusalem in the north to Kadesh-barnea in the south, the kingdom stretched only about 110 miles north and south.

To compare the size to something familiar, Judah was a little larger than Delaware or about twice the size of Rhode Island. During those periods when Judah controlled the Negev from Beersheba to the Gulf of Aqaba, Judah had an additional area of about 4,700 square miles, roughly equal to the land area of Connecticut.

Step Four: Delve Into the History

As a part of this step, you begin to obtain a working history of the Jewish people and knowledge of the chronological order of events in the nation of Israel. This type of understanding is integral to a deeper understanding of the book of the Bible. Several questions to consider for this step are: "What caused this event that I am studying?" or "How did history affect the passage I am studying?" or "How did history affect the people I am studying?" As you study history, it increases your awareness of God's control over the progress of history. For the particular period of Judah during the lifetime of the prophet Habakkuk, I've included my historical research here.

The only explicit time reference in Habakkuk is to the Babylonian invasion as an imminent event. (verses 1:6, 2:1, and 3:16) Some scholars suggest that Habakkuk was written during the reign of Manasseh (686–642 B.C.) or Amon (642–640 B.C.) because of the list of Judah's sins in verses 1:2–4. However, the descriptions of the Chaldeans indicate that Babylon had become a world power, and this was not true in the time of Manasseh when Babylon was under the thumb of Assyria. It is also unlikely that this prophecy took place during the time of King Josiah (640–609 B.C.) because the moral and spiritual reforms of Josiah do not fit the situation (verses 1:2–4). The most likely

> **Proceed with Caution**
>
> Encourage your group not to overestimate what is involved in studying the Bible. The Bible is not a complex database requiring highly skilled technicians to decode; there are no such passwords or special codes to be learned. The spirit in which we approach the Bible is far more important than our ability to use even the most sophisticated Bible study tools.

date for the book is in the early part of Jehoiakim's reign. (609–597 B.C.) Jehoiakim was a godless king who led the nation down the path of destruction. (2 Kings 23:34–24:5 and Jeremiah 22:17)

The Babylonians began to rise to power during the reign of Nabopolassar (626–605 B.C.), and in 612 B.C., they destroyed the Assyrian capital of Nineveh. By the time of Jehoiakim, Babylon was the uncontested world power. Nabopolassar's successor, Nebuchadnezzar, came to power in 605 B.C. and carried out successful military expeditions in the west, advancing into Palestine and Egypt. Nebuchadnezzar's first invasion of Judah occurred in his first year, when he deported 10,000 of Jerusalem's leaders to Babylon. The nobles who oppressed and extorted from the poor were the first to be carried away. Since Habakkuk prophesied before the Babylonian invasion, the probable date for this book is 607 B.C.

Step Five: Study the Culture

Part of learning about the Bible is to understand the lifestyle of these ancient people. The clothing, professions, music, manners, and family life are only a few of the cultural considerations. For each book that you study, ask the question, "How do all these things affect the message and the people about whom I am studying?" As an example of some material about the culture of Judah during the lifetime of the prophet Habakkuk, I've included my research.

> **Potent Quotables**
>
> "Even though the fig trees have no blossoms, and there are no grapes on the vine; even though the olive crop fails, and the fields lie empty and barren; even though the flocks die in the fields, and the cattle barns are empty, yet I will rejoice in the Lord! I will be joyful in the God of my salvation." (Habakkuk 3:17–18, NLT)

The size of the houses in Judah at this time were generally smaller and less imposing for the middle and lower classes. Their dwellings retained the rectangular shape, but the house itself frequently consisted of a courtyard open to the sky and divided by stone pillars, with one or two rooms at the rear. In some instances, as at Beersheba, the back room became a part of the casemate wall surrounding the town. A variation of this arrangement is a small room in the front of the street that may have served as a shop or workshop. Behind this lay an open courtyard, with a family room or two adjacent. The courtyard contained a clay baking oven, grinding stones for producing flour, wooden weaving looms, and sometimes a very small olive or grape press. Cisterns or lavatories were rarely found. The water supply usually came from nearby springs or wells. A man and a woman and three or more children crowded into such small quarters.

Families had little furniture. A great many of the poorest simply sat on the floor on mats of reeds or skins to do their work or to eat, and they slept on the floor on bedrolls. Those who could afford them had stools or simple chairs with backs, small tables, and wooden bed frames with mattresses supported by wooden slats or ropes.

Step Six: Consider the Political Background

One of the keys to understanding the background of a particular era in Bible history is to know that many times other nations and their kings and politics affected the Jewish people. Many times they lived under foreign rule or in exile from the Holy Land. Yet throughout every season in history, God is always in control of every political situation. It will deepen your understanding and reading experience to know the political background of the situation. My research on Judah during the lifetime of the prophet Habakkuk is here.

Habakkuk prophesied during the fall of Nineveh in 612 B.C. and the rise of Babylon as the Neo-Babylonian Empire. By 605 B.C., Assyria and Egypt had been defeated by Babylon at Carchemish. Judah's days were numbered, and Babylon's power was rapidly expanding. In addition, the death of King Josiah in 609 B.C. brought an end to an era of religious reform in Judah. It seemed that the wicked were prevailing both inside and outside Judah. Habakkuk cried out against the violence, lawlessness, and injustice he saw all around him.

Step Seven: Summarize Your Insights

In the last few steps, you have been compiling some specific research data from your reference books. For this step, you take a look at all of this gathered information (steps three through six) and begin to summarize the research and draw some conclusions about the affect of the background on the writings. I've drawn these conclusions for Judah during the days of the prophet Habakkuk here.

The people of Judah in the days of Habakkuk seemed to ignore God and be filled with godless activity and wicked people. After the religious reform from King Josiah, this era among the Jewish people ended and each of the kings who followed during Habakkuk's prophecies generally turned away from God and toward evil.

Because of the central location of Judah and the importance of the land, the power of Judah waned and Babylon rose in strength and moved toward conquering Judah.

Step Eight: Plan a Personal Application

As I've mentioned in the other study methods, the information in the previous steps is more than simply adding to your knowledge. Particularly with background studies, it would be easy to leave the study with the knowledge element. Instead, this step takes the study into the practical application area. Each person's application will be different than my personal application. I've written my application from this study here.

Proceed with Caution

Don't try to complete these lessons or studies using only your own strength, energy, or power. The Bible is a spiritual, supernatural book written by the hand of God, so ask for his help. Ask the Lord to give you his "Spirit of wisdom and revelation so that you may know him better." (Ephesians 1:17)

If I put on my spiritual glasses and look at my world, I find that it's not too different from the world at the time of Habakkuk. Evil reigns, and I begin to wonder how God can allow it to continue. How can God use some of the evil nations to bring more evil, as Babylon did to bring down Judah? These frank questions were what Habakkuk asked, and God encouraged this honest dialogue. I need to walk to a different beat than my neighbors and others who don't have a personal relationship with Jesus Christ. It's the stance that Habakkuk took in his world as a prophet, and I can also move to take this different stance. It takes courage, so I need to ask God to daily give this strength and courage to me.

Ideas for the Judah Background Lesson

Now that we've completed the Old Testament study using the Bible Background Method, this section turns and provides some specific insights for you as you discuss this material with your small group. One of the keys is not to turn the session into a lecture where you talk about the information you have discovered. Instead, let the various members of your group talk about what they have discovered. Work hard to draw these individuals into the discussion.

Lead the group in a discussion about the differences and the similarities between Judah and our world. Who is the voice of Habakkuk crying in the middle of our world? How did Habakkuk acknowledge his world yet determine to walk to a different drumbeat in his lifestyle and choices? How can we do the same and gain encouragement from his actions as we learn about the background of his world? Use these questions as conversation starters, and create other follow-up questions to use with the members of your group.

A Lesson About Ephesus (the Book of Ephesians)

The first step in the method is to select a subject or the setting of a book from the Bible. Because the last example was from the Old Testament period, I selected the city of Ephesus which was the background for the New Testament Book of Ephesians. The Apostle Paul wrote the church at Ephesus and you can increase your understanding of this letter from Paul by knowing more about the Bible background. Let's get started.

Step Two: Gather Your Reference Tools

For this section, you list the resources that will be the greatest help to learn the Bible background of the topic you selected in the previous step. Also, listing these resources will help you refer to them in future background studies. The resources for this particular study on Ephesus are included below.

- *Eerdmans Handbook to the Bible*, by David and Pat Alexander (editors), Wm. B. Eerdmans Publishing Co., 1993.
- *The New Unger's Bible Dictionary*, R. K. Harrison (editor), Merrill F. Unger (editor), Moody, 1988.
- *The Zondervan Pictorial Encyclopedia of the Bible*, by Merrill C. Tenney, Zondervan Publishing House, 1975.

Step Three: Explore the Geography

To understand the background of the Bible, you will need to begin to learn about the geography of Palestine and the Near East in general. Make a point of getting acquainted with the various types of land, names of mountains and areas, and bodies of water like Galilee. In particular for this study on Ephesus, you need to understand the Apostle Paul made missionary travels throughout the region. Ephesus was just one of the active cities in the Roman Empire. As you study geography, ask yourself, "What is the effect of the surrounding geography for the book that I am studying?" I have answered this question for Ephesus in the space here.

The city of Ephesus was situated on the western coast of Asia Minor at the mouth of the Cayster River, one of the four major east-west valleys that ended in the Aegean Sea. It was at the beginning of a major highway that went eastward across Asia Minor into Syria and then into Mesopotamia, Persia, and India.

Ephesus was a large port city and had a population of around 400,000 in the Apostle Paul's time. It was the most important city in the Roman province of Asia. Its strategic location caused it to be the meeting place of the land and sea trade routes in that part of the world in those days.

Teaching Tips

From time to time in your group, remind everyone that they should be ready to obey. Jesus said, "If anyone loves me, he will obey my teaching. My father will love him, and we will come to him and make our home with him." (John 14:23, NIV) We don't want to be like the person who studies his face in the mirror and then goes away and forgets what he looks like: Instead we want to do what the Bible says and so be blessed. (James 1:22–25, NIV)

Step Four: Delve Into History

For a deeper understanding of a particular Bible book, you will need to have a working knowledge of the Jewish people and a chronology of the major events in this history. In particular, it's important to know the historical background surrounding Paul's missionary journeys. One of the places he traveled was Ephesus. My research on Ephesus and the historical background is included here.

Ephesus was an ancient city whose origins are lost in the midst of antiquity. It was known as an important port city in the days of the ancient Hittites (early 1300s B.C.).

Around 1080 B.C., the Greeks captured and colonized the city from across the Aegean Sea, introducing Greek ways. Five centuries later, the legendary King Croesus conquered it and restored Asian influence to the city.

The Romans took the city in 190 B.C., and it remained in their hands or in the hands of their allies until the days of Paul and later. It became the major city in the Roman province of Asia, although Pergamum remained the capital.

Step Five: Study the Culture

Culture is a constant affect on the events and lifestyles of the ancient people from the Scriptures. As you begin to research and understand more about the people's clothing, professions, trades, music, false religions, languages, art, family life, etc., then the information will enrich your study. As you research, you consistently ask the question, "How do all these things affect the message and the people about whom I am studying?" My cultural research on Ephesus follows.

From the time that the Greeks took the city in 1080 B.C., cultural conflict existed between the Asian and Greek ways of life. The original religion included the worship of the mother goddess whom the Greeks later called Artemis (Diana in the Roman system). Here the original goddess had a shrine, and the Greeks later built a grand temple that became known throughout the whole Mediterranean world.

At the crossroads of Europe and the Orient, the city had an international flavor; peoples of many backgrounds, particularly traders and sailors, mixed freely. Thus, it was a cosmopolitan city, primarily Greek in culture, but with Asian underpinnings. It had all the conveniences of a modern Roman city—a gymnasium, a stadium, theaters, and a central marketplace.

Proceed with Caution

God has taken the trouble to have his truth written down and preserved for us over the centuries. We should not be casual or loose about the way we read and understand the Bible. It is important to interpret the Bible honestly, carefully, and consistently instead of simply picking out verses that support what we would like the truth to be.

Step Six: Consider the Political Background

Many of the events of the Bible were related to the politics of the rulers of the Roman World for Jesus and Paul. The political systems affected the way people lived, yet we must recognize that God is always in control of the political situation. Even the pagan king Nebuchadnezzar verbalized this fact. (Daniel 4:34–35) In the section that follows, I've included my research about the political background of Ephesus as a practical illustration of this step in the Bible Background Method.

As a city loyal to Rome in Paul's day, Ephesus was governed by the Roman proconsul from Pergamum. Thus, it was allowed to have its own government and was divided into "tribes" according to the ethnic composition of its population. In Paul's time, there were six of these tribes; the representatives to their gathering elected the "town clerk," who was responsible for all public meetings. Other government officials included the Asiarchs, municipal officers of Rome and the Neokoros, the temple officials.

Step Seven: Summarize Your Insights

Now that you've gathered some background data, return to steps three through six, and examine this information in order to summarize the research. Ask these questions: How does this background information help me better understand what I am studying? What influence did any of these factors have on the subject (or book) that

I am studying? My particular response to these questions related to the city of Ephesus follows.

The city of Ephesus was an important city. Because of its strategic value, Paul and his team headed there on their second missionary journey. Paul later ministered there again for some time (on his third journey).

Teaching Tips

Remind yourself and your students that it's important to be humble. God gives wisdom and grace to the humble. (Proverbs 3:34 and 11:2) Be willing to have your old opinions and assumptions challenged, and to be shown sins that you need to repent and be forgiven of.

Because of its cosmopolitan population, here was an opportunity to minister to many different kinds of peoples—Romans, Greeks, and the people of that part of Asia. A ministry also could be fostered with the travelers and traders who came both by land and by sea.

Ephesus's history and geography made the city strategic for planting churches and then spreading the news of the Gospel throughout the whole territory around it, as well as to many other places through the caravans and shipping routes.

Create a Personal Application

Our motivation for learning the Bible background is not just to increase the number of facts that we can spout about it. Every study and teaching method brings you toward a personal application. My personal application for this study on Ephesus is here.

As the world continues to become overpopulated today, it is my responsibility to witness to Jesus Christ in the strategic places of the world. This means that in my town, I need to find out where the strategic gathering centers are located. Then I should plan to go there, both by myself and with my church, to testify to the grace of God and his salvation. I will talk with Harry and Frank about this, and we will make plans for evangelizing our community.

Ideas for Teaching the Ephesus Lesson

As the group gathers to talk about Ephesus. Make sure you ask if anyone had any difficulties with the research process. Some people take much more naturally to finding information than others, and as a group you might walk through some of the specifics and which books are the most valuable in this process. Then turn to Ephesus. Everyone will have learned different geographical, historical, cultural, and political background information. Through the group process, each individual will increase their knowledge and background through the discussion session. Spend at least part of the time talking about their personal application from the study.

Blank Bible Background Method Form

Here's a blank form for you to fill in the Bible Background Method material on new studies that you and the members of your group will create.

1. Subject: ____________________
2. Reference tools used: ____________________
3. Geographical background: ____________________
4. Historical background: ____________________
5. Cultural background: ____________________
6. Political background: ____________________
7. Summary of insights: ____________________
8. Personal application: ____________________

The Least You Need to Know

- The Bible Background Method offers ways to gain interesting perspectives on a Bible passage.
- Learning the political, cultural, geographical, and historical setting helps us to gain a deeper understanding of the text.
- This chapter includes two examples of the Bible Background Method of teaching the Bible. One example is from the Old Testament, and the other is from the New Testament. These lessons are detailed as though you completed the lesson, and the information is ready for you to use or to follow for a new study.

Chapter 22

Two Sample Lessons on the Overview Book Method

In This Chapter

- Getting the big picture with the Overview Book Method
- Looking at the Book of Jonah through the Overview Book Method
- Gaining insight into the Book of Ephesians using the Overview Book Method
- Tips to help students use the Overview Book Method

The Overview Book Method consists of six distinct steps:

1. Read the book. Chapter 12, which covers this method in depth, includes seven different suggestions for reading the Scriptures.
2. As you read, make some observations.
3. Do a background study, as covered in detail in Chapter 11. In this step, you want to discover the historical and geographical setting of the book.
4. Make a horizontal chart of the book's contents. In chart form, diagram the layout of the book's contents on one or two pages for a

visual picture of the book. This horizontal chart has three parts: the major divisions of the book, the chapter titles, and the paragraph titles.

5. Make a tentative outline of the book, looking for major divisions, subdivisions, and the important points under the subdivisions.
6. Write out your personal application from the overview book study.

Just in Case

If your group appears to be stuck in a rut, here's something to re-energize yourselves. Differentiating between the actual Bible and all of the study helps you understand and apply biblical truths. Many Bibles have notes scattered throughout the text written by fallible authors. Be careful not to read those sections as "gospel truth." Only the Bible text itself is inspired by God and carries his authority.

A Lesson About the Book of Jonah

Some people may think this story is more fiction than fact but most scholars believe the story is fact. The short book of Jonah is tucked into the minor prophets of the Old Testament and will be the Old Testament book selected for the practical example of the Overview Book Method.

To help you see how this study method works, I've chosen the Book of Jonah. This book has four chapters.

Step One: Read

The first step is to read the book. Believe it or not, some people spend all of their time reading *about* the book without reading the Bible text itself. In your study Bible, read the book repeatedly; also read it in different Bible translations.

Step Two: Make Notes

As you read, write down facts that you discover in nine different areas: category, first impressions, keywords, key verse, literary style, emotional tone, main themes, structure of the book, and major people.

Category: Old Testament minor prophet letter.

First impression: The book is more than a story about Jonah and the whale; it is a picture of God's compassion.

Keywords: "Get up" and "go."

Key verse(s): "But Nineveh has more than 120,000 people living in spiritual darkness, not to mention all the animals. Shouldn't I feel sorry for such a great city?" (Jonah 4:11, NLT)

Literary style: Known as the Bible "fish tale" and a historical story of the prophet Jonah. The book centers on the story itself instead of the prophet's words to the people.

Emotional tone: Vivid storytelling, yet a solid picture of God's compassion for anyone who doesn't believe in him.

> **Teaching Tips**
>
> Often we forget to pray. Before you begin to read your Bible, pray. Invite God's Spirit to open your eyes and heart to spiritual truth in God's word. 1 John 2:27 promises, "But you have the Holy Spirit, and he lives within you, in your hearts, so that you don't need any one to teach you what is right. For he is teaching you all things, and he is the Truth, and no liar; and so, just as he has said, you must live in Christ, never to depart from him." (Living Bible)

Main theme(s): God's sovereignty: Although the prophet Jonah tried to run away from God, God was in control. By controlling the stormy seas and a great fish, God displayed his absolute, yet loving, guidance.

God's message to all the world: God had charged Jonah with a purpose, which was to preach to the great Assyrian city of Nineveh. Jonah hated Nineveh, so he responded with anger and indifference. Jonah had yet to learn that God loves all people. Through Jonah, God reminded Israel of its missionary purpose.

Repentance: When the reluctant preacher went to Nineveh, there was a great response. The people repented and turned to God. This was a powerful rebuke to the people of Israel, who thought they were better but refused to respond to God's message. God will forgive all those who turn from their sins.

God's compassion: God's message of love and forgiveness was not for the Jews alone. God loves all the people of the world. The Assyrians didn't deserve it, but God spared them when they repented. In his mercy, God did not reject Jonah for aborting his mission. God has great love, patience, and forgiveness.

Structure: The book has two key divisions. In verses 1:1–2:10, Jonah forsakes his mission. Then in verses 3:1–4:11, Jonah fulfills his mission.

Major people: Jonah, the great fish, God, the people of Nineveh.

Reference books used:

- *Life Application Study Bible* (Tyndale, 1996)
- *Holman Bible Dictionary* (Holman Bible Publishers, 1991)

Step Three: Delve Into the Background

In this step, each person digs into the background of the book. In the section that follows, I complete this step for Jonah.

Jonah means "dove" in Hebrew and the Book of Jonah preserves the story of part of the prophet's ministry. The Book of Jonah is unique among the minor prophets: It consists of a short story about a prophet and confines the message to a sentence (verse 3:4).

The hero—or, rather, antihero—is mentioned in 2 Kings 14:23–29 as active in the reign of Jeroboam II (about 785–745 B.C.). His prediction of national expansion for the Northern Kingdom, evidently made early in the reign, expressed God's longing to save his people, wicked though they were. This theological background is important for the book.

A series of cumulative arguments suggests that the book was written at a comparatively late date, probably the fifth century B.C., though many Bible students think the book came from about 750 B.C. Its Hebrew language is marked by Aramaic features, some of which can be paralleled only in Imperial Aramaic, current in the Persian period. There appear to be deliberate echoes of Jeremiah 18:7, 8, and 11 (Jonah 3:8, 10) and of the postexilic Joel 2:13 and 14 (Jonah 3:9 and 4:2). The title "king of Nineveh" (verse 3:6) seems to imply that the city was the capital of Assyria, which it became only at the end of the eighth century. The book appears to be loosely tied to history and presents later theological reflection.

Some have regarded the book as an allegory: Jonah then stands for Israel swallowed in Exile by the Babylonian sea monster (compare Jeremiah 51:34, 44). Yet God used the fish not to punish Jonah, but to rescue him. Instead, the book is to be regarded as a satirical parable intended to criticize and correct its readers' attitudes (compare 2 Samuel 12:1–6 and 14:1–11, and Isaiah 5:1–7). It builds on an earlier phenomenon, as the parable in Luke 19:11–27 builds on Archelaus's visit to Rome. The book's extraordinary features—the seemingly exaggerated size of Nineveh (verse 3:3); Jonah's survival with a song in the fish's interior, digestive juices notwithstanding; and the suddenly appearing/disappearing plant (verses 4:6–7)—are meant to rivet the reader's attention and to enhance the purpose of the book, sort of like the fantastic debt in Matthew 18:24 did. Jonah is presented as a caricature of Elijah, who obeyed God the first time (1 Kings 17:8–10, and Jonah 1:1–3 and 3:1–3) and had reason for despair (1 Kings 19:4 and Jonah 4:3).

> **Teaching Tips**
>
> Encourage members of your group to persist in Bible study. Most of us know the challenge of beginning a new diet program or exercise regimen. During the first few weeks, most of us lose interest and get discouraged by the lack of results. Encourage consistent and deliberate Bible study.

The two halves of the book have a dual focus, on pagans (verses 1:4–16 and 3:3b–10) and on the Israelite prophet (verses 1:17–2:10 and 4:1–11), and their respective relationships to God. The portrayal of pagans in a positive light as sensitive and submissive to God's will recognizes their worth and potential in his sight. Jonah is shown to be inconsistent: After praising God for rescuing him from threat of death, he complained when God did the same for pagans. Two creedal statements represent God as the universal creator (verse 1:9) and as the preserver of the lives of pagans in an extension of his covenant grace (verse 4:2; compare Exodus 34:6 and Psalms 145:8, 9, 15, and 16). He so loves the world: The book has a premissionary role in defining a theological truth, God's relation to the world outside the sheepfold of faith. Even the Assyrians' later destruction of Israel (2 Kings 17) and their tyrannical imperialism (2 Kings 18:22–24; Nahum 3:1–4, 19), which the book appears to presuppose, could not separate them from God's loving concern for their survival.

Step Four: Create a Horizontal Chart

Jonah Runs from the Lord	Jonah's Prayer
The Lord said, "Get up and go to Nineveh." (1:1) Jonah got up and went the opposite direction. (1:3)	Lord you threw me into the sea. (2:3) I lost hope but turned to the Lord. (2:7)
The Lord arranged for a great fish to swallow Jonah and he was inside three days and three nights. (1:17)	I will fulfill all my promises for my salvation comes from the Lord. (2:9) The Lord ordered the fish to spit up Jonah on the beach. (2:10)

Proceed with Caution

From time to time, remind the members of your group about the overall purpose of studying the Bible: God gave us the Bible to communicate to us and to change our lives through the knowledge of him. It's not just a bound set of facts and figures, plot lines, and poems.

Jonah Goes to Nineveh	Jonah's Anger at God's Mercy
God told Jonah to go to Nineveh and deliver a message of judgment. (verse 3:1)	Jonah was upset at God's mercy and asks to be dead. (verses 4:1–4)
Jonah obeyed. (verse 3:3)	God questions Jonah's anger. (verse 4:4)
The people of Nineveh repented. (verses 3:5–9)	God made a plant for shade then a worm to eat the plant. (verses 4:7–9)
God saw the people had changed and had mercy on them. (verse 3:10)	God shows compassion and love to Jonah. (verses 4:10–11)

Create a Tentative Outline of the Book

For the next step in the Overview Book Method, each person creates a tentative outline of the book. You need to reassure the members of your group there is no right or wrong way to construct this outline. Everyone will do it differently. My version of the outline for Jonah follows.

I. People with bad reputations can be pious and know God. (verses 1:1–16)

II. God hears the distress calls of his people. (verses 1:17–2:10)

III. In his compassion, God turns away from judgment when any people repent. (verses 3:1–10)

IV. God's people should mirror God's compassion for all people. (verses 4:1–11)

Potent Quotables

"But Jonah got up and went in the opposite direction in order to get away from the Lord. He went down to the seacoast, to the port of Joppa, where he found a ship leaving for Tarshish. He bought a ticket and went on board, hoping that by going away to the west he could escape from the Lord." (Jonah 1:3, NLT)

Make a Personal Application

Each person in your group will make a personal application from studying the Book of Jonah. Everyone will have a different application into their life from the study. My personal application is follows as an example.

Instead of running from God, I need to listen to his voice; when God says to go, I need to go. The message of God's love is not just for one race or one people, but it's for everyone. I need to keep that in mind and pray for the peoples of the world, even people who are considerably different than I am. Just as God accepts everyone from different backgrounds and ethnic groups, I need to have the same sense of love (God-given) for others in my life.

Teaching the Book of Jonah

In your small group, this book is ripe for discussing a number of critical questions:

- How do we hear God's voice? The Bible is the predominate method that God speaks today.
- How do you respond when you receive some guidance from the Lord?
- Have you sometimes run from God's guidance? What happened?
- How do we learn again of God's compassion through the story of Jonah? What hope or encouragement does it give us today?

Prepare a Lesson About Ephesians

Here's another lesson to use with the Overview Book Method. This time, let's examine Ephesians, which has six chapters.

Step One: Read

As usual, the first step in using this technique (or almost any technique, when you get right down to it) is to read the book—and more than once. Aim to read it at least five times.

Step Two: Take Notes

For this second step, take notes on your observations from reading the Book of Ephesians. My notes follow as a practical example of this step.

Category: New Testament letter.

First impression: This is a book that strengthens my faith and challenges me in my responsibilities. It's strongly doctrinal in teaching.

Keywords: "in Christ" and "walk."

Key verse(s): Verses 1:3 and 4:1.

Literary style: A general letter that is punctuated by two worshipful prayers.

Emotional tone: Calm, with the intention of teaching the readers and challenging them in their responsibilities.

Main theme(s): What we are because of Jesus Christ ("in Christ") and the responsibilities that are ours because of our standing.

Structure: Two main divisions separated by a "therefore." In the first part, two prayers are recorded.

Major people: Paul, the Ephesian church, evil forces, and Tychicus.

Reference books used:

- *Eerdmans Handbook to the Bible* (Wm. B. Eerdmans Publishing Co., 1993)
- *William Hendriksen's Ephesians* (Baker, 1979)
- *The New Unger's Bible Dictionary* (Moody, 1988)

Just in Case

What do bandages and the Bible have to do with each other? If you cut your hand, it needs a bandage. If that bandage is sitting on the counter in its wrapper, it's not doing any good. The bandage helps only when you apply it to the wound. The same is true with the Bible. All of us are wounded, and we don't always do what's right even when we really want to. God has given us a bandage with a built-in antibiotic called the truth of God. It's up to us to apply that bandage and find the healing that is there.

Step Three: Delve Into the Background

In this step, each person researches the background of the Book of Ephesians. I've written my research on this book follows.

Paul had founded the church in Ephesus on his second missionary journey and left Aquila and Priscilla there to follow up with the new Christians. While there, they had an influence in Apollos's life.

At the beginning of this third mission, Paul returned and taught in the city for a lengthy time, during which the good news about Jesus Christ spread throughout the province of Asia.

Then after Paul was imprisoned in Rome, he wrote a letter to a church. He wanted to simply strengthen the church both doctrinally and practically. He wrote it to build up believers' opinions of themselves (in light of the other powerful religious influences in the city, such as the temple of Artemis) and encourage them to carry out their responsibilities as Christians in their community.

Teaching Tips

Applying the Bible means taking it personally. If the Bible says that God desires our obedience, it's up to us to say, "Then how should I obey?" If the Bible tells a story about a man who is unmerciful and lives to regret it, it's up to us to say, "How do I measure up in the merciful category?"

Many references in the book pertain to the original readers because the background is the city of Ephesus and its culture, government, and history. (For more information, take a look at Chapter 21, which explores the Bible Background Method.)

Create a Horizontal Chart

Chosen by God	Saved by Christ	Empowered by the Holy Spirit
Three worshipful Praises separate the work of the Trinity: ◆ Father (1:4–6) Son (1:7–12) Holy Spirit (1:13–14)	The work of Christ is seen as a work of grace which we receive by faith. ◆ Redemption (2:1–10) Reconciliation (2:11–22) (The results of each are seen here.)	The ministry of the Holy Spirit is to make all believers of all backgrounds one in Christ. This was a mystery before.
Paul's first prayer (1:15–23)		Paul's second prayer (3:14–21)

Teaching Tips

Remind members of your group how important consistency and accountability are when it comes to Bible study. It doesn't matter when you study the Bible, as long as you set aside the time to consistently study it. In addition, most people find it helpful to have someone keep them accountable. It's hard to neglect your Bible study when you know someone will call on you.

Responsibilities	Relationships	Conflict
Verses 4:1–5:21 "Therefore ..." 1. We are to have a united walk. (verses 4:1–16)	Verses 5:22–6:9 The specifics are now given: 1. Husbands and wives (verses 5:22–33)	Verses 6:10-20 The reason we have difficulties in our responsibilities and relationships
2. We are to have an understanding walk. (verses 4:17–32)	2. Parents and children (verses 6:1–4)	is because of our spiritual warfare. But we have God's armor to protect us.
3. We are to have a holy walk. (verses 5:1–14)	3. "Employer" and "employee" (verses 6:5–9)	Paul's closing greetings, Tychicus sent (verses 6:21–24)
4. We are to have a Spirit-led walk. (verses 5:15–21)		

Create a Tentative Outline of the Book

This step involves making a tentative outline of the entire book. Each person in your group will create a slightly different outline. I've created an example of this with the book of Ephesians below.

I. Who the members of the church are (chapters 1–3)

   A. They've been chosen by God (chapter 1) (ends with a prayer)

   B. They've been saved by Christ (chapter 2)

   C. They are empowered by the Holy Spirit (chapter 3) (ends in a prayer)

II. What the members of the church are to do (chapters 4–6)

   A. Their responsibilities (verses 4:1–5:21)

   B. Their relationships at three levels (verses 5:22–6:9)

   C. Their conflict with satanic powers (verses 6:10–20)

   D. Concluding remarks (verses 6:21–24)

Teaching Tips

By working hard to ask good questions and listening with insight to the members of your group, you'll raise the members' ability to retain and understand the Bible passages.

Make a Personal Application

As with every method, one of the most critical sections is the personal application. It's where the Bible becomes much more than head knowledge when each individual applies it to his or her own life. I've written my own personal application from the overview on Ephesians.

What strikes me about the book is the close relationship between believing and acting. If I believe in Jesus Christ, I am supposed to act in a Christian way. Because of who I am in the sight of God, certain actions are required of me in all my relationships.

Because I have reconciled with others (chapter 2), I should forgive in the same way Christ forgave me (verses 4:32). I have not always been that forgiving and have held grudges and resentment. I will search my heart and make sure I have forgiven everyone who may have "done me wrong"—truly or just imagined. Then, if necessary, I will go to these people and ask *their* forgiveness. As a check on myself, I will memorize Ephesians 4:32.

Teaching the Book of Ephesians

This book from Paul has many key areas to examine and discuss as a group:

- Look at how Paul explains God's purpose. Ask the participants to examine their lives to see if they are committed to fulfilling God's purpose.
- Paul discusses the position of Christ as the center of the universe and the focus of history. If you take this perspective to heart, how does it change your daily priorities?

Potent Quotables

"How precious to me are your thoughts, O God! How vast is the sum of them! Were I to count them, they would outnumber the grains of sand. When I awake, I am still with you." (Psalms 139: 17–18, NLT)

- This book also describes the function of Christ's living church. It's important for each individual to function within the local church. Discuss with the members of your group their roles in the local church and how consistent they are with their service to God.
- Numerous other smaller themes arise throughout the Book of Ephesians. Personalize each one for the members of your group, and always encourage them to apply these themes in a personal way.

Teaching Tips

Encourage members of your group to stick to attending their discussion groups. If the group is oriented toward discussion questions, it strengthens the Bible study skills of the individuals. When week after week they hear questions that direct them to read the Bible for answers, they'll gradually learn how to think about a Scripture passage.

Blank Overview Book Method Form

The following section is a blank form for the Overview Book Method. You can photocopy this form and give it to the members of your group. Or you can teach the various steps and have each person write it into a notebook, or put it into a computer file and give it to each participant. Every time you use the method, you will need a new form.

Book: ______________________ Chapters: ______________________

1. Number of times read: ______________________
2. Notes on the book: ______________________
   - Category: Old Testament minor prophet letter
   - First impression: ______________________
   - Keywords: ______________________
   - Key verse(s): ______________________
   - Literary style: ______________________

- Emotional tone: ____________________
- Main theme(s): ____________________
- Structure: ____________________
- Major people: ____________________
- Reference books used: ____________________

3. Background of the book: ____________________

 ____

4. Horizontal Chart: Make a Horizontal Chart, as I made for Jonah and Ephesians, for each study you create.

5. Tentative outline of the book:

 ____

 ____

6. Personal application:

 ____

> **Teaching Tips**
>
> Make sure you've created an environment of caring in your small group. This is one of the critical factors when it comes to encouraging members to learn.

The Least You Need to Know

- The Overview Book Method is a means of quickly grasping the themes and big picture of a particular book of the Bible.
- A four chapter book in the Old Testament filled with drama and insight about human nature is the Book of Jonah. It is included in detail as an example from the Old Testament for how someone can complete the Overview Book Method.
- The Apostle Paul loved the church at Ephesus and wrote the Book of Ephesians. This chapter uses Paul's letter to the Ephesians as a New Testament example of the Overview Book Method.

Chapter 23

In-Depth Study of a Single Bible Chapter: Two Sample Lessons

In This Chapter

- Learn the In-Depth Chapter Method with the short yet powerful psalm that begins The Hymnbook of the Old Testament
- Gain insight into teaching this method in a group setting
- The Apostle Paul explains the Great Purpose for Our Lives in the first chapter of his letter to the Ephesians

One of the most manageable units of the Bible for consistent study is the chapter. Although the first written Bible had no chapters, Cardinal Hugo introduced the modern chapter system in the middle of the thirteenth century. Many Christian leaders feel that the length of a chapter and the limited themes that each chapter contains make it a perfect unit to study and teach.

In this chapter, you'll see examples of this method that I've put together, and you'll get some ideas about teaching a chapter this way to your members of your study group.

A Review of the In-Depth Chapter Method

The In-Depth Chapter Method involves seven different steps:

1. Write a chapter summary after reading and rereading the chapter many times. You can write the chapter summary in one of three ways: paraphrase it, outline it, or rewrite it without the modifying clauses.
2. List your observations about the chapter by looking carefully at every sentence and word, and then writing down what you see.
3. Ask interpretive questions that will help you discover the biblical writer's purpose and message. List difficulties—those difficulties that you personally struggle with in the chapter and also the possible difficult questions about the text—and then try to find the answers to your interpretative questions by checking the context, defining words and phrases, studying the structure of the sentences, comparing translations, or studying the background. As a last resort, consult a commentary for answers.
4. Next, correlate your chapter with other Scriptures. Scripture best explains Scripture, so use other parts of the Bible as an explanation through cross-referencing. For more details on this step, see Chapter 13.
5. Create ways to apply to your own life the lessons you've learned by studying this chapter in-depth.
6. While they're fresh in your mind, write down some concluding thoughts about the chapter.
7. Finally, select one personal application and write it down, making sure that it's not only personal, but also practical, possible, and measurable.

> **Potent Quotables**
>
> "Oh, the depth of the riches of the wisdom and knowledge of God! How unsearchable his judgments, and his paths beyond tracing out! Who has known the mind of the Lord?" (Romans 11:33, NIV)

> **Just in Case**
>
> If the class discussion gets heated and out of control when you're talking about a doctrine or social issue, call a halt to the discussion and allow for a time of cooling down. Don't allow personal attacks or a harsh tone of voice. If the topic merits further discussion, ask the various viewpoints to prepare remarks with time limits that they can give during the next meeting. Others in the group can ask questions. Encourage everyone to "agree to disagree," to keep arguments to a minimum.

An In-Depth Lesson About Psalm 1

Psalm 1, which I have called "A Wisdom Psalm," begins one of the longest books in the Old Testament. Much of Psalms is written in the Hebrew poetic style of couplets. For example, you say a statement, then slightly change the words and repeat it again for emphasis. This type of poetry is evident from the first Psalm and carried out in the entire book. The first Psalm is relatively short yet shows a powerful contrast between good and evil.

Step One: Summarize the Chapter

The first step in the In-Depth Chapter Method is to summarize the contents in an outline format. I've outlined Psalm 1 as a practical example of how to complete this study.

Introduction (verses 1:1–2)

I. Blessed is the man who avoids wickedness. (verse 1:1)

  A. His delight is in God's law, and he meditates continually. (verse 1:2)

  B. The wise man's abiding is compared to a tree. (verse 1:3)

    1. Planted by streams of water

    2. Fruit yielded in season

    3. Leaf that doesn't wither

    4. Prosperous and productive

II. The destructive path of the wicked. (verse 1:4)

  A. The wicked are compared to chaff. (verse 1:5)

    1. The wind blows away chaff.

  B. The wicked will not stand in judgment. (verse 1:6)

  C. The wicked will not be in the assembly of the righteous (verse 1:6)

Teaching Tips

Remember that your Bible study group isn't like a business or civic group. One of the distinguishing factors is the nature of the relationships. Team building should be a natural part of the time together. Make sure that the relationships set your group apart as decidedly Christian.

III. God watches both the righteous and the wicked.

   A. The Lord protects the righteous. (verse 1:7)

   B. The Lord punishes the wicked. (verse 1:7)

Step Two: Make Your Observations

The second step to examine a chapter in-depth involves asking the question, "What does it say?" For every verse in the chapter, you will saturate yourself with the contents of the Bible passage. Verse by verse for Psalm 1, I've completed this exercise as a practical example.

Step Three: Interpret the Passages

For the next step in the method, you are going to turn to interpretation of these verses in the chapter. What does each verse mean? These steps aren't executed in isolation of each other but are interconnected. I've put these steps in two columns with each verse from the psalm aligned with the appropriate verse. For example, the rephrasing of the verse Psalm 1:1 is across from the interpretation, "There is joy in obeying God and his law." As a practical example of this In-Depth Chapter Method, I've written my answers to these two steps.

Part One

	2. Observation **What does it say?**	**3. Interpretation** **What does it mean?**
(Psalms1:1)	Blessed is the man who doesn't walk in the way of the wicked or stand in the way of sinners or sit in the seat of mockers.	There is joy in obeying God and his law. The godly don't live like sinners. The godly don't join in with scoffers.
(verse 1:2)	But his delight is in the law of the Lord and on his law, the godly meditate day and night.	The godly's joy is in God's law or the Scriptures. The godly man thinks about the law or Scriptures day and night.

	2. Observation What does it say?	**3. Interpretation What does it mean?**
(verse 1:3)	He is like a tree planted by streams of water which yields its fruit in season and whose leaf does not wither. Whatever he does prospers.	The godly put down deep roots in God's law, like a tree planted by a stream of water. The life of the godly is fruitful and doesn't fade, and will prosper.
(verse 1:4)	Not so the wicked!	This type of relationship isn't true for the wicked.
	They are like chaff that the wind blows away	The ungodly are like the worthless chaff, which is scattered by the wind.
(verse 1:5)	Therefore, the wicked will not stand in judgment, nor sinners in the assembly of the righteous.	The ungodly won't be able to withstand the wrath of God at the day of judgment.
(verse 1:6)	For the Lord watches over the way of the righteous, but the way of the wicked will perish.	God controls the destiny of the godly and also knows that the wicked will be punished.

Just in Case

Stand back from your Bible teaching sessions and ask yourself, how much time are you spending in prayer during the session? If you determine that you are not spending very much time in prayer, you could close the study time with intercessory prayer. Invite the members of the group to ask others to pray for them about a specific matter, or ask another individual to pray for that need. Be open in the group about your own specific prayer needs and your actions will encourage the same sort of transparent honesty from others.

Correlation

The entire Bible is interrelated and connected. Different Bible themes, for example, appear throughout Scripture. For the fourth step in the In-Depth Chapter Study, you will consider the cross-references or correlation between the particular chapter and other parts of the Bible. These other verses relate to the verses in Psalm 1 and also help you explain and understand these verses. My practical example of Psalm 1 follows.

Application Related to Each Verse in the Passage

The time studying a single chapter isn't for simply increasing your knowledge about that chapter. The entire purpose of any Bible study is for personal application. The application step in this Method is coordinated with your understanding of each of the various verses—which is why the chart is aligned in this manner. In isolation, you can't see the particular pattern of the Psalm and how it fits together as easily as you can in a chart form. As a practical example of this method, I've included my personal application and response to these verses from Psalm 1 in the space below.

Part Two

	4. Correlation **Where else is it explained?**	**5. Application** **What will I do about it?**
Psalms		
1:1	Deuteronomy 33:29 Psalms 40:4 Job 21:16 Proverbs 1:22 Isaiah 28:14 Hosea 7:5	1 There is joy in obeying God's laws, and I must refuse to be with anyone who doesn't listen to God or who ridicules the Lord.
1:2	Psalms 112:2 Psalms 119:1 Romans 7:22 Psalms 19:7 Ezekiel 11:20 Ezekiel 18:17 Genesis 24:63	2 The more I delight in following God and his law, the more fruitful I will become.
1:3	Psalms 52:8 Psalms 92:12 Psalms 128:3 Jeremiah 11:16 Zechariah 4:3 Isaiah 33:21 Numbers 24:6 Job 14:9	3 When I soak up God's Word, I will be good and will receive God's approval and produce actions that honor God because I have God's Word in my heart.

	4. Correlation **Where else is it explained?**	**5. Application** **What will I do about it?**
1:4	Job 13:25 Isaiah 40:24 Jeremiah 13:24	4 The ungodly are treated like worthless chaff.
1:5	Psalms 5:5	5 God condemns the ungodly, and they will be lost forever.
1:6		6 God watches my path if I follow the Lord, and the ungodly are destroyed.

Teaching Tips

Are you making your questions to the group personal and practical? Asking questions that come straight from your heart and reveal practical implications can help other members of your small group do the same. Did you find some reasons to give the members of your group praise and encouragement from the Bible text? If so, members of your group can do the same. Did you connect a particular verse to your own prayer life? Then so can the members of your group. The most productive questions draw the reader back to the spiritual meaning for studying the Bible and will also work well during the group meeting. Find room for them in your discussion plan.

Draw Your Conclusions

In this step of the method, you write some general conclusions from the study of the chapter. It allows you to step outside the bounds of the particular verse and structure of the previous points and instead make some general conclusions from your study of this chapter. I've written my conclusions from Psalm 1 here.

This psalm shows a clear contrast between the godly and the ungodly—those who follow God and love his Law or the Scriptures, and those ungodly people who do not follow God's ways and are on the path of destruction.

The proper response is to love the law of the Lord and the Scriptures.

Create a Personal Application

The final step of this method is to apply the lessons from the chapter to your daily life. This application will be different for each person in your group (including yourself). The personal application is where the study of Scripture becomes more than information but something that God can use for the spiritual transformation of your life. I've included my personal application from Psalm 1 as an example.

I need to increase my daily commitment to follow God and love the Scriptures. Only when I set my mind on the Scriptures am I more in touch with God and can meditate and think about God's presence in my life to a greater degree than currently in my thinking.

I will read the Scriptures in the morning and take a few minutes at my lunch break to read part of the Bible. It will allow the law of God to fill my day and help me to meditate on it to a larger degree in my life.

Potent Quotables

"Long ago, even before he made the world, God loved us and chose us in Christ to be holy and without fault in his eyes. His unchanging plan has always been to adopt us into his own family by bringing us to himself through Jesus Christ. And this gave him great pleasure." (Ephesians 1:4–5, NLT)

Teaching the In-Depth Look at Psalm 1

Have the group discuss the difference between the godly and the ungodly. Is the difference always clear, or does it sometimes fall into a gray area? What does it mean to the various members of the group to meditate on the law of the Lord? How do they practically accomplish this in their day-to-day living? As they walk with the Lord and meditate on his Word, what type of results have they experienced and what are they promised to experience?

An In-Depth Study Lesson of Ephesians 1

This section begins the second practical example of how to complete the in-depth study of a chapter from the Bible. I selected the first chapter of the Apostle Paul's letter to the church at Ephesus. It is clear from the Scriptures (the Book of Acts in particular) that Paul dearly loved the Christians in this city. In the first chapter of this book, which I called God's Great Purpose for Our Lives, I've handled each of the six steps for this method as a New Testament practical example.

Chapter title: "God's Great Purpose for Our Lives"

Step One: Summarize the Chapter

For this first step, you are reading the chapter numerous times and creating a general outline of the chapter and the verses which distinguish your outline. As an example for how to complete this step, I've completed the exercise for Ephesians 1 here.

Introduction (verses 1:1–2)

I. The revelation of the purpose of God (verses 1:3–14)

 A. The summary statement: what he has given us (verse 1:3)

 B. The basis of our salvation (the work of God the Father) (verses 1:4–6)

  1. Chosen to be holy and blameless (verse 1:4)

  2. Adopted as his sons (verse 1:5)

  3. Grace freely given us (verse 1:6)

 C. The benefits of our salvation (the work of God the Son) (verses 1:7–12)

  1. He sacrificed himself for us (verse 1:7)

  2. He lavished grace on us (verse 1:8)

  3. He revealed his will to us (verses 1:9–10)

  4. He made us part of his inheritance (verses 1:11–12)

 D. The gift of our salvation (the work of God the Holy Spirit) (verses 1:13–14)

  1. He revealed Christ to us (verse 1:13)

  2. He sealed us as God's children (verse 1:13)

  3. He guarantees our inheritance (verse 1:14)

II. The response of prayer to God (verses 1:15–23)

 A. The foundation of the prayer (verses 1:15–23)

  1. For the faithful and loving believers (verse 1:15)

  2. To a faithful and loving God (verses 1:16–17a)

 B. The formulation of the prayer (verses 1:17b–20a)

  1. Prayer for wisdom (verse 1:17b)

  2. Prayer for enlightenment (verse 1:18a)

  3. Prayer for experiential knowledge (verses 1:18b–20a)

C. The finale of the prayer (verses 1:20b–23)

Acknowledgement of …

1. Christ's resurrection (verse 1:20b)
2. Christ's dominion over all (verse 1:21)
3. Christ's headship over all (verse 1:22)
4. Christ's lordship over the church (verse 1:23)

Teaching Tips

When you reach the personal application section of a Bible study, plan questions designed to draw out anecdotes from group members. Ask them to provide personal examples; these experiences will convey in story form the benefits of obeying a truth from the passage or the consequences of ignoring the spiritual truth. Personal experiences catapult people from the comprehension level of learning to the changed-life level.

Step Two: Make Your Observations

In this section, you begin a verse-by-verse analysis of the chapter. Through observation you are going to examine each phrase and sentence of the chapter in depth, writing down each observation. The key question which you will be asking throughout this step is "What does it say?" Saturate yourself with the contents of this chapter and read it repeatedly. Don't rush this part of the process but understand each verse. As a practical example of this step in Ephesians 1, I've completed my observations verse-by-verse for the entire chapter.

Step Three: Ask Interpretive Questions

For this third step, you return to a verse-by-verse examination of the entire chapter but instead of observation, you are asking interpretive questions and looking for answers. The key question here is "What does it mean?"

In two columns, I've aligned the observations and the interpretations for Ephesians 1. When you complete any In-Depth Chapter Analysis, you will want to create two columns so you can gain much more from the experience than in a single column. My interpretations of Ephesians 1 follow.

	2. Observation What does it say?	**3. Interpretation What does it mean?**
Ephesians		
1:3	God has blessed me with *every* spiritual blessing.	3 God thinks the world of me.
4	God chose me to live a life of holiness.	4 I must obey God and his commandments.
5	God has adopted me into his family.	5 This means that I belong to him forever.
7	Through Christ I have been forgiven.	7 Christ is the only one who can forgive sins.
9	God has revealed his will to us through Jesus Christ.	9 Christ is God's total revelation of himself.
11	I am made an heir of God through Christ.	11 I have all the privileges of being an heir.
13-	The Holy Spirit in me is	13 This means that I am important,
14	a guarantee of my salvation and acceptance.	14 that God gave me so great a guarantee.
16	Paul prays for the Ephesians.	16 I need to pray for fellow Christians.
18	Paul prays for others' enlightenment.	18 I need to pray that others may know God's will.

Teaching Tips

In addition to soliciting anecdotes from members' past experiences, ask them to apply those past experiences to current lessons in a particular passage. What will their new application with this additional insight from Scripture look like? The ideas that your group offer won't fit every person, but when application ideas saturate their minds, the Holy Spirit has fuel to work with after the group meeting concludes.

Step Four: Correlate

Because the Bible was written by many different men, God used different men to communicate his message, and various themes are consistent throughout Scripture.

We gain insight into the verses that we are studying by looking for "cross-references" or correlating the verses in the chapter with other Bible passages. In this step, you look for appropriate verses which give insight into the specifics for a verse in the chapter. As a practical example from Ephesians 1, I've included my cross-references in the left-hand column in the following table. The key question that is answered in this step is "Where else in the Bible is this verse explained?"

Step Five: Create an Application

The final part of this verse-by-verse study of the chapter involves listing some possible applications. The applications are coordinated with the particular verse in the chapter. The overall goal of any Bible study is personal application. In this section, you are listing some of the many possible applications for the contents of a chapter from the Bible. I've listed my possible applications verse-by-verse in the right-hand column of this chart. The key question which you are asking yourself verse-by-verse in this step is "What will I do about the truth that I've learned in this verse?"

Part Two:

	4. Correlation **Where else is it explained?**	**5. Application** **What will I do about it?**
Ephesians		
1:3	1 Peter 1:3 2 Peter 1:4	3 Thank God for what he has done for me.
4	Romans 8:29 Exodus 26:1-17	4 I must make sure I'm leading a holy life.
5	Galatians 4:5 Philippians 2:13	5 I need to act as though I belong to God's family.
7	Mark 10:45 Romans 3:25	7 I must thank God for the totality of his forgiveness.
9	Galatians 1:15 Ephesians 3:9 Hebrews 1:1–2	9 Bible study is essential if I'm going to know God's will.
11	Romans 8:16–17 Acts 20:32	11 I should thank God for this great gift.
13	John 3:33	13 I need to live my life in
14	Ephesians 4:30	14 such a way that I do

	4. Correlation Where else is it explained?	5. Application What will I do about it?
	2 Corinthians 5:3	not offend the Spirit who lives in me.
16	Philippians 1:3 Romans 1:8–10	16 I need to pray for Bill, Mark, and Jane.
18	Acts 26:18	18 I need to pray for Steve and Mona.

Step Six: Draw Your Conclusions

For this step, the reader returns to the chapter and re-examines everything that they have learned about the chapter to this point. Then you draw some general conclusions: not verse-by-verse, but more global conclusions that capture some of the principles in the entire chapter. For this New Testament chapter of Ephesians 1, I've drawn some conclusions.

This chapter shows what God has given his people: He has blessed them with every spiritual blessing there is. The chapter continues listing many of those blessings in the Trinitarian work of salvation. This is what God the Father, God the Son, and God the Holy Spirit have done for us. Reading a section of Scripture like this one should give us a real sense of worth because this is God's commentary on what he thinks of those who belong to him.

The proper response to this grand revelation should be a prayer of thanksgiving, adoration, and praise, which is exactly what Paul does at the end of the chapter.

Proceed with Caution

As the teacher or facilitator for your Bible study, you are the person who leads the others into the biblical text. Guard against speculative questions. These are questions that push the discussion beyond what you can know from the text and ask you to speculate on an answer. A speculative question seeks information not disclosed in the Bible passage and tries to satisfy curiosity about a fact that God figured we didn't need to know. Also, it promotes conjecture about the Bible rather than investigation and analysis of it. Watch carefully and avoid speculative questions.

Step Seven: Apply the Lesson Personally

The entire In-Depth Chapter Method has been building to this final point. It is through the personal application that you and each of the participants in your study gain insight and application into your everyday lives. The Scriptures are to be studied to spiritually enrich your daily life. It's key to put the application into the present tense as something that you can do right now—not in the future. Ask yourself, "What am I going to do about this now?" As an example of how to fill in this step, I've included my personal application from Ephesians 1.

I need to develop more of the spirit of prayer, as Paul does here. He is so overwhelmed by what God has done for us that he spontaneously prays. I need to meditate on what God has done for me and respond to him with a prayer of adoration and praise.

To start this process, I will reread Ephesians 1 five times, substituting *I* and *me* for the pronouns in the chapter. I will then spend time praying without asking for myself, but directing all my requests toward God and his glory.

Ideas for an In-Depth Study of Ephesians 1

Spend some time in your group talking about God's purpose for your lives. When we respond to God's love by trusting him, his purpose becomes our mission. Have you committed yourself to fulfilling God's purpose?

Blank In-Depth Chapter Study Form

Now that you've seen two completed examples of this In-Depth Chapter Study Method, you are ready to select your own chapters for individual study and for your group to study. The following form is included as another tool, which you can photocopy or have the members of your group write by hand or type into your computer and reproduce with each new chapter to be studied.

Chapter: ____

Chapter title: ____

1. Chapter summary:

Introduction

I.

A.

Part One:

2. Observation What does it say?	3. Interpretation What does it mean?

Part Two:

4. Correlation Where else is it explained?	5. Application What will I do about it?

6. Conclusions: ____

7. A personal application: ________________________________

The Least You Need to Know

- The In-Depth Chapter Method is a means of digging deep into a small section of the Bible.
- Psalm 1 is a stark contrast between good and evil with the application for the reader to constantly turn to God for spiritual insight and strength. I've included detailed analysis of this Old Testament chapter using the In-Depth Chapter Method.
- The Apostle Paul loved the church at Ephesus and wrote the Letter to the Ephesians. The first chapter from Ephesians is used as the New Testament example of how to study a chapter in-depth. This section includes detailed answers to each step of the method, which you can use to stimulate ideas and action as you study other chapters in the Bible.

Chapter 24

Two Sample Lessons: Comprehensive Study of a Particular Bible Book

In This Chapter

- Tie a whole book of the Bible together in a way that makes sense
- A Comprehensive Study of Jonah
- Insight about how to teach the Comprehensive Study Method of the book of Jonah to your small group
- Some additional tips and ideas

For the final chapter of *The Complete Idiot's Guide to Teaching the Bible*, it seems appropriate to include a comprehensive study of two books of the Bible: one from the Old Testament and one from the New Testament. The method takes some of the results from the Chapter Analysis Study Method and the Overview Book Survey Method and combines them so that you can see the whole picture of a particular Bible book.

The Comprehensive Study Method: A Review

The Comprehensive Study Method involves six simple steps. One of the keys to achieving success with this method is to complete the in-depth Chapter Study and the Overview Book Survey methods before using this method. Your group will want to use the chapter and book overview methods first, and then follow up with the Comprehensive Study Method. Keep the forms from the other methods handy as you complete this method.

Here are the six steps:

1. Reread the book several times. Use a modern translation, but do not refer to any commentaries.
2. Write out a detailed, final outline of the book. In this step, compare the work you did on the book overview to the in-depth chapter study.
3. Write a descriptive book title.
4. Summarize your insights.
5. Write down a personal application and, in the process, review the various personal applications you wrote in the Overview Book Survey Method and the in-depth Chapter Study Methods.
6. Tell others about the results of your study, and take the information to your group for dialogue and interaction as you teach the Bible to others.

Just in Case

Prayer is a key part of any Bible group. Some people feel uncomfortable praying aloud, so encourage prayer in different ways and pray at different times of the study. For example, try "popcorn prayer," in which the individuals pop in a sentence whenever they choose.

Preparing a Lesson About the Book of Jonah

This section and the ones that follow will present a practical example of the Comprehensive Method as applied to the Book of Jonah. This small book contains four chapters in the Old Testament and because of the shorter length makes an excellent model for this method.

Step One: Read the Text

For the first step of the Comprehensive Method, you need to get intimately acquainted with the contents of the single book which you have selected. In this example, I have chosen Jonah. I suggest that you read the chapter at least five times to gain the most insight.

Step Two: Create a Detailed, Final Outline

Next, create a final and detailed outline. I've completed this step below for the book of Jonah.

I. The prophet's flight from his commission to go to Nineveh (verses 1:1–2:10)

  A. The commission to go to Nineveh (verses 1:1–2)

  B. The flight to Tarshish (verse 1:3)

  C. Jonah in a storm (verses 1:4–8)

  D. Jonah's proclamation of faith in the Lord (verse 1:9)

  E. Jonah thrown into the sea (verses 1:10–16)

  F. Jonah in the great fish (verses 1:17–2:1)

  G. Jonah's prayer of praise (verses 2:2–9)

  H. Jonah's deliverance from the great fish (verse 2:10)

II. The prophet's reluctant obedience to his commission to go to Nineveh (verses 3:1–4:11)

  A. A new commission to go to Nineveh (verses 3:1–2)

  B. Jonah's proclamation in Nineveh (verses 3:3–4)

  C. The deliverance of Nineveh (verses 3:5–10)

  D. Jonah's sorrow over Nineveh's deliverance (verses 4:1–8)

  E. Jonah's debate with the Lord 4:9; the proclamation of the Lord to Jonah (verses 4:10–11)

Teaching Tips

As you work through the Scriptures with the members of your group, remind them to pray for the Holy Spirit to counsel, teach, and remind them of Christ's commands. This conscious nudging was one of the primary roles of the Holy Spirit. "But when the Father sends the Counselor as my representative—and by the Counselor I mean the Holy Spirit—he will teach you everything and will remind you of everything I myself have told you." (John 14:26, NLT)

Step Three: Create a Descriptive Title

Because you have read the particular book numerous times and created an outline, now you think of an original title which describes in a few words what the book is all about. For the book of Jonah, I created the title "Much More Than a Fish Story—Don't Run from God," I named it in this way because Jonah is about a prophet running from God who was swallowed by a great fish and then spit up and went to preach to the people of Nineveh. It summarizes the overall content of this book.

Step Four: Devise a Summary of Insights

Return to your chapter summaries for this book and summarize the major themes and conclusions of the book. This summary step is the fourth part of the Comprehensive Study Method. I've written my version of these insights about the Book of Jonah here.

- God's sovereignty: Although the prophet Jonah tried to run away from God, God was in control. By controlling the stormy seas and a great fish, God displayed his absolute, yet loving guidance.
- Running from God isn't the answer. Instead, I need to trust God for my past, present, and future. When I or someone I know says "no" to God, it quickly leads to disaster. Yet when I or someone I know says "yes" to God, it brings a new understanding of God and his purpose in the world.
- God's message to all the world: God had charged Jonah with a purpose: to preach to the great Assyrian city of Nineveh. Jonah hated Nineveh, so he responded with anger and indifference. Jonah had yet to learn that God loves all people. Through Jonah, God reminded Israel of its missionary purpose.
- So often it's easiest to stay within our own group and never expand our horizons. God doesn't want us to limit ourselves in this area. God wants his people to proclaim his love in words and action to the whole world. He wants us to be his missionaries wherever we are and wherever he sends us.
- Repentance: When Jonah, the reluctant preacher, went to Nineveh, there was a great response. The people repented and turned to God. This was a powerful rebuke to the people of Israel, who thought they were better but

> **Teaching Tips**
>
> In general, Christians are enamored with the promises of God throughout the Bible. Although it's important to lean on these promises, it's equally important not to neglect God's commands scattered throughout Scripture. Emphasize the commands of God in Jonah and how they can be applied to everyday life.

refused to respond to God's message. God will forgive all those who turn from their sins.

- God doesn't honor pretense or sham. He wants the sincere devotion of each person. It is not enough to share the privileges of Christianity. We must ask God to forgive us and to remove our sin. Refusing to repent shows we still love our sin. It took drastic action for Jonah to repent.
- God's compassion: God's message of love and forgiveness was not for the Jews alone. God loves all the people of the world. The Assyrians didn't deserve it, but God spared them when they repented. In his mercy, God did not reject Jonah for aborting his mission. God has great love, patience, and forgiveness.
- Through the compassion of God shown in Jonah, we learn that God loves each of us, even when we fail him. But he also loves other people, including those not of our group, background, race, or denomination. When we accept his love, we must also learn to accept all of those whom God loves. We will find it much easier to love others when we truly love God.

Step Five: Make a Personal Application

Review all of the personal application material that you wrote from the book survey and the chapter analysis studies. If any of your applications haven't been completed, then write those applications into this section. If you have completed all of them, then choose another personal application that is specific and measurable. In the case of this study on Jonah, I've written my personal application. Every person in your small group (including yourself) will have a distinct personal application.

Recently, my life and my work and even the world seem out of control. The Book of Jonah reminds me that God is firmly in control of the details of my life. When Jonah refused to follow God, it quickly led to disaster. I need to be more aware of God's work in my daily life. In consistent prayer, I will turn to God, acknowledge his work in my life, and ask for him to be even more involved in the details of my work, home, and world.

> **Proceed with Caution**
>
> Don't try to cut corners: You must study the chapters and write the lessons yourself before teaching them to others. If you fail to prepare, you can't be effective as a teacher.

Step Six: Sharing the Study

While Bible study is food for your personal growth, it should also be told to others. You can tell your personal application in two different ways: first with another person one-on-one. Or you can tell the experience to your entire Bible study group. As with the other parts of this Comprehensive Study Method, I've written my response to this section about the study of Jonah. As for me, I will share this study with Bill and James, who are co-workers and the members of my Bible study group.

Ideas for Teaching the Book of Jonah Lesson

Now that the study is completely finished, I turn to the teaching aspects in this section. We explore the predominate themes of Jonah and I list them so they can be discussed in the group setting.

As you teach the Book of Jonah, return to the four "megathemes" of the book: God's sovereignty, God's message to all the world, repentance, and God's compassion. Take time in your small group to go through each of these themes. Explore where they are pinpointed in Jonah and, most important, how they are applied in the lives of the members of your small group.

Teaching Ephesians Through the Comprehensive Study Method

This part begins the New Testament example of the Comprehensive Study Method. For this second example, I selected Ephesians because we've used this letter from the Apostle Paul in other chapters. Normally you would have studied all six chapters of Ephesians separately, then pulled together this information for the Comprehensive Study.

Step One: Read Ephesians

Reading the entire book in one sitting in a recent translation is an important part of this process. You should read the book five different times, and through each reading something new will jump into your mind. Ephesians has six chapters. I suggest that you read them several times and keep track of each time you read a chapter.

Step Two: Create a Detailed, Final Outline

After you read Ephesians numerous times, you will create a detailed and final outline of the entire book. Be sure to make use of the material that you have created chapter by chapter in the In-Depth Chapter Analysis. My final outline for Ephesians is here.

Introduction (verses 1:1–2)

1. The author (verse 1:1)
2. The recipients (verse 1:1)
3. The salutation (verse 1:2)

I. God's plan for the church; who we are in the sight of God (verses 1:3–3:21)

  A. The selection of the church (verses 1:3–21)

    1. The revelation of the purpose of God (verses 1:3–14)

      a. The summary statement (verse 1:3)

      b. The basis of our salvation: the work of God the Father (verses 1:4–6)

      c. The benefits of our salvation: the work of God the Son (verses 1:7–12)

      d. The gift of our salvation: the work of God the Holy Spirit (verses 1:13–14)

    2. The response of prayer to God (verses 1:15–23)

  B. The salvation of the church (verses 2:1–10)

    1. The work of Christ in regeneration (verses 2:1–10)

      a. What we were (verses 2:1–3)

      b. What Christ did (verses 2:4–9)

      c. What Christ made of us (verses 2:19–22)

  C. The secret of the church (verses 3:1–21)

    1. The revelation of the "mystery" (verses 3:1–13)

      a. All saved people are heirs together (verses 3:1–6)

      b. This needs to be preached to everyone (verses 3:7–13)

Teaching Tips

As the group's teacher, make sure you consistently acknowledge your own limitations. You can set the stage for the group discussion, but the members of the group are the participants. All members are responsible to God for their own growth and learning from the study. You are a facilitator; always ask God to move in the hearts of the participants, including yourself.

2. The response of prayer to God (verses 3:14–21)
   a. Praying for others to know this (verses 3:14–21)
   b. The doxology (verses 3:20–21)

II. The conduct of the church; our responsibilities before God (verses 4:1–6:20)

A. The responsibilities of the church (verses 4:1–5:21)
1. To have a united walk (verses 4:1–16)
2. To have an understanding walk (verses 4:17–32)
3. To have an unselfish walk (verses 5:1–4)
4. To have an unblemished walk (verses 5:5–21)

B. The relationships within the church (verses 5:21–6:9)
1. Marital relationships (verses 5:21–33)
2. Family relationships (verses 6:1–4)
3. Employment relationships (verses 6:5–9)

C. The resources of the church (verses 6:10–20)
1. The admonition (verse 6:10)
2. The adversaries (verses 6:11–12)
3. The armor (verses 6:13–17)
4. The access (verse 6:18)
5. The ambassador (verses 6:19–20)

D. Conclusion (verses 6:21–24)
1. The messenger (verses 6:21–22)
2. The greeting (verses 6:23–24)
3. Descriptive title: "Christian, You Are Somebody! Now Live It!"

Teaching Tips

No matter what else happens during your group session, make sure prayer is a key element. You are asking God to accomplish what no amount of teaching can do: prick their consciences, alter their attitudes, and bend their wills in the direction of biblical standards. Rely on God through prayer for every life change that occurs during your time of teaching the Bible.

Step Three: Create a Descriptive Title

In this part, you need to think of an original title that will capture the overall theme of the book. For Ephesians, I wrote the title, "Christian, You Are Somebody in Christ. Now live the Christian life." Paul exhorted the Christians in Ephesus about the importance of unity and understanding who they were since Christ had transformed their lives.

Step Four: Summarize Your Insights

If you studied each chapter using the Chapter Analysis Study Method, then you would have created six different summaries and insights. Return to these studies and review them, then take the major themes and conclusions and write them down. I've written my insights for Ephesians. You and every other person in your study would have different thoughts, which will be some of the key things to discuss when together.

- God is the author of salvation. He planned it from the very beginning. And because it is his plan, it works!
- Jesus Christ is the one who redeems us from our sins and reconciles us to God and to one another. There is no way that people of varying backgrounds, races, religions, and cultures can be reconciled to one another except through Christ.
- The Holy Spirit is the one who lives in us and enables us to understand what we are in Christ. He is the guarantee of our salvation and the enabler for us to live our lives in God's way.
- Because of who we are in God's sight, we have the responsibility to live holy lives: We have the responsibility to become like him. What God has done is described in chapters 1–3; what we are to do is described in chapters 4–6. We must take these responsibilities seriously.
- The plan of God is for all his people to be involved in the work of the ministry. Because all of us have been given spiritual blessings, all of us have the responsibility of ministry to others: to share the Gospel, lead people into a relationship with Christ, and then teach them the disciplines of the Christian life.
- God expects a certain type of behavior from all Christians in our most intimate relationships. This includes in marriage, within the family, and at work. Thus, the responsibilities for all these relationships are carefully spelled out. Our faith is to be expressed through the basic relationships of life.

- It is impossible for us, in our own strength, to live the way God wants us to. That's why he gave us the Holy Spirit and his armor to help us live his way. The resources of God are ours in addition to the blessings. We must put on the whole armor of God in order to live victoriously.

- This book is tremendously encouraging to us when we begin to feel sorry for ourselves. Here God tells us what he thinks of us. There can be no higher or greater recommendation than God's in terms of what he thinks of us.

> **Potent Quotables**
>
> "Jesus Christ said, 'A student is not greater than the teacher. But the student who works hard will become like the teacher.'" (Luke 6:40, NLT)

Step Five: Make a Personal Application

Each of the Bible study methods in this book leads to this critical step—the personal application. Studying the Bible leads to nothing if it doesn't impact your spiritual growth. One of the ways you take the knowledge from the Scriptures is to include a personal application. Each person should create a personal application that is concrete and measurable and practical. What you write for your application will be different than my application and anyone else in your group.

This book spells out what my responsibilities as a Christian are in all areas of life. I know that God expects me to be a good and diligent worker. I am to obey him and submit to him in the name of Jesus Christ.

I have not always been the best worker. This passage (Ephesians 6:5–9) has convinced me of my responsibilities to be a better employee. I will determine, by the help of the Lord, to be the best employee possible. Also, when the opportunity arrives, I will share my faith and the good news about Jesus and how it has changed my life with the vendors who come into our office. But I know these vendors will have to see it in my life first before they will listen to what I have to say to them.

So that I will carry out this application, I will ask David, a Christian with whom I work, to help me be the kind of worker that God wants me to be. I will ask him to meet with me each week to pray that both of us might have that kind of testimony. This may be an opportunity for me to begin working with David on a one-on-one basis.

Step Six: Choose People to Share With

As you spend time studying the Bible and learning new information, you feed your personal spiritual growth. This information and insight should be shared with others. Like many things, if we don't plan to tell others and make it intentional, it doesn't get done. With this step, you select the people who you will share the results of your Bible study. My answer in relation to this study of Ephesians is below. I will share this with the people in my Bible study group.

Teaching the Book of Ephesians

When teaching Ephesians, it will be significant to return to the major themes of the book and emphasize the application. For example, one of the themes emphasized is God's purpose. According to God's external, loving plan, he directs, carries out, and sustains our salvation. Ask the members of your group to discuss how God's purpose becomes our purpose when we respond to Christ's love by trusting him. How are you fulfilling God's purpose in your life?

Blank Comprehensive Study Method Form

You will have other studies beyond the two in this chapter that you will want to do using the Comprehensive Study Method. I've included this blank form for you to either photocopy or have the members of your group write in a notebook or put in a computer file so you can print copies for the different studies.

Book: ________________________ Chapters: ____________________________

1. Number of times read: ____
2. Detailed, final outline: ____
3. Descriptive title: ____
4. Summary of insights: ____
5. Personal application: ____
6. People with whom I will share this study: ____________________________

   ____

The Least You Need to Know

- The Comprehensive Study Method is the most complete means of grasping the themes and gaining a big picture of a particular book of the Bible.
- The short Book of Jonah is used as an Old Testament example of the Comprehensive Study Method in this chapter.
- Paul's letter to the Ephesians is the New Testament example of the Comprehensive Study Method included in this chapter.

Appendix A

Bible Character Study: Questions to Ask

This is a list of 70 questions that you can use in the fifth step of the Bible Character Study (see Chapter 7). There's no need to try to answer every question in every single study; depending on the depth of your study and the time you have, simply select the questions you'd most like to resolve.

I've categorized the questions into seven major divisions. If you think of other questions, add them to this list. Also, please note that I've attempted to be gender-neutral by alternating the pronouns. You can ask these questions about men and women equally.

Standing in the Community

- Who wrote what we know about this person?
- What did people say about him? What did his friends say?
- What did her enemies say about her?
- What did her family (husband, children, brothers, sisters, parents) say about her?
- What did God say about him?
- Why do you think God allowed this person to be mentioned in the Bible?

Character Testing

- What were this person's aims and motives?
- What was he like in his home?
- How did she respond to failure? Did she get discouraged easily?
- How did she respond to adversity? Did she handle criticism well?
- How did he respond to success? Did he appear and act proud when praised?
- How did he respond to the mundane and trivial things in life? Was he faithful in the little things?
- How quickly did she praise God for the good/bad things that happened to her?
- How quickly did she obey God when told to do something?
- How quickly did he submit to God's ordained authority?
- What was he like when he was alone with God?

Background

- What can you discover about this person's ancestry and family?
- What does her name mean? Why was she given that name? Was it ever changed?
- What was his home life like? How was he raised? Where was he raised?
- What were the characteristics of his parents? Did they influence him?
- Was there anything special about her birth?
- Where did she live? What was her everyday life like?
- Was he exposed to other cultures? Did they affect him in any way?
- What was the condition of his country—politically and spiritually—during his lifetime?
- What kind of training did she have? Did she have any formal schooling?
- What was her occupation?
- How long did he live? Where did he die? How did he die?

Significant Events

- Was there any great crisis in this person's life? How did she handle it?
- What are the great accomplishments for which he is remembered?
- Did she experience a divine "call"? How did she respond to it?
- What crucial decisions did he have to make? How did they affect him? How did they affect others?
- Did any recurring problem keep coming up in her life?
- Where did she succeed? Where did she fail? Why?
- How did the environment and circumstances affect him?
- What part did he play in the history of God's plan?
- Did she believe in the sovereignty of God or that God has control over every event?

Relationships

- How did this person get along with other people? Was he a loner? Was he a team person?
- How did she treat other people? Did she use them or serve them?
- What was this person's spouse like? How did he influence her?
- What were his children like? How did they influence him?
- Who were her close companions? What were they like? How did they influence her?
- Who were her enemies? What were they like? How did they influence her?
- What influence did he have on others? What influence did he have on his nation? What influence did he have on other nations?
- Did he take care of his family? How did his children turn out?
- Did her friends and family help or hinder her in serving the Lord?
- Did he train anyone to take his place? Did he leave a "Timothy" or disciple behind?

Personality

- What type of person was she? What made her the way she was?
- Was her temperament phlegmatic, sanguine, melancholic, or choleric?
- What were the outstanding strengths in his character? What traits did he have?
- Did her life show any development of character as time passed? Did she grow and progress?
- What were her particular weaknesses and faults?
- What were his particular sins? What steps led to those sins?
- In what area was his greatest battle: lust of the eyes, lust of the flesh, or pride of life?
- What were the results of his weaknesses and sins?
- Did she ever triumph over her particular weaknesses and sins?
- What qualities made her a failure or success?
- Was he in any way a type of Christ?

Spiritual Life

- What personal encounters did this person have with God that are recorded in the Bible?
- What was his purpose in life? Did he try to bring glory to God?
- What message did she live and preach? Was her life a message against or for Christ/God?
- Did he live a separated life or a life set apart for holiness and depth with God?
- What did she believe? What great lessons did God teach her?
- Why do you think God dealt with him in the manner in which he did?
- What was her attitude toward the Word of God? Did she know the Scriptures?
- What kind of prayer life did he have? Did he have close fellowship with God?
- Was he bold in sharing his testimony? Was he a courageous witness in times of persecution?

- How big was her faith in God? How did she show it? Did God give her any specific promises?
- Was he a good steward of what God had given him—time, talents, and wealth?
- Was she filled with the Spirit? What were her spiritual gifts? Did she use them?
- Was he eager to do God's will, willingly and without question?

Appendix B

A Partial List of Bible People to Study

The following lists provide characters or people to study in the Bible.

The Principal Patriarchs

Enoch

Noah

Abraham

Isaac

Jacob

Leaders in Early Hebrew History

Joseph

Moses

Aaron

Joshua

Principal Judges

- Othniel
- Deborah
- Gideon
- Jephthah
- Samson
- Eli
- Samuel

Kings of the United Kingdom

- Saul
- David
- Solomon

Kings of Israel (All Evil)

- Jeroboam I
- Nadab
- Baasha
- Elah
- Zimri
- Omri
- Ahab
- Joram
- Jehu
- Jhoahaz
- Joash
- Jeroboam II
- Zechariah
- Shallum
- Menahem
- Pekahiah
- Pekah
- Hoshea

Kings of Judah

Evil

- Rehoboam
- Abijah
- Jerhoram
- Ahaziah
- Athaliah
- Amaziah
- Azariah or Uzziah
- Ahaz
- Manasseh
- Amon
- Jehoahaz
- Jehoiakim
- Jehoiiachin
- Zedekiah

Good

- Asa
- Jehoshaphat
- Joash
- Jotham
- Hezekiah
- Josiah

Poets

Ethan
Heman
Job

Principal Prophets

Balaam
Elijah
Elisha
Nathan
Isaiah
Jeremiah
Ezekiel
Daniel
Hosea
Joel
Amos
Obadiah
Jonah
Micah
Nahum
Habakkuk
Zephaniah
Haggai
Zechariah
Malachi

Other Prominent Men of the Old Testament

Abel
Absalom
Adam
Ahasuerus
Xerxes
Ben-Hadad
Bezalel
Cain
Caleb
Dathan
Abiram
Eleazar
Aaron
Esau
Ezra
Gehazi
Goliath
Haman
Ish-Bosheth
Ishmael
Jesse
Jethro
Joab
Jonadab
Jonathan
Judah
Korah
Laban
Levi
Lot
Melchizedek
Mephibosheth
Mordecai
Naboth
Nadab
Nehemiah
Pharoah
Phinehas
Sennacherib
Assyria
Shadrach
Uriah
Hittite
Zerubbabel

Prominent Men of the New Testament

Jesus Christ

The Twelve Apostles

Peter
Andrew
James
Zebedee
John
Philip
Bartholomew
Thomas
Matthew
James
Alphaeus
Thaddaeus
Simon
Judas Iscariot

Other Men of the New Testament

Agrippa
Annas
Apollos
Aquila
Aristarchus
Augustus
Barnabas
Bartimaeus
Caesars
Caiaphas
Cornelius
Epaphroditus
Felix
Festus
Gaius
Gamaliel
John the Baptist
Joseph, the husband of Mary
Joseph of Arimathea
Lazarus
Luke
Mark
Nicodemus
Onesimus
Paul
Philip
Pontius Pilate
Silas
Simon, the leper
Simon, the Pharisee
Stephen
Timothy
Titus
Trophimus
Tychicus
Zechariah
Zebedee

Prominent Women

Women of the Old Testament

Abigail
Athaliah
Bathsheba
Deborah
Esther
Hannah
Huldah
Jael
Jezebel
Leah
Michal
Miriam
Naomi
Queen of Sheba
Rachel
Rahab
Rebekah
Ruth
Sarah
Vashti

Women of the New Testament

Anna
Bernice
Dorcas
Elizabeth
Eunice
Herodias
Martha
Mary, mother of Jesus
Mary, mother of John Mark
Mary of Bethany
Mary Magdalene
Priscilla
Salome
Sapphira

Appendix C

A List of Positive and Negative Character Qualities

This list of positive and negative characteristics will be useful in completing Step 6 of the biographical study in Chapters 9 and 19.

Positive Characteristics to Look for in a Person

Thriftiness
Good stewardship
Resourcefulness
Observation
Industry
Creativity
Enthusiasm
Optimism
Capacity to love
Kindness
Patience
Self-denial
Capacity to give of oneself
Willingness to sacrifice
Compassion
Meekness
Sympathy
Generosity
Forgiveness
Gentleness
Mercy
Capacity to make peace

Submission
Agreeability
Consideration
Self-control
Passionate devotion
Honesty
Integrity
Dependability
Loyalty
Dedication
Faithfulness
Trustworthiness
Sincerity
Diligence
Order
Righteousness
Fairness
Obedience
Courtesy
Respect
Reverence
Deference
Thankfulness
Wisdom
Discernment
Sensitivity
Perspective
Discretion
Carefulness
Cautiousness
Discipline
Characteristics of the Beatitudes
Sense of humor
Actions of a servant
Uncompromising
Flexibility
Uncomplaining nature
Contentedness
Tolerance
Independence
Quiet
Calm
Humility
Durability
Bravery
Courage
Boldness
Confidence
Cheerfulness
Modesty
Cleanliness
Purity
Chastity
Moderation
Balance
Earnestness

Zeal

Energy

Stability

Determination

Negative Characteristics and Sins to Look for in a Biographical Study

Inability to forgive

Prejudicial attitude

Negligence

Insensitivity

Unkindness

Malice

Selfishness

Cruelty

Wastefulness

Forgetfulness

Carelessness

Idolatry

Talkative nature

Foolishness

Shortsighted approach

Ungratefulness

Disobedience

Tyrannical nature

Nosiness

Rebelliousness

Rudeness

Coarseness

Insulting behavior

Unfairness

Dishonesty

Deceitfulness

Crafty/sly behavior

Hypocritical behavior

Shallowness

Laziness

Flattering behavior

Compromising behavior

Backbiting behavior

Tendency to gossip

Slandering behavior

Libelous behavior

Unreliability

Unfaithfulness

Tendency to forget God

Love for men's praise

Independent spirit

Doubt

Shame of Christ

Anger without cause

Legalistic

Profane

Presumptuousness
Fear of men
Apostasy
Undisciplined
Self-righteousness
Lust for power
Joy in evil
Worry
Bigotry
Manipulation
Disrespect
Argumentative behavior
Procrastination
Complaints
Violence
Bitterness
Blasphemous behavior
Scornfulness
Sarcastic behavior
Envy
Jealousy
Vanity
Dogmatic behavior
Arrogance
Fearfulness
Stinginess
Greed
Covetousness
Fornication
Adultery
Immorality
Drunkenness
Gluttony
Immodesty
Sensuality
Boastfulness
Stubbornness
Conceit
Pride
Wavering behavior
Double-mindedness
Fickleness
Humorlessness
Impulsiveness
Cop-out behavior
Cowardliness
Idleness
Apathy
Irritating behavior
Annoying behavior
Harsh behavior

Appendix D

Ideas for Topical Study

The following is a random list of possible topics for study:

Anger	The Holy Spirit
Citizenship	Humility
Courage	Integrity
Discipleship	The lordship of Christ
Evangelism	Love
Faith	Marriage
Fear	Obedience
Follow-up	Parent/child relationships
Fruitfulness	Patience
Giving	Prayer
Godliness	Priorities
God's guidance	Purity
The Gospel	The quiet time
Grace	Salvation
Holiness	Self-discipline

Sin

Steadfastness

Thankfulness

Wealth and possessions

Witnessing

The Word of God

World vision

Worship

Appendix E

A Suggested List of Keywords

The following words are a list of key biblical words that could be used for the Word Study Method (see Chapter 20 for more on this method).

Adoption
Adversary
Apostle
Atonement
Baptize
Believe
Bless
Body
Call
Chasten
Christ
Church
Confess
Covenant
Death
Disciple
Emmanuel
Everlasting
Evil
Faint
Faith
Favor
Fear
Fellowship
Flesh
Good

Gospel
Grace
Hear
Hell
Holy
Hope
Iniquity
Jehovah
Jesus
Judgment
Kingdom
Know
Law
Laying on of hands
Life
Light
Lord
Love
Lust
Manifest
Marriage
Mediator
Meek
Mercy
Mind
Minister
Miracle
Mystery
Name
Obey
Passover
Peace
Perfect
Perish
Preach
Propitiation
Reconcile
Redeem
Remnant
Repent
Rest
Resurrection
Righteous
Sabbath
Sacrifice
Saint
Sanctify
Save
Servant
Sin
Soul
Spirit
Temptation
Trial
Truth
Understand

Vain

Vision

Watch

Wisdom

Witness

Word

World

Worship

Index

A

B

C

D

E

I

J

K–L

M

P

Q–R

S

T

U–V

W

X-Y-Z